The Edible Sea

The Edible Sea

Paul J. and Mavis A. Hill

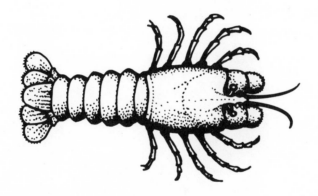

South Brunswick and New York: A. S. Barnes and Company
London: Thomas Yoseloff Ltd

A. S. Barnes and Co., Inc.
Cranbury, New Jersey 08512

Thomas Yoseloff Ltd
Magdalen House
136-148 Tooley Street
London SE1 2TT, England

Library of Congress Cataloging in Publication Data

Hill, Paul J.   1921-
  The edible sea.

  Includes Index.
  1. Cookery (Sea food).   2. Sea food.   I. Hill,
Mavis A., 1922-   joint author.   II. Title.
TX747.H54 1975   641.6'9   74-9186
ISBN 0-498-01550-5

PRINTED IN THE UNITED STATES OF AMERICA

To our three daughters;
Carol and Julie,
who will try anything that relates to the sea,
and in memory of Jennie,
who loved the sea but looked often
"at the trees and flowers and the fields . . ."

Contents

Preface

Such pastimes as beachcombing, skin diving, boating, and fishing are bound to create the desire for ever deeper knowledge about our creatures of the sea. Skin and scuba divers, especially, are caught up in efforts to seek more information about how they can make use of the various forms of sea life with which they find themselves surrounded in our underwater world. Just how much of this sea life besides fish and shellfish is edible? How are those unfamiliar species prepared for the table? Which of the ocean's creatures are toxic to eat? And what are the nutritional values of seafood? Most divers, as inherent students of nature as well as avid seafood fans, will try anything—as long as they know it's safe to eat. Therefore it wasn't long after we brought our first abalone to the surface in 1957 that we began to research and experiment with almost everything we found in our underwater world. During our research of the subject, however, we found a great void regarding accessible material on edibles of the sea. Many marine biologists couldn't help us and even seafood gourmets were found lacking in knowledge of exotic seafoods except where their own ethnic backgrounds were concerned. Consequently we began, literally from the bottom of the ocean and working our way to the surface, to ferret out information from foreign cooks and foreign cookbooks. Meanwhile we experimented on our own with many species after first determining from toxicologists that these were safe to consume.

9

The deeper we dug, the more surprised and delighted we became, determining, finally, that almost every living thing in our Mother Sea is edible. Further, all these things were delicious and nutritious once one knew how to prepare them. The sea is a veritable "bouillabaisse!"

Spurred on by our many diving friends and others in the water-sports world, we soon found ourselves well into writing *The Edible Sea*. Acquiring the information was rewarding and fun—but not easy. No single publication was found that explained the use, much less the preparation, of all edible species in our oceans. Almost all seafood cookbooks written to date are directed at seafood lovers and cooks who will buy fish or shellfish at the local supermarket. A few with a foreign flair mention sea urchin roe and even sea cucumber but the written word apparently hasn't been found necessary to natives of some areas in the world who have lived their whole lives eating such things as sea anemones, sea hare, jellyfish, and sea snakes, to mention only a few. Recipes for shark meat, for instance, are rare, including recipes for the very common angel shark of California and Europe, yet this is one of the most delicious fish in the ocean.

Since we began work on *The Edible Sea*, many occurrences have added to our feeling of urgency in getting it before the general public. Talk of pollution, world protein shortages, and rising prices of red meat (even our old economy-related stanbys, liver, chicken, and hamburger) made us realize that everyone who is able to wield a fishing rod, wander along the seashore, or learn to dive can take advantage of the great benefits, both nutritionally and budgetwise, that seafood of all kinds can bring to them. The tremendous growth in the interest of skin diving has generated a whole new industry, and Caribbean and South Pacific islands are now literally peppered with diving resorts. The same is true in many other areas of the world including the cold Nordic countries. Further, air travel has become more comfortable and convenient so that diving and fishing travel has mushroomed. These people now find that they can enjoy the warm waters of exotic islands over a four-day weekend or short week's vacation with no strain on their time. It is important, therefore, that these travelers have access to information about what is safe to eat from our oceans and how to prepare it, either in a modern kitchen or in the wilds.

The Edible Sea was written for divers, fishermen, boaters, seafood cooks, marine-life instructors and students, and all nature lovers in general. The first chapter covering seafood nutrition, aphrodisiacs, freezing seafood, smoke-cooking, toxic sea life, and the wine list at the back of the book will educate and entertain anyone with an interest in the sea and its relation to man. The recipes for both the commonly known and exotic species cover animals and algaes from the shallow littoral zones to the abyssal depths. A great many of these recipes are our own. Those recipes that have come from others have been tested either by us or by authorized cooks to ensure your future enjoyment and success with them.

Go down to the sea again. Take advantage of the bounty offered by our Mother Sea in her delicious, economical bouillabaisses, our nutrition-laden oceans.

Acknowledgments

As with most books of this type, the number of people who contributed to the finishing of the work are too many to mention. It is impossible to recall, much less list, all the devoted seafood lovers who contributed either directly or indirectly to the compilation and research of so much information and so many recipes. Many of these people, in discussing seafood with us, merely gave us a *feeling* of a better way to do things. Some of our best information came to us by way of casual remarks cast forth by fishermen on the beach, divers, boaters, or others we met briefly in our travels or at-home dives. All have our gratitude and their rightful place in this book.

We are most grateful to the California Department of Fish and Game for the use of their library and their help with classification of fish; the California Department of Public Health; and Fletcher Harvey, packer of Lake Dark Harbour Brand Dulse for his help in that area.

We are especially indebted to Mr. John Olquin, Director of the Cabrillo Beach Marine Museum in San Pedro, California, for his time and help with information on Cetacea and grunion; and to Dr. Bruce W. Halstead of World Life Research Laboratory, Grand Terrace, California, for the time given us in consultation about toxic sea life.

For their personal time as guides and acquainting us with seafood cultures around the world we would like to thank Stu Stinchfield of Divers

World, Silver Spring, Maryland; John Baldi of South Shore Divers, Quincy, Massachusetts; Wilbur and Dottie Trask, Ipswich, Massachusetts; Herb and Sylvia Strunk of Savage, Maryland; and Bill Crawford of Key Largo Diving Headquarters, Key Largo, Florida. Also Willard and Mavis Manus (Greece); Walter Deas and Valerie and Ron Taylor (Australia); Masamitsu Sekine (Japan); Dave and Pat Nicholson, Bob Soto, and Mrs. J. A. Dailey (the Cayman Islands); and Leo Zanelli of *Sub Aqua Magazine* and the British Sub Aqua Club (England). Our special thanks also go to Bud and Josie Smith of *Dive Magazine*, who flew us into Mexico and introduced us to some of the finest home-style seafood cooks in that country. We cannot leave this area without thanking the many dive stores and dive clubs who aided us in ways too numerous to mention.

For their personal help and general encouragement we would like to extend our gratitude to Larry and Sharon Canfield and the rest of the Sea Sabre Dive Club in California; Robert Marx, who was of great benefit in responding to our calls for help with various aspects; Chuck Buchanan; Herman Russ; Robert D. Scoles; Roy Hauser of the dive boat *Truth*, San Pedro, California, for taking his personal time and efforts in toting back huge pieces of elk kelp for our experiments and for waiting for us to bring sea cucumbers and other sea life aboard before throttling off for home; Eddie Tsukimura of the dive boat *Golden Doubloon*, San Pedro, California, for his help in research of sea cucumbers; Jim and Joyce Milner of Milner's Charter Service, San Pedro, California; Alice Hollenbeck and Bob Frank of Southern California for their help with information on preparing sea urchin roe; Ed Brawley, of Brawley's, Inc. in Northern California; Roy Brizz of Brizz Advertising; James Stewart, Scripps Institution of Oceanography; and Sus Yasada and others at Meijis Market, Gardena, California.

Let us not forget our little dog, Muff, who bravely tested many unresearched species for us and is healthier at fourteen years old than she was as a puppy!

Introduction

The Edible Sea is meant to be used as a guide to edible sea life in all oceans and as a reference for basic and gourmet recipes from around the world. The text identifies edible and toxic sea life with comprehensive illustrations and photographs, and includes current information from leading world toxicologists.

The text is written in an easy-to-understand style and contains very few scientific terms except for the inclusion of scientific names for the various species to facilitate proper identification. The information is presented so that it can be utilized by those who are interested in seafoods, good nutrition, marine sciences, and even aphrodisiac foods; also for those who want new and interesting ways of preparing common seafoods and simple ways of preparing unusual or exotic seafoods. Many rare or little-known seafoods are included for the adventurous reader.

Chapter 1 deals with general information and introductory material and should be read first, since this information applies to all following chapters. After a brief introduction, the nutritional benefits of the sea are discussed. Aphrodisiacs are then covered, followed by methods for freezing and smoking seafood. The chapter is concluded with a discussion on toxic sea life and pollution.

The remaining chapters cover phyla or specific groupings of sea life. The opening text of each chapter begins with a short discussion of the edible qualities of the group and goes on to present detailed information of the various species. The chapter progresses with the identification, geographical location, description, and how to clean and prepare the edible parts, followed by recipes for the group. Toxic sea life is then covered. For quick reference, an asterisk (*) precedes each paragraph covering toxic sea life. Equipment tips for catching or gathering are at the end of the text for each particular group. Some sea life can be taken only by skin or scuba diving. If you are not a certified scuba diver, do not attempt to dive without first acquiring proper instruction from a reliable agency.

The information on edible sea life in this book can be used for survival purposes where a specific species and locality is identified. Students of diving or zoology will find the contents organized in the index and table of contents for quick reference to help them in their studies.

The Edible Sea is a complete seafood instruction book and also is intended as a form of entertainment for those who love the sea. We urge you to experiment on your own with various species after you have determined these species are safe to consume. The sea is yours, for fun and for nourishing sustenance. Enjoy it.

The Edible Sea

SOME USEFUL AMERICAN, ENGLISH, AND METRIC EQUIVALENT MEASURES

U. S. Liquid Measures	*Metric*
1 gallon	3.785 liters
1 quart	.946 liters
1 fluid ounce	29.573 mililiters

U. S. Dry Measures	*Metric*
1 quart	1.101 liters
1 pint	.550 liters
1 teaspoon	4.9 cubic centimeters
1 tablespoon	14.8 cubic centimeters
1 cup	236.6 cubic centimeters

U. S.	*English*
1.032 dry quarts	1 quart
1.201 liquid quarts	1 quart
1.201 gallons	1 gallon
1 English pint	20 fluid onces
1 American pint	16 fluid ounces
1 American cup	8 fluid ounces
8 American tablespoon	4 fluid ounces
1 American tablespoon	½ fluid ounce
3 American teaspoons	½ fluid ounce
1 English tablespoon	⅔ to 1 fluid ounce (approx.)
1 English tablespoon	4 teaspoons

The American measuring tablespoon holds ¼ oz. flour

1

The Edible Sea

"You ain't gonna *eat* them ugly things? Gawd, I just threw two a' them back this mornin'!"

The leathery face of the surf fisherman wore a wry expression as he stood above our dive club gathered around a two-foot ray that lay on the beach. Ideas for cooking the ray were being exchanged by the divers and several members of the club turned their attention to a pile of whelks, sea urchins, and scallops that also lay nearby.

"We like whelks pickled and sea urchins with melted cheese on toast," said someone. Our onlooker, the line fisherman, winced, took a firmer grip on his fishing rod, and walked away down the beach, shaking his head in disgust. We divers, along with some of the more knowledgeable fishermen, know that looks are only scale deep and we have been pleasantly surprised time after time at how delicious some grotesque-appearing sea creatures can be when properly prepared and thrown into a frying pan, baked, or even eaten raw.

Actually, the sea is a veritable supermarket. The world's oceans cover approximately seventy percent of our planet and can be compared to a vast bouillabaisse. This nutritious stew is just waiting for us to dip in and extract our favorite tidbits from its broth. As with the shells and bones

19

in a bouillabaisse, however, there are a few inedibles with which to contend that must be sorted out. Most of the contents of the seas are delicious and the very ultimate in good nutrition. Indeed, even the "broth" of this bouillabaisse, seawater itself, can be extremely healthful when taken in very small amounts under certain conditions.

Noted biologists estimate that the seas swarm with twenty thousand species of plant and animal plankton that could be our salvation as a protein source in the future if we find efficient methods of harvesting it. Some plankton, with little processing, tastes like lobster, shrimp, and even Wheaties, they say. In addition, there are about one hundred thousand species of marine invertebrates and probably twenty-five thousand species of fish. Seafood is plentiful and will continue to be so, providing that we learn to farm the sea, improve our catching techniques, control the catching of those that are becoming extinct, control pollution, and make use of more edible species.

Today, half the world's population lives in chronic protein starvation, a deficiency that destroys man's ability to work efficiently, shortens his life span, and stunts his children's growth and minds. In addition, probably within the next fifty years, the earth will face a severe animal protein deficiency. Knowing what sea life is edible and nutritious and how to prepare these species for human consumption may mean the difference between vibrant health or sickness and abundance or want.

We hope the information presented here will open the door to the utilization of other seafoods besides those now commonly used by the general public so that the popular species will not be so intensely pursued. We hope, too, that the information in *The Edible Sea* will help you to take advantage of the ocean's great seafood potential and add interest and variety to your table; therefore adding to your enjoyment of our water world as well as to your abundant health.

Healthfoods of the Sea

Seafood is a storehouse for most of the nutrients essential to the body for proper functioning; it is delicious, easily digested, and a welcome variety for meals. Seafood combines the high quality and complete protein unique to the animal kingdom with the soft fats characteristic of the vegetable kingdom and also contains useful amounts of minerals and vitamins. An average serving of most seafoods furnishes more than enough animal protein to meet the usual daily requirements of the body, yet the fat content is very low. The latter makes seafood a dieter's delight as it helps solve the problem of getting required nutrients without extra, unwanted calories. The small amount of fat in seafood is unsaturated, easily digested, and is used readily by the body tissues. This property of unsaturated fat in most seafood is what prompts nutritionists to recommend increased consumption of these foods. Nonoily species of fish such as sole, whiting, rockfish, perch, and sheephead contain less than two percent fat in the flesh. This is also the case with turtle meat and most of the shellfish (mollusks and crustaceans) including lobsters, crabs, scallops, abalone, and conch. Weight for weight, even the fatty fish such as mackerel and salmon contain fewer calories and less total fat than most other comparable protein foods.

Vitamins

Fish-liver oils are exceptionally high in vitamins A and D. A 3.5-ounce serving of fat fish provides about ten percent of the daily requirements of vitamins A and D. A similar serving of most fish would satisfy about ten percent of the thiamine, fifteen percent of the riboflavin, and fifty percent of the niacin requirements. Vitamin content of an average serving of eel or swordfish is almost fifty percent of daily requirements. Eel and oysters are high in thiamine and riboflavin. Seaweeds are a valuable source of vitamins and minerals—all the elements required for nutrition are represented, including niacin, vitamin B_{12}, vitamin D, vitamin C, thiamine, riboflavin, and carotene, from which the body manufactures vitamin A.

Minerals

Most fish will provide the body with more nutrients than a porterhouse steak. Also, the mineral content of fish includes satisfactory sources of magnesium, phosphorous, iron, copper, and smaller amounts of other minerals. Shellfish such as clams, abalone, scallops, and oysters also have an abundance of these minerals, in most cases more than milk. Oysters, shrimp, and clams are about twice as rich in available iron than beef and lamb; while cod, perch, trout, and most other fish are a little poorer source. Clams are rich in calcium; lobster, crabs, and oysters are also a good source of calcium. One large oyster may supply about 0.5 milligrams of copper. Seafoods rich in phosphorus are fish, lobster, crabs, oysters, and shrimp; clams also supply a fair amount of this mineral. Sea urchin roe is high in potassium and protein and is also well supplied with other nutrients. Filtered or sterilized seawater is a good source of all the trace elements known to be essential to gocd, vibrant health, while seaweeds are far richer in organic iodine and potassium than any vegetable source (refer to "Seaweeds and Seawater").

Protein

Seafood is an excellent source of high-quality protein that ccntains generous amounts of amino acids. The quality of oyster protein is superior to that of most fish and beef, however the protein content is relatively low. A four-ounce serving of lean fish will supply about half the daily requirement of protein. The highest recorded protein content for any animal food was for tuna caught off Cape Verde Islands. It is interesting to note that fish feeding off plankton generally have the highest protein value.

Although some seaweeds are high in protein (red algae thirty-six percent), there are some deficiencies in amino acids here, and the value of proteins is classified in terms of their amino acid composition. Most naturally occurring proteins contain eighteen amino acids.

Proteins have been called the "building blocks" of nutrition because their main function is to build and repair tissue. When more protein is consumed than our body needs, however, the excess is slowly changed chemically into sugar and stored as body fat.

Cholesterol

Cholesterol levels in the blood are raised by the combinations of saturated fats and large amounts of cholesterol in the diet. Increasing the amount of polyunsaturated fat, while reducing saturated fats and cholesterol intake, acts to bring down blood cholesterol. Seafoods are much lower in fats than other meats. The fats that they do have are soft and mostly polyunsaturated. If eaten several times a week, seafood will neutralize the harmful effects of saturated fats from other foods in the diet and actually reduce body cholesterol.

Heart specialists are particularly interested in the nutritional benefits of fishery products because a high proportion of polyunsaturates in the diet may help to decrease the incidence of arthereosclerosis. Animals of the sea, like all creatures in the animal kingdom, do contain some cholesterol. Most fish are lower in cholesterol and higher in total fat, however, than shellfish (crustaceans and mollusks.) Crustaceans are suspected at times of containing high levels of cholesterol, according to The International Oceanographic Foundation of Florida. There is mounting evidence that sterol levels vary with the state of the animals (soft-shelled crabs contain a much higher level than hard-shelled ones). This would indicate that crustaceans which are molting would contain a higher level of cholesterol. Many doctors concerned about heart problems warn their patients away from cholesterol altogether. Eating fish several times a week could maintain safer levels of cholesterol while insuring an adequate intake of high quality protein, at the same time adding variety to your diet.

Digestibility

Fish is more easily digested and less stimulating than the flesh of mammals or birds. For this reason it can play a major role in the diets of young children, elderly people, and invalids with weak digestive powers. White-fleshed fishes contain very little fat and are very easy to digest. Among these are the sole, whiting, most flatfishes, rockfishes, and sheephead. Those with very delicate digestions should not eat herring, mackerel, trout, eel, other fat fishes, or fish fried in fat. The edible qualities of fish are greatest just before their spawning periods.

Lobster, crab, shrimp, prawns, and barnacles are highly nutritious but not as digestible as fish. Lobster meat is more delicate and more digestible than crab, and the meat of the claws and legs are more tender and delicate than the tail. Fresh-water crayfish are very delicate. It may be of interest to some that rheumatic and gouty individuals may sometimes develop toxic symptoms after eating crustaceans.

Oysters are very digestible when eaten raw and in season, but not as easy to digest when cooked. The muscle, or hard part of oysters, should not be given to invalids with weak digestive ability. Small oysters are more delicate and are easier to eat than large ones. The adductor muscles of clams are also more digestible raw. Scallops are easier to digest raw and will become tough and fibrous if cooked more than a few minutes. Seaweeds are a little more difficult to digest than other proteins. Sharks, skates, and rays are easier to digest if they have aged several days in the refrigerator or freezer.

Germ Killers

Doctors at the National Institute of Health, Bethesda, Maryland, have found that the juices and meat of oysters, abalone, clams, and other mollusks contain a rich source of a substance that destroys disease germs. It is also reported that the feeding of oysters and clams to mice that have been infected with polio virus has reduced their death and paralysis rate by twenty-five percent. Protection against influenza viruses and cold-sore virus was also demonstrated, and staphylococcus bacterial germs were also hit hard by the mollusk substance. The search for new medications from under the sea has turned up an anticancer drug that is effective against a certain tumor in laboratory mice. Called *stoichactin*, the new drug is an extract from a Tahitian sea anemone. The University of Hawaii is presently conducting research with this agent. Research is being conducted constantly to find other medical uses for sea life.

Seafood Aphrodisiacs

Much to our delight, science has now proclaimed seafood to be a proven aphrodisiac. One scientist, Dr. Nicholas Vinette, has put it rather poetically by stating in his writings, "Those who live almost entirely on shellfish and fish . . . are more ardent in love than all others." Similarly, Dr. Joseph Reusch, president of the German Lifesaving Association, says that male divers are sexier than the average man. Divers, of course, are avid seafood lovers. They are also very prolific and produce many healthy children. Well! Let's hear it for the oyster!

Dr. Reusch discovered that divers get a boost in their sex lives also from the remarkable quantity of oxygen that accumulates in the blood when they dive. He proposes taking patients into recompression chambers to 120 feet to restore virility.

Since man first began delving into his environment and the effect of one element upon another, he has steadfastly held that seafood contributes to his sexual potency—even before the word *aphrodisiac* was invented. Generations of experience have shown us positive results that now are backed by these scientific facts. People of the Mediterranean countries have long been identified as powerful and virile lovers—the French, Italians, Greeks, Spanish; also of course, the Scandinavians—all of whom utilize seafood extensively, partaking of it daily in some form or another.

British explorer Captain Cook, known as a real swinger with the young beauties (and uglies) of the South Pacific Islands, was virtually the creator of "free love" in that area, if we can believe reports that he held a record of ten native girls every day. Where did he achieve this amatory energy? Why, he gorged on a special shrimp dish every morning, just to keep in shape! And this is by his own admission, according to factual accounts on record.

Lord Byron and the great Casanova both swore by the effects of devouring plenty of seafood as homework during off hours of pursuing and indulging in their favorite "hobby." Madam Pompadour was famous with Louis XV because she cooked Filet of Sole ala Pompadour before each romantic interlude. All these great lovers, and many more too numerous to mention here, learned from experience and used without question a method that to them was a fact of life but that professors today are just finding to be a scientific truth!

Octopus stewed in its own ink is famous in Spain for its aphrodisiac properties; the French take to oysters for the most part along with sea urchins; while the Greeks favor prawns. Bouillabaisse has been recognized the world over (albeit behind cupped hands and chuckles of admitting to a belief in a "superstition") as a bestower of sexual prowess. Cod, salmon, shark, shellfish of all kinds, seaweed, and seawater itself have long been consumed diligently by those seeking added virility. Now, rather than believing that good results are caused by psychological reasons, the opposite view is taken—that is, if you eat plenty of seafood and don't get the desired results, you obviously have a mental block against amorous interludes!

Among the most important minerals and elements that contribute to efficient functioning of the sex glands are phosphorous, iron, copper, and iodine; seafood is rich in all of these. Vitamin A nourishes the mucous membranes that lubricate the sexual organs. Vitamin B-1 (thiamine) produces and supplies hormones to the pituitary gland, which stimulates the sex glands. Vitamin D is known to increase sexual desire.

The fact that sea animals feed from surroundings that contain all the elements needed for balanced nutrition, and the fact that they have prodigious reproduction abilities, are two more reasons they have been cited for their aphrodisiac propensity. Large gamefish and salmon are in great favor in this regard, it is said, due to their power and bravery, which steps up overall health in the glandular system, both in the fish and the person who eats them. Fish roe ranks high on the list of aphrodisiac foods. Such things as sea urchin, sea cucumber, limpets, periwinkles, all crustaceans are great aphrodisiacs. They are "bottom dwellers" for the most part and partake of foods low on the food chain, rendering them potent examples of those creatures imbibing on high amounts of basic elements. Seaweeds themselves, which make up the diet of most gastropods, are very high in phosphorous, one of the elements responsible for the aphrodisiac qualities in sea food, as mentioned above.

More study is being conducted to pinpoint exactly the scientific basis for this beneficial result from eating seafood, but whatever it is, it's having its effect on divers, almost all of whom are hot-blooded seafood enthusiasts. They are healthy, virile, animated, ebullient, vibrant, and vigorous, among other things, and will tell you themselves that they are, in addition, quite handsome. They are among the happiest of nature's children—for they partake of nature and what she has to offer as they find her—in the raw and in the wild, following their ancestors' paths, investigating a new frontier and foraging for wild food in the bosom of the sea. The vast majority of divers, as well as most other seafood gourmets of the world, prefer their scallops eaten raw or cooked just slightly, and the same goes for their preference in eating oysters. Recipes for raw abalone and conch dishes are becoming very popular also.

One diver we know, using a take-off from a motto of the Oyster Institute of America, said it best with "Eat Seafood—Love Longer!" How about that for a bumper sticker?

How To Freeze Seafoods

Any fish or other seafood that has been taken from the ocean recently may be frozen. Freezing will preserve the freshness of your catch if you follow a few basic rules:
1. Seafood to be frozen should be in prime, fresh condition.
2. All air must be excluded from the meat during freezing and storage. Packages must be both moisture and vapor proof.
3. Freezing and holding temperature should be 0° F or below.
4. Thawed seafood should be prepared promptly for eating and should not be refrozen.

Bacteria cannot be completely eliminated, but its growth can be kept to a minimum. Illness-producing bacteria grow at room temperature. Freezing temperatures drastically retard bacteria growth. Temperatures of 170° F and above will kill most bacteria.

Preparation Before Freezing

Proper care in the field is absolutely essential for freshness of seafood to be frozen later. All seafood to be frozen should be placed on ice, in a refrigerator, or at least in a wet burlap bag as soon as practical after catching. Fish should not be kept in a bucket of water because the water may eventually become warm and increase bacteria growth and spoilage. In any case, seafood should not be allowed to become warm. Further, it should be cleaned before freezing.

Large fish should be filleted or cut into steaks. Small fish may be frozen whole after cleaning. In any case, the preparation should be such that the fish are ready for cooking without further cleaning. Commercial practice indicates that it is a good idea to give fish steaks and fillets a twenty- to thirty-second dip in brine before wrapping and freezing.

This treatment markedly reduces the leakage or "weep" which occurs when the fish is thawed. The desired brine solution may be made by dissolving one quarter cup of salt in one quart of water. Filtered seawater may be used for this if convenient.

Lobster tails may be frozen fresh, uncooked, Lobsters should be alive when the tails are twisted off to insure their freshness. The intestinal vein may be removed by using one of the lobster antennae, inserting the larger end of the antenna into the anal canal, and twisting as you pull it out. The intestinal cord will come out with the antenna. Large legs can be twisted off and frozen. The body cavity may be frozen also by first removing the stomach and intestinal tract. Lobster meat can be cooked first, if desired, then frozen quickly and kept until ready to use.

Abalone, conch, and scallops may be frozen uncooked by removing the shell and entrails. Do not trim the meat but freeze it as it is so that in case freezer burn develops it will be on the trimmings you later remove. Abalone also may be sliced ready for pounding and cooking if you don't intend to keep it frozen too long. This will save some work just before dinner but it is well to remember that sliced ab meat will not keep as long as the whole ab in the freezer.

Clams, mussels, and oysters are best taken right out of the shell and placed into liquid-tight containers for freezing. Freeze quickly, reserving the juices in the refrigerator, then pour the juices over the frozen meat and return it to the freezer. This method freezes the meat in a block of ice and will preclude early freezer burn.

Sea urchin roe should be removed from the test, or shell, and placed in a liquid-tight container, then covered with its own juices or a saline solution and frozen immediately.

Seaweed fresh from the ocean may be cut into pieces small enough to fit a container and frozen in a saline solution.

Packaging for Freezing

A large mass of meat will take a long time to cool in the center and will allow up to several hours for growth of bacteria. Therefore, seafood should be packaged in quantities and sizes no larger than will be cooked at one time. Place two pieces of wax paper or freezer paper between steaks, fillets, and pieces. This will prevent the pieces from freezing together and they will separate easily when taken from the freezer for thawing. Label each package as to date, kind of seafood, and weight or number of servings or pieces. Use colored tape or colored pencils to speed package identification: i.e., red for lobster, blue for fish, green for abalone, etc.

Packages must be both moisture and vapor proof. Proper packaging keeps food from drying out and prevents air from entering the package and causing oxidation or "freezer burn." The air in freezers has a low humidity due to the condensation of its moisture in the form of ice on the freezing surfaces, and because of this relatively low humidity, frozen foods held in storage will dry out quickly unless they are protected by a moisture-vapor proof wrapper or package. Products that dry out in storage quickly become rancid, take on foreign flavors, become tough, and are dry when cooked.

Suit the packaging to the shape and size of the meat and the storage time. Materials may be waxed cartons, plastic containers, plastic bags, aluminum foil, tin cans, and so forth. For short storage such as one month, a double wrapping of meat with freezer wrap may be used; or simply slip it into a plastic bag and seal it. For longer storage times, up to one year, the water seal method is best. Use leak-proof containers or plastic bags and fast freeze overnight. Later, fill the container to within one inch of the top with water, preferably salt water. The flesh should be completely covered. In this way, the ice cap formed by the "water seal" effectively excludes all air. Cover the top with freezer wrap or other type lid. This method is also the top "flavor-keeper" procedure.

Fat fish, such as salmon and albacore, should be eaten within three months for best flavor. Lean fish, such as halibut, bass, rockfish, and lingcod, should be eaten within six months for best flavor. Lobster, crab, and shrimp are best eaten within three months. Long storage tends to toughen these crustaceans.

Although fish and abalone are especially susceptible to freezer burn, the water seal method of packaging will usually prevent any unfavorable flavor changes for periods of up to twelve months. Eventually, the ice will dehydrate with about a year of storage. Air pockets will form and get to the meat unless the ice is sealed air tight.

For large pieces or whole fish, freeze, then dip in ice water to glaze. Refreeze, repeating the dipping and freezing several times until a thin, solid layer of ice has formed. Wrap carefully in freezer wrap.

Freezer Procedure

When seafood is packaged for the freezer it should be placed immediately into a 0° (or lower) freezer. Care should be taken not to place one package on top of another or even in close contact with another in the beginning. Good circulation around the packages accelerates freezing.

It is best to place the unfrozen packages against a refrigerated surface. Arrange them so that they do not touch any frozen packages stored in the freezer. If necessary, use corrugated carton material between the frozen packages to prevent them from coming in contact with each other. After new packages are thoroughly frozen, they may be stacked in any convenient manner in the freezer.

Freezing temperatures above 0° F result in large ice-crystal formation and considerable cell-wall breakdown within the flesh of seafood. This is particularly undesirable in that it produces a softening effect noticeable when improperly frozen fish is thawed. Freezing temperatures of 0° F or below cause little change in the consistency of frozen fish. Bacterial action is stopped at about +20° F and enzymatic action greatly retarded at 0° F. Thus frozen food holding temperatures should be at least this low for satisfactory results.

Thawing Frozen Seafood

It is not necessary to thaw fish and some other seafoods completely before cooking, although uniform cooking is more likely to occur if fish is at least two-thirds thawed before applying the heat. Additional cooking time must be allowed if fish is frozen. When fish are to be breaded and fried it is more convenient to thaw them first for ease in handling.

Thaw frozen seafood in the refrigerator in its original wrappings. If seafood was frozen with a water seal, leave the container at room temperature for about an hour. Remove the container from the block of ice and chip off the ice cap. Put the seafood on a refrigerator rack and place a container under the rack to catch the melting water or juices. Use any other method you can devise for this procedure, but however you do it, remember that it is important not to let the seafood soak in the thawed liquid, which will give it a spongy, lackluster quality and may destroy a lot of flavor.

Meat may be thawed much more rapidly at ordinary room temperature than fish. At 70° F, approximately two hours time is required per pound. This time can be reduced to approximately forty-five minutes per pound by placing the packaged meat in front of an electric fan. Frozen fish is best defrosted in the refrigerator because it loses its natural juices more readily when thawed at room temperature. Also, the surface area of the fish would reach room temperature too quickly and provide perfect conditions for bacteria growth.

For best quality, cook thawed fish immediately, although thawed fish can be kept in the refrigerator for two or three days and still be edible. Do not refreeze seafood once it has been thawed completely. The meat will suffer in flavor and texture if refrozen. Be sure to inquire about the freshness of any seafood you buy if you intend to freeze it.

Cold Storage

If you do not intend to freeze your catch, you should preserve it by refrigeration or some other method of cold storage. Keep fresh or thawed seafood refrigerated below 40° F and preferably at 32°. Fish will retain its flavor for about two days at this temperature. Fresh seafood can be kept for about a week in a good refrigerator and still be edible but not as flavorful as it will be when very fresh. The danger zone for bacteria growth is from 40° to 140° F.

Seafood dishes should be served as soon as they are cooked, or they should be cooled rapidly to 40°. Leftovers should be put into the refrigerator while they are still hot. If seafood is allowed to cool to room temperature and then let stand, bacteria can begin to grow again quickly.

Raw meat from crabs, shrimp, lobster, and oysters should not be held unrefrigerated for more than an hour. Failure to refrigerate cooked shrimp for four to six hours before serving may cause gastrointestinal problems.

Smoke Cooking

Almost any type of fish or other seafood can be smoked successfully, although the oilier type fish achieve a somewhat better flavor

Smoke cooking. Loading a smoker with a rack full of abalone (from top) and a pan of pulverized hickory (on burner at bottom). Left to right, Melanie Culverhouse, Sharon Canfield, and Rose Ann Lane get ready to serve up a treat to the Sea Sabre dive club at Campland, Mission Bay, San Diego, California.

under this cooking and preserving process. Oysters, clams, prawns, shrimp, lobster, eel, octopus, scallops, mussels, and abalone all have been smoked with excellent and sometimes unique results as to flavor and originality of the finished product.

In pioneer days during long, cold winters, the food supply had to hold out until spring. Smoking or salt curing were methods used to preserve meat. Today, emphasis has shifted toward smoking as a means of flavor variety and enhancing the flavor of some meats rather than as a method of preservation exclusively.

Smoking Methods

Food can be smoked in three basic ways, the hottest and fastest method of which is called *smoke cookery* and is done at temperatures from 200° to 400° F. This is nothing more than cooking and smoking with a backyard barbecue equipped with a cover and with hardwood chips sprinkled over the charcoal. This method enhances the flavor of the meat but does not improve its preservation qualities.

The second type of smoking is *cold smoking*. Here the meat is placed on racks a good distance from a slow, smouldering fire and cured below 90° F from several days to as long as four weeks, depending on the length of preservation desired. This method removes most of the moisture from the meat and preserves it for periods of over a year. A common product of this method is ham and beef jerky.

Third, we have what is called *hot smoking*. This is done at temperatures running between 100° and 190° F and allows the meat to be cooked while adding the smoke flavor. Some moisture is removed in this process and meat preservation is improved. This, of course, is the method most used in commerically smoked fish and game, either to your order or for sale over the counter. This is also the method we are most concerned with in home smoking your own seafood.

Equipment for Home Smoking

Smokers vary in complexity from a cardboard box to large steel, thermostatically controlled ovens. Knowing the requirements for an efficient smoker will help you select one or build your own. You will need a smoke source, an area to confine the smoke, a draft to move the smoke, baffles to disperse the smoke, and meat racks or hooks. The smoke source can be electric, gas, or charcoal with a metal pan of hardwood chips or sawdust. A slow-burning, smoky hardwood fire will do also. The area to confine the smoke can be made of any noncombustible material. Combustible items such as a cardboard box, wooden box, or canvas tent or even green tree boughs may be used if the area will receive low heat from 80 to 85 degrees. For hotter smoke sources of 100 to 190 degrees you can utilize such items as an old refrigerator, stove, shed, barrel, garbage can (new!), or even metal foil bent to shape.

Top and bottom draft holes are essential to keep the smoke moving over the food. Stagnant smoke will impart an objectionable flavor. Temperatures can be roughly controlled with adjustable draft holes. Baffles to disperse the smoke can be made of a piece of metal perforated with many holes and mounted between the smoke source and smoke area. A drip pan will also serve double duty as a baffle.

A very compact, lightweight but sturdy portable smoker is available from Luhr Jensen & Sons, P. O. Box 297, Hood River, Oregon. This "Little Chief" smoker costs about thirty-five dollars and is just two feet high and one foot square with a handle for easy transport. It can be utilized on the patio or even in an apartment fireplace and will smoke up to twenty pounds of meat with professional efficiency.

Curing for Flavor and Storage

In smoking sea foods, curing is an important step that will extend the storage period and improve the flavor, texture, and appearance of your end product. Curing draws the water out of meat, making for more desirable conditions that retard spoilage. Micro-organisms that cause meat fermentation or spoilage need water to flourish. More moisture is removed by the heat from the smoker, and chemicals from the smoke also have a preservative effect. In the "dry cure" method, salt is rubbed into the meat and the meat is left to stand for a time before smoking. This method may cause the meat to shrink and have a saltier flavor. The "brine soaking" method, wherein the meat is soaked for a given time in a mixture of water, salt, and sugar, allows less shrinkage and leaves meat moister with a little more flavor than the dry cure method. Whenever possible, use premixed curing salt sold at most butcher shops and packing houses. Otherwise try to get the "dairy fine" grade or "three quarters" ground salt. Pure salt has fewer chemical impurities. As a last resort, table salt can be used. Sugar is used in all brining mixtures to reduce the hardening effect of the salt. Brown sugar or molasses may be substituted according to your taste.

Strength of Brine

The amount of salt to use depends upon the amount of water needed. A 100% saturated solution is about 1¼ cups of salt to 1 quart of water. Fish brine should be between 60 and 90%. One cup of salt to one quart of water makes a 90% saturated solution. One-half cup makes 60% solution. The solution is about right when it will just float an egg. Salt may also be measured by weight; the standard measuring cup will hold about 10 ounces by weight of salt.

Hot Smoking Procedure

Mix in a brine container (not aluminum):
For every quart of water:

¾ cup regular or brown sugar
¾ cup curing salt
¼ cup rock salt
1 teaspoon lemon juice

The above amount is about right for up to ten pounds of fish. For larger quantities, increase portions accordingly. For flavor variations, seasoning can be added to the brine such as onion, garlic, tarragon, pepper, crab boil spice, bay leaves, or soy sauce. To bring out the flavors of the brine, mix eight hours in advance and leave out the rock salt. For better flavor, double the brining time and reduce salt by one-half.

Cut fish chunks about four inches wide and submerge into the brine with a weight such as a large dinner plate. Cure (one hour for fillets that are skinned and two hours if the skin is left on) in the refrigerator. For saltier flavor, large fish can be cured up to five hours. After curing, rinse off the brine solution and place skin side down on paper towels, patting off excess moisture with more towels. Allow fish to air dry about an hour, then place on oiled smoker racks.

Woods that can be used for fuel are maple, apple, cherry, birch, oak, manzanita roots, nut trees, grape vine trimmings, leaves, seaweed, corn cobs, coconut husks, and the best of all—old-fashioned kiln-dried hickory. Refill the smoke pan every one and one-half to two hours.

After seafood has been in the smoker for about five hours, begin checking for doneness every hour. When it is close to being finished, the outside will have a bronze glazed appearance that's similar to the outside of a roast turkey. Gently break a couple of pieces open, checking to see that they are done in the center. The meat should flake apart easily. When smoked fish is taken from the smoker, let it cool at room temperature for a half hour, then refrigerate in air-tight containers before serving. Refrigerated smoked fish will last three weeks or more. The drier it is the longer it will keep. Frozen smoked fish will keep a good year.

The smoking time varies depending upon the size of the pieces and amount of heat. A little experimenting will tell you what length of smoking time will satisfy your palate.

Oysters, clams, scallops, mussels, squid, and octopus should be brined from thirty minutes to one hour and smoked about one hour or to suit your taste. Shrimps and prawns are precooked about five minutes, brined for two hours, and smoked for one and-a-half hours. Double the brining time and smoking time for lobsters. For smoking abalone, brine for two hours and smoke for two hours (refer to Mollusk chapter for smoked abalone recipe details). For an outstanding secret recipe (until now!) for brining and curing, refer to Cleveland's Smoked Fish in the Fish chapter.

Toxic Sea Life

Some people, for one reason or another, cannot tolerate seafood of any kind or are allergic to certain fish or specific shellfish. Some diseases will cause various types of reactions to certain seafoods. For instance, the consumption of crustaceans may cause toxic symptoms to develop in rheumatic individuals or people suffering from gout.

Aside from causing allergy illnesses in a small percentage of people, seafood must be handled properly and cleaned as soon as possible after catching. It spoils easily and should be kept cool by putting it on ice or in a wet sack right after it is caught. It should then be refrigerated, frozen, or eaten as soon as possible.

Of course in addition to the above cautions, it must be pointed out that some sea life is just naturally toxic to man and should not be eaten at any time. In some cases only parts of an otherwise edible and nutritious animal is toxic. Eating toxic sea life can produce various results; from a mild upset stomach to death, with steps in between that can be extremely unpleasant, so it is important that seafood lovers realize what is safe to consume and what is not. Tropical waters carry most of the sea life that is found to be toxic, however, and temperate and cold waters are relatively free of poisonous sea life.

Various marine biotoxins are briefly discussed in the following chapters where applicable to specific sea life. These aspects are not covered in detail, however, as the purpose of this book is to present the "edible" sea, not the "inedible" sea.

Biological Contamination

A recently discovered cause of food poisoning that is recognized as a significant contributor to gastrointestinal outbreaks in the United States is a microorganism called *Vibrio parahemolyticus*. Cooked seafood is responsible for most of the episodes, according to Dr. William H. Barker, Jr., of the United States Center for Disease Control. Errors in refrigeration, cooking, or food-handling hygiene lead to the incidents, and most often involved as the "carriers" for the organism are crab, shrimp, lobster, and oysters. Diarrhea is the dominant symptom, and abdominal cramps, nausea, and vomiting also occur with relative frequency. Some of the food handling errors contributing to outbreaks include:

1. Raw crab and raw oysters held unrefrigerated long enough to allow organisms to proliferate to very large numbers.
2. Undercooking of shrimp and oyster meat that has been left unrefrigerated for several hours.
3. Failure to refrigerate cooked shrimp for four to six hours before serving.

4. Leaving oysters unrefrigerated overnight and then roasting and eating in a "half raw" state.
5. Placing cooked seafood in containers previously exposed to raw seafood.

The organisms multiply rapidly, and in three to four hours ten organisms can become almost one million. The organism may survive in seafood cooked at temperatures of up to 176 degrees Fahrenheit.

Pollution Poisoning

Some toxic sea life is caused by pollution, and though scientists continue to gather evidence and issue warnings to the effect, the amount of sea life affected by pollution is steadily increasing. Actually, however, the amount of sea life seriously affected is infinitesimal and most seafood at this time is perfectly safe to eat. Although some environmentalists would have us believe that the ocean is completely polluted; most ocean water is less polluted and cleaner than most tap water. The above notwithstanding, one should never eat shellfish from water into which untreated sewage flows. Untreated sewage almost always contains some infectious hepatitis. Many cases of hepatitis have been caused by pollution poisoning of shellfish beds, and contamination of millions of acres of shellfish beds has caused them to be closed. Pesticides also are the cause of toxic oysters, mussels, clams, and crabs; and some fish can store up pesticides at concentrations as high as 790 ppm while shrimp and some fish will die from as little as 0.0003 ppm before they can affect man.

Chemical Pollution

Of all the pollutants, toxic chemicals are the worst. The introduction of a metallic compound in the environment of previously edible fish has been known to trigger a chemical reaction that renders the fish toxic (called ciguatera poisoning). Toxic chemicals are dumped into rivers and the ocean by many industries such as mining, dyeing, plating, smeltering, oil, agricultural and electrical industries, and manufacturers of chemicals, pharmaceuticals, pesticides, paper and pulp, glass, rubber, ceramics, etc. It was a plastic plant that caused mercury poisoning at Minimata Bay in Japan and killed forty-seven people from 1953 to 1961. The Japanese incident, however, was caused by a concentrated amount of mercury in the small bay adjacent to the plant and affected only people who ate seafood from that one area; also many of those affected were people who worked in the plastic plant and were exposed to the mercury from other sources inside.

The Mercury Scare

Pollution, of course, is a serious threat to our oceans, and constructive measures are very necessary before the situation becomes irreversible.

Such things as the mercury poisoning scare of 1972 in the United States, however, have been overemphasized and do nothing to help the problem; instead, this type of hysteria causes negative attitudes that only serve to delay progress on the real answer. Frederick Stare, M.D., Chairman, Department Nutrition at Harvard University, after exhaustive study ridicules the stories that the public has become subjected to in regard to the terrible things found in foods, things from DDT to mercury, zinc, lead, and infinitum. "Tomorrow it may be gold," he says, "who knows what? In part, this is because scientific techniques to analyze foods have improved greatly in recent years and one can now find traces of most anything! Is any food safe to eat?" Dr. Stare feels that the guideline of safe mercury levels used by the FDA is arbitrary and may be at least twice as low as it could be.

Jack Kevokian, Senior Research of Saratoga General Hospital in Detroit, blamed part of the mercury scare on ignorance and emotion. He said the mercury content in the human body seems to be decreasing instead of increasing. Kevokian has criticized the United States Food and Drug Administration (FDA) for the standard of 0.5 ppm of mercury in fish and stated there was nothing in the way of scientific study to support that figure. The standard for Japan and Sweden is 1.0 ppm. It has been calculated that a man would have to eat eighty pounds of fish containing 0.5 ppm of mercury (much higher than most fish) within a period of a year to be in danger of illness. This is about eight times the average consumption of any fish in the United States. (Mercury half life is seventy days.) Further, a recent University of California study concluded that samples of fish pickled almost one-hundred years by the Smithsonian Institute revealed that the open sea was laden with as much mercury then as it is today!

"Mercury occurs in our environment naturally; in the sea, the soil, and food—all foods," says Dr. Stare. "It has probably always been in our environment. The important thing for us to do is lessen and prevent increased pollution of the environment, not only with mercury but with other substances." Dr. Stare added that the chances of becoming ill from mercury or other contaminants in fish or other foods are infinitesimal compared to the hazards of too many calories and too much saturated fat and cholesterol, a warning with which we are all familiar.

The world continues, however, to dump pollutants into the sea and man will, eventually, contaminate his future perfect food supply. Increasing world pollution can eventually change the many under-the-sea Gardens of Eden that are full of life into barren, hostile deserts. "The false concept of the ocean as unlimited, endless, of infinite fecundity, providing reserves of food for mankind until the end of the world, must be changed," said Jacques Cousteau in an interview. He concluded that the fate of the ocean depends upon man and the fate of man depends on the oceans.

The following chapters cover the edible qualities of seafood, and paragraphs that cover toxic seafood are preceded with an asterisk (*).

2

Crustaceans

Paradoxically, the ugliest creatures in the sea to most people are also the most popular of all seafoods. These are the crustaceans, rela-

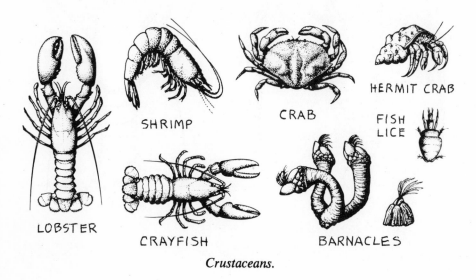

Crustaceans.

tives of the spider. The class includes lobsters, crabs, barnacles, shrimp, crayfish, prawns, sand fleas, fish lice (copepods), and a major part of the ocean's plankton. Class Crustacea comes under the Arthropoda phylum, which includes most insects as well as the spider mentioned above. There is also a minor class of marine Arthropods called *Archnida* that includes the horseshoe crabs and seaspiders. The eggs of the horseshoe crab are eaten in Asia, but some species are toxic. Generally speaking, all crustaceans are edible but some species are so small or meatless that they have little to offer by way of food for man.

Lobsters

There are two major groups of lobsters. Usually, these are referred to as the spiny lobster and the clawed lobster. Spiny lobsters (genus *Panulirus*) are called rock lobsters in most areas and a few call them "crayfish." The clawed lobster of the United States (genus *Homarus americanus*) is usually referred to as the New England lobster. Crayfish and lobster are basically all the same in Australia. Recently the official

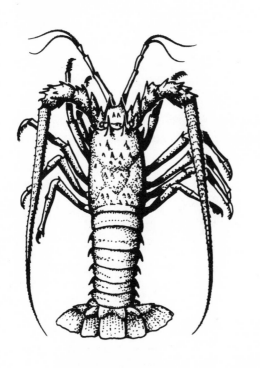
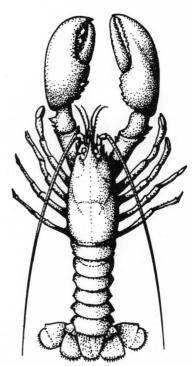

SPINY LOBSTER

CLAWED LOBSTER

Lobsters.

Spiny lobster. COURTESY ROBERT B. EVANS.

name of the Australian crayfish was changed to rock lobster to minimize export confusion. Western Australia is the greatest producer of frozen rock lobster tails and the United States is the largest consumer.

Spiny Lobsters

Spiny lobsters can be distinguished readily from the clawed lobster by the absence of large claws, the presence of many prominent spines on the body and legs, and their very long antennae. Spiny lobster tails are a favorite in many parts of the world and though the whole lobster is just as edible and delicious as the clawed lobster, it is not popularly served whole in restaurants. This is due to the fact that the numerous sharp spines would make this dish a real prickly plateful and very hard to handle.

An oddball in the lobster family is the shovel-nose lobster, sometimes called the scaly slipper. Scientifically known as *Scyllarides,* this funny-looking bug has a fat body, shorter legs than most lobsters, and no claws or antennae—presenting a picture that makes lobster lovers feel he has all his equipment missing! The shovel-nose is found in the tropical Pacific, Indian Ocean, tropical Atlantic, and South African waters. The

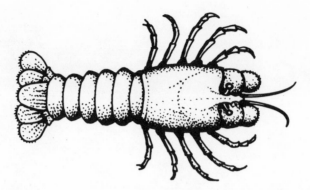

Shovel-nose lobster.

"cigalle" shovel-nose of the Mediterranean at Spain's Costa Brava is the *Scyllarus latus* and is very prolific. Its meat is very delicate and preferred in Spain over other lobsters.

Clawed Lobsters

The clawed lobster of the east coast of Canada, the United States, and northern Europe has large claws, a smooth body, and looks very much like its first cousin, the freshwater crayfish. (Tribe Astacura includes all clawed lobster and clawed freshwater crayfish.) This lobster is recognized as the king of all crustaceans by many people and is classed among the most highly prized of all shellfish for eating.

An important species in Norwegian waters is a long, skinny relative (*Nephrops norvegicus*). There is also a clawed lobster (*Eniplometopus occidentalis*) that lives in the warm areas of the tropical South Pacific, Hawaii, and the Indian Ocean. This species, however, lives in the colder depths of one-hundred feet or more on the outer sides of reefs. He is uniquely patterned with white spots against a brilliant salmon-red shell.

Cooking Lobsters

The lobster is versatile and can be baked in or out of its shell, can be boiled whole, and its meat can be removed either before or after cooking for use in various dishes. Lobsters should either be boiled or frozen while still alive for best results. A lobster will live longer if you keep him cool in the refrigerator, on ice, or in a wet bag. A lobster that dies will spoil fast from seepage of intestinal fluids into the meat and should be eaten as soon as possible. A second choice, should the lobster die, is to freeze the tail. If the lobster dies while being transported, the tail should immediately be removed and kept cool on ice prior to freezing or cooking.

Clawed lobster. This one weighed fifteen and a half pounds and had six-inch claws. It was caught in ninety feet of water near the East Glouchester Breakwater. COURTESY BILL SURETTE, *Framingham News* MASSACHUSETTS.

Removing Lobster Meat

When removing the meat from a lobster, watch for the red-orange "coral," or roe, which is the egg mass; and don't miss the "tomally," or liver—both of these are not only edible but delicious and are considered very tasty by gourmets. Meat near the head and around the joints is often missed if one is not aware of the succulent morsels to be found in these areas. The bulk of lobster meat, of course, is found in the tail, legs, and body. Small (barely legal size) bugs have little meat other than the tail meat that is worth going after, and it is best to twist off the tails of these, roll them into a neat ball, and pop them into an airtight plastic bag for freezing.

BOILED LOBSTER

Drop live lobster into boiling salted water in a pot that has a lid and is large enough so the water will cover the whole lobster. Place the lid on the pot, bring the water back to a boil, and cook 10 minutes for small lobsters or 15 minutes for medium sized lobsters and 20 minutes for large ones (8 pounds or over.) Remove the lobster with tongs and hold under cold running water a few seconds, but do not soak. Soaking will render the meat watery and spongy and it will lack flavor. Serve hot and whole or remove the meat for creamed dishes or salads. If served hot and whole, furnish individual dishes or melted butter or our "Scrumptedelicious Sauce," which follows:

SCRUMPTEDELICIOUS SAUCE

This is the "king's choice" instead of plain melted butter as a dip for boiled lobster. We will refer to it throughout the book also for use with other shellfish. In our opinion it is unsurpassed as a butter substitute in these cases. We use it often and call it "Scrump" sauce.

Melt 1 stick of real dairy butter (dairy butter is a *must* for this). Add 4 crushed garlic cloves, 1 teaspoon lemon juice, ⅛ teaspoon finely crushed tarragon, 1 tablespoon finely chopped parsley, and 4 teaspoons chopped chives. Mix all together well and keep warm for several hours for the flavors to coalesce. Keep refrigerated in a covered container between uses. (It will solidify in the refrigerator, but you need only to melt it down, slowly, again.)

Cleaning and Eating Clawed Lobster

1. Twist off the claws.
2. Crack the claws with a nutcracker, lobster-crackers, pliers, mallet, or what have you. Tasty chunks of solid meat are inside.
3. Separate the tail piece from the body by arching the lobster's back until it cracks, then twist and pull.
4. Bend back and break off the flippers from the tail.
5. Insert a small fork or finger into the meat where the flippers broke off and push out the meat. Remove the intestinal vein. Cut the tail meat into bite-size pieces and dip into melted butter or favorite sauce.
6. Unhinge the back shell from the body.
7. Remove and discard the stomach sac behind the eyes. The remaining parts (liver and white meat, and the roe of the female lobster) are edible except for the spongy gills. The liver is called "tomally" and turns green when it is cooked. Some people consider the tomally best eating of all.
8. Crack open the lower part of the body. There is a lot of white meat in this section.
9. If you're still hungry you may eat the legs. Place a leg end in your mouth and suck out the meat as if the leg were a straw. This is delicious and is one of the fun parts of eating clawed lobster.

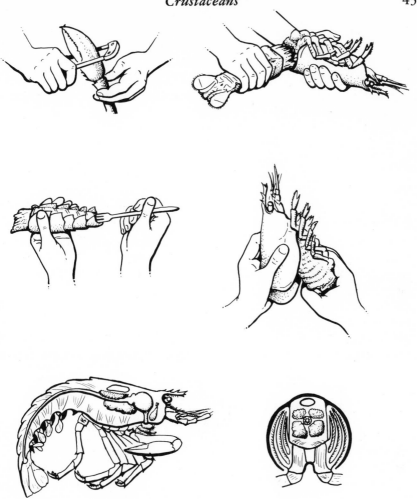

Cleaning and eating clawed lobster.

Cleaning and Eating Spiny Lobster
1. Twist off the antennae at the base (you may need gloves to protect your hands from the spines).
2. Crack the antennae with a nutcracker or mallet. Tasty chunks of meat are inside the base of the antennae.
3. Separate the tail piece from the body by twisting half way around and pulling.
4. Split the underside of the tail lengthwise with a sharp knife.

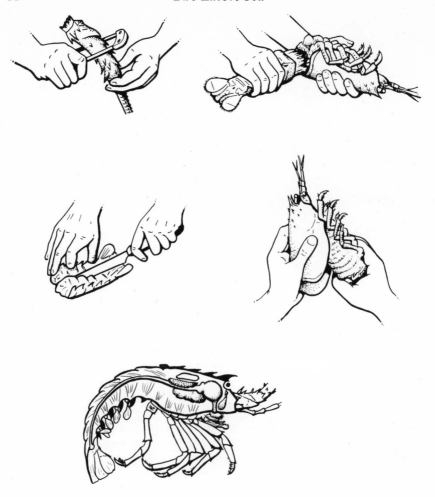

Cleaning and eating spiny lobster.

5. Break open the shell by bending it backwards and pull out the meat. Remove the intestinal vein. Cut the tail meat into bite-size pieces and dip into melted butter or your favorite sauce.
6. Unhinge the back shell from the body.
7. Remove and discard the stomach sac behind the eyes. The remaining parts (liver, white meat, and roe of a female lobster) are edible except for the spongy gills. Be sure to get all of the white meat around the head and antennae.
8. Crack open the lower part of the body. There is a lot of white meat in there.
9. On a large lobster, crack open the legs. This is the best part. The

huge chunks of butter-tender leg meat are like the claw meat of a northern bug; there is more of it, pound for pound, and it's every bit as good. The leg meat of a small spiny lobster is scarce, hard to get at (due to the hard, spiny shell), and is hardly worth the bother— unless you are really hungry and have plenty of time and patience.

BROILED LOBSTER

Use lobster tails or whole lobster split lengthwise. Place cleaned lobster on rack with shell side up about 4 inches from heat. Cook half-pound tail or a one-pound lobster 6 minutes, then turn. Brush meat with melted butter and cook 8 minutes more or until golden brown. Previously boiled lobster can also be used and should be brushed with melted butter and cooked just until meat is heated through— about 5 minutes. Sprinkle with paprika (optional) and serve with melted butter. Wrapping the tails in foil will keep them moist and prevent burning. Add 5 minutes more to the cooking time if you use the foil method.

BROILED LOBSTER TAILS PIGGYBACK

Insert scissors between hard shell on back of lobster tail and meat. Clip shell down center, leaving the fantail and underside membrane intact. Carefully open shell, gently separating it from the meat, and lift the meat to the *outside* through the split shell, so that the meat rests on top of the shell and leaving the fantail end of the meat still attached. Brush the meat with melted butter (or "Scrumptedelicious Sauce" under Boiled Lobster) and broil about 4 inches from the heat; 6 minutes for 2-ounce tails, 10 minutes for 4-ounce tails, 14 minutes for 6-ounce tails,

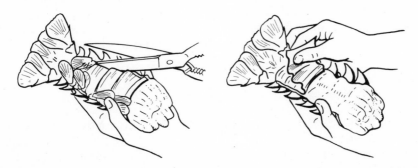

Preparing lobster tails for broiling. Before broiling, either split the underside of the tail lengthwise with a sharp knife, or cut away the underside membrane (including swimmerettes) with scissors, cutting along each side of the tail and peeling off the soft undershell.

and 18 minutes for 8-ounce tails. Serve with "Tangy California Sauce" if desired (refer to chapter 8, under "Sauces").

BARBECUING LOBSTER IN FOIL

This method will give you juicy, succulent white meat that will come out of the foil dripping with nectar and sending up a pleasant swirl of tempting, aroma-filled steam. With the coals all ready for barbecuing and the grill about 3 or 4 inches above the coals, wrap the lobster tail snugly in foil and place on the barbecue. Cook a one-half pound tail or a one-pound whole lobster about 15 minutes with the shell side down. Turn and cook another 10 minutes. Remove lobster tail from foil and serve. For a nicely browned appearance, place the tail on the grill flesh side down after removing the foil and cook for 2 or 3 minutes until lightly browned. If you like lobster meat with a lightly scorched or burned taste, leave the foil off and cook first with the flesh side down 5 minutes, then turn to the shell side and continue to cook 15 minutes more. Serve with plenty of melted butter.

SEA SABRE COMBINATION PLATE

Bring your steak, salad, and garlic bread along on the boat with you. Jump in and grab your bug, then help set up the boat barbecue. Have your buddy standing by with the steak and put the lobster on the grill first, cooking it 5 or 10 minutes before placing the steak on the heat, for you will find lobster meat takes longer to cook than steak. When both are almost ready, toss a couple slices of garlic-buttered french bread on the barbecue and toast them on both sides. Meanwhile stumble across the rolling deck to find your plate, fork and knife, salad, and, of course, your bota bag! Make your way back, find a steady place to sit (preferably leaning on your buddy) and have at it. King Neptune himself never had a banquet like this and you did it all yourself!

VIRGIN ISLAND LOBSTER BOATS

Ellsworth Boyd, diver and author of diving articles, gave us this very unique and effective recipe. It was given to Ells and his friends Bob Allen and Jim Kelly by an old native at St. Thomas, Virgin Islands, who traded it for a bottle of rum. We say it was well worth the price! The only things you'll need are a lobster apiece, aluminum foil, canned chunk pineapple, plenty of rum, butter, and a broiler.

Cut lobster meat into bite-sized chunks. Form little individual "boats" using a double thickness of foil for each one and making sure the sides are at least three inches higher than the amount of filling you plan to place into them. Make sure that the "boat" is leak proof, then fit lobster chunks neatly into each one. Don't pile the chunks on top of one another; make a single layer. Now for each boat use two ounces of rum—pour one ounce over each boat's goodies—and drink the other ounce (ah, this is going to be fun.) Now pour 1½ ounces of the syrup from a can of pineapple over the "cargo" and place pineapple chunks over the lobster meat, making sure you don't completely cover the meat—let the lobster show through (with all that rum it needs some air!). Place a thin sliver of butter on the meat and broil the boats for about 12 to 15 minutes for an average-sized lobster tail, longer for larger ones. Eat right from the boats, spearing first a piece of lobster, then a piece of pineapple, and swirling each in the succulent juices. Have another rum drink, proposing a toast to the old native who concocted this tantalizing taste treat!

LOBSTER A LA NEWBURG

(Serves 4 for company or two gluttons!)

This is the "ultra" Lobster Newburg and if you have a chafing dish, be sure to use it, for this dish is very beautiful and impressive prepared at the table before your guests. (Let them sip a little wine while you do this and use candlelight.) Lobster à la Newburg, however, tastes every bit as good prepared in a double boiler.

You Will Need
2 cups lobster meat, cut into ½-inch chunks
4 tablespoons butter

½ teaspoon paprika	4 egg yolks
½ cup sherry wine	1 tablespoon cognac
1 cup cream	Hot toast points

Beat the egg yolks together with the cream. Melt butter in the blazer pan of your chafing dish or top of a double boiler. Add lobster meat and sauté directly over the flame about 3 minutes. Sprinkle with paprika and add the wine, then cook 3 minutes more.

Place the water pan under the blazer pan or top of double boiler. Bring the water to a simmer, then add the cream and egg mixture. Stir tenderly until sauce is thickened. (If you want it a little thicker, add a tablespoon arrowroot mixed with a little wine.) Add cognac, stir, and serve over hot buttered toast points. Nice with a green vegetable mixed with slivered almonds, and a mixed green salad.

JOYCE MILNER'S FRIED LOBSTER TAIL

Remove lobster tail from rest of lobster. Split tail lengthwise and remove the intestinal tract. Get your skillet very hot (use no butter at this point) and lay the lobster tail halves in the skillet, shell side down. Now dot with butter and sprinkle with salt and garlic salt. Cover and cook until meat is white. Place 2 tablespoons butter in skillet, turn lobster tails so that meat side is down and cover. Cook until meat pulls away from shell easily (watch carefully and if it begins to get too brown, turn the tails over again). Pull out meat with fork or serve on the shell.

FRENCH FRIED LOBSTER TAILS

(Serves 6)

You Will Need

6 lobster tails, 5 or 6 oz. each	Salt and pepper
2 beaten eggs	½ cup flour
¼ cup Half 'n Half	½ cup bread crumbs

Cut tails in half lengthwise and remove meat in one piece. Combine eggs, Half 'n Half, and seasonings. Combine flour and crumbs. Dip lobster meat in egg mixture and roll in crumb mixture. Use basket in your deep fat fryer and fry in deep fat at 350° for 3 to 5 minutes, depending on size of tails. Drain on paper towels. Dip in favorite sauce, or use Tahitian Lobster Sauce given below:

Tahitian Lobster Sauce

1 cup mayonnaise	½ teaspoon grated onion
½ cup sour cream	¼ teaspoon dijon mustard
¼ cup chopped parsley	¼ teaspoon chopped tarragon
1 tablespoon lemon juice	1 clove garlic, crushed
1 teaspoon anchovy paste	

Mix all ingredients together well. Makes about 1½ cups sauce.

LOBSTER THERMIDOR
(Serves 6 and utilizes shells)

You Will Need

6 lobster tails (size depends on your catch and your eating habits!)

¾ cup butter	¼ teaspoon pepper
⅓ cup dry sherry	⅛ teaspoon nutmeg
⅓ cup dry white wine	Grated parmesan cheese
⅓ cup flour	3 fresh mushrooms, sliced (or 2 oz. can)
1½ cups milk	1 tablespoon salad oil or melted butter
½ teaspoon salt	

With scissors cut along each side of the membrane on the underside of the shell and remove the tail meat. Cut into bite-sized chunks. Remove moisture from shells with paper towel.

Melt ½ cup butter in large skillet and dip shells in this. Heat a moment, turning to coat all over—this gives a shiny luster to the shells. Arrange tails in a shallow baking pan, spreading out the tail fan. Add lobster meat to the butter in the skillet and sauté lightly, stirring slightly as it cooks. Add the wines and continue to cook until it is cooked down slightly. Set aside.

In another pan, melt the remaining ¼ cup butter and blend in flour to make a "roux" (refer to chapter 8, under "Sauces"). Blend in milk, salt, pepper, and nutmeg, stirring and cooking mixture until thickened. Pour the sauce over the lobster and wine mixture and mix lightly. Spoon into shells and sprinkle with the parmesan cheese. Dip sliced mushrooms in oil or butter and arrange 2 or 3 slices on top of each serving. Bake in moderate (350°) oven for 10 minutes or until heated through.

EAST INDIAN LOBSTER
(for curry lovers!)

You Will Need

½ cup seedless raisins	1 egg yolk
½ teaspoon curry powder	½ cup Half 'n Half (milk/cream)
¼ teaspoon paprika	1 tablespoon sherry
2 tablespoons butter	1 tablespoon chopped pimiento
1 tablespoon flour	1½ cups cooked lobster meat
½ teaspoon seasoned salt	4 baked patty shells
½ cup chicken broth	

Mix and beat together egg yolk and Half 'n Half. Cook raisins, curry powder, and paprika in butter a few minutes. Blend in flour and salt, slowly blending in broth. Cook, stirring until sauces begins to thicken. Stir egg yolk and half-and-half mixture into sauce and cook a few minutes longer. Blend in wine, pimiento, and lobster meat.

Spoon mixture into patty shells. Nice to serve these with sliced green onions, shredded coconut, and crumbled, crisp bacon.

SOUTHERN DELIGHT
(Serves 4)

You Will Need

1 pound lobster meat	½ teaspoon paprika
4 tablespoons butter	Cayenne pepper

2 tablespoon flour	1 cup cooked peas
1 cup cream	½ cup sherry wine
½ teaspoon salt	2 beaten egg yolks

Cut lobster meat into 1-inch chunks. Melt butter in blazer pan of chafing dish and blend in flour, salt, paprika, and cayenne. Add cream gradually, then cook and stir until sauce thickens. Fold in peas and lobster meat and cook five minutes. Mix egg yolks with sherry, remove pan from flame, and stir in sherry-egg mixture. Serve at once on hot buttered toast points.

NEW ENGLAND STUFFED SHIRT

One lobster serves two people. Use either clawed or spiny lobster. Do not precook.

Place lobster on its back and cut it in half lengthwise. If you prefer to kill it first, sever the spinal cord where the tail meets the body shell. Remove the intestinal vein down the back of the tail and the stomach sac behind the eyes and discard. Also discard the spongy gills. Save the liver (tomally) and the roe (coral) and meat from the thorax cavity for the stuffing. If you are using the clawed lobster, crack the claws.

You Will Need

4 live lobsters, 2 lbs each	1 tablespoon crushed thyme
1 large onion	½ cube butter, melted
1 clove garlic	Freshly ground salt & pepper
4 cups fine breadcrumbs	½ cup dry sherry wine
Capers	

Grind onion and garlic and mix with bread crumbs, liver, coral, and one-half the melted butter. Moisten while mixing with a little sherry. Add salt and pepper to taste. Heat lobsters in broiler 5 minutes, remove and stuff the thorax cavity with the mixture. Place capers in tip of shell at head. Place lobsters on rack, tucking the tail ends under the wire to keep them from curling. Bake at 350° in oven for about 30 minutes, then drip the rest of the melted butter over the stuffed section and serve with more melted butter.

LOBSTER CURRY

You Will Need
2 cups lobster meat
1 tablespoon butter
1 tart apple, peeled and grated
1 teaspoon to 1 tablespoon curry powder (to taste)

1 minced onion
1 tablespoon cornstarch (or more, if needed)
1 cup cream
   Boiled,white rice

Sprinkle grated apple with lemon juice and set aside. Melt butter in blazer pan. Add onion and grated apple and cook until apple is soft and onion is transparent. Add enough curry powder to suit your taste. Mix a little cream with the cornstarch to make a liquid and add, then add remaining cream. Stir until smooth and well cooked. Add lobster meat and heat thoroughly. Serve over cooked rice, either in a community dish or as individual servings.

LOBSTER AUSTRALIAN
(Serves 4 and utilizes lobster shell)

You Will Need
2 lobsters, medium size
1 cup Half 'n Half
1 cup fish stock (refer to sauces)

¼ pound fresh mushrooms
Cayenne pepper
Mashed potatoes
Lemon juice
Grated cheddar cheese

Boil lobsters. Remove legs and split lobster from head to tail. Remove tail and thorax meat. Slice the meat. Make a thick sauce of 50% Half 'n Half and 50% fish stock, heating the two liquids and thickening with the flour or cornstarch made into a liquid with a little water. Add a touch of wine.

Spoon about 1 tablespoon of the sauce into the lobster shell and sprinkle with chopped mushrooms. Add a little lobster meat over the sauce, then more mushrooms and a dab of lemon juice and cayenne pepper to bring out the mushroom flavor. Now add some more sauce. Pipe each serving around the edges with mashed potatoes forced through a pastry tube. Sprinkle lightly with grated cheddar cheese and broil until browned and hot.

LOBSTER BISQUE

You Will Need
1 lobster, about 5 ounces, minced
   Butter
1 tablespoon flour
½ cup heavy cream

½ cup light cream
¼ teaspoon salt
Dash cayenne pepper
Paprika
Dash of sherry (if desired)

Brown minced lobster in butter over moderate heat for about 3 minutes, stirring constantly.

Stir in 1 tablespoon flour and add both the creams, ¼ teaspoon salt,

and cayenne pepper. Cook, stirring constantly until soup is slightly
thickened and very hot. Divide into bouillon cups and sprinkle with
paprika. Add a dash of sherry if desired.

"MAYHEW'S MARVELOUS MIXTURE"
LOBSTER-CRAB BISQUE

Robert Cahill, representative for the state of Massachusetts, veteran
diver, and published author, says "A friend of mine, State Representative Gregory Mayhew of Martha's Vineyard Island, Massachusetts, gave
this recipe to me. His ancestor was the first white man to own and settle
the Vineyard, Nantucket, and the Elizabeth Islands; and the recipe, with
a few revisions to facilitate its preparation, has been handed down for
generations." We can testify from first-hand experience that this bisque
is easy to prepare and absolutely unsurpassed on a cold, stormy night
around the fire. It's delicious and will give you a little glow too!

You Will Need

1 can green pea soup	2 cans evaporated milk
1 lobster, cut into bite-sized chunks	1 can tomato soup
1 can crab meat	1 small bottle dry sherry wine

Mix all together and heat just to boiling point but do not boil. Serves
from 6 to 10 people.

DICK ANDERSON'S "FAVORITE RESIPEE"

(Bull Lobster Legs—we think)

Dick Anderson is Will Rogers, Bob Hope, and Mack Sennett all
poured into one wet suit. He's the diving world's answer to Stanley
Livingston, Albert Schweitzer, and "Seldom Seen Slim" (the latter of
whom he most resembles). A wreck diver and gold diver, among other
things, Dick is most well known throughout the entire world of diving
for his side-splitting diving films and magazine articles. Below is his
"Favorite Resipee" (for lobster?) as he gave it to us: (Dick hastens to
admit that his spelling is "simply abdominal").

In my long association with the sea I've eaten almost everything but a
mermaid. One time when I was stranded on California's San Miguel
Island for ten days I even resorted to sea urchin roe and boiled abalone.
The resipee for sea urchin roe is simple enough. You get a sea urchin and
crack it open and eat the yellowish, seedy looking roe. It tastes kind of
sweet and salty and is considered by some to be a delicacy. In small doses it
probably is but as daily sustenance it is a genuine bummer. Too much of a
good thing, as they say.
Strips of abalone boiled in a tin can over a driftwood fire sounds romantic

but as daily sustenance it falls even below urchin roe. The consistancy is that of silicone-rubber and after a few days of this diet one could easily choose starvation as the desired alternative. However, one need not live by boiled abalone alone. And, before we get into the real resipee, you should know something about various resipees for stranded divers. Like all islands, San Miguel has seagulls. If you ever tried to catch a seagull you know that it's impossible. However, hunger has a way of breaching the unbreachable breach. With seagulls it's best to breach the unbreachable breach on the beach.

Seagulls are the scavengers of the sea and they will go after anything that is remotely edible. A handful of limpets or a few cracked urchins or abalone guts or any food scraps will attract them like ants to a picnic.

To catch one, all it takes is a length of monofilament fishing line or any fishing line. Monofilament line is universal and it can be found wherever folks fish. It is often mixed up on bundles of kelp that float up on the beach. Such was the case at San Miguel.

To catch the gull, you simply make a big slip-knot and place it on the sand with the bait. When the gulls collect to munch the morsels or mussels you simply yank on the line and PRESTO, you have a gull by the leg. The gull does not take kindly to this and takes off. The effect is like flying a kite with a mind of its own. You don't even need a good breeze. This sounds kind of cruel but since you're going to eat the fowl critter anyway the action is utilitarian and not intended for sport.

As you pull in the gull you'll find that he has a mouth big enough to swallow a grapefruit and he will try to eat you before you eat him. If he gets you by the eyeball it could ruin your entire meal. I'm kind of opposed to killing but if you have to eat a seagull it is probably most humane to kill it first. Just lop off his head like the Christmas goose.

A seagull is easier to clean than a rattlesnake. The skin and feathers just peel right off like unwrapping a package of meat. The guts fall out in an individual wrapper. What's left is all dark meat. Poke a stick through the bird and hold it over the hot coals of a fire. The length of time required for cooking depends upon how hungry you are. When the bird is done you simply rip off a piece and start chewing. It tastes sort of like scorched seagull. But it's better than boiled abalone.

So is fox. On San Miguel I caught one stealing one of my seagulls. Hunger drives men mad and I've got to confess that in a moment of hungry panic, anger, and desperation, I once dispatched a pilfering fox with a crude bow and arrow at shamefully close range. I won't go into the resipee for fox because it's the same as the resipee for cat or dog.

Now we come to the real resipee. Actually it's more of a disclosure than a resipee, but to be really honest, the only thing I can cook is fried potatoes and since this is a seafood book that suggestion was turned down.

Of all the delicacies from the sea, the legs of the California bull lobster is the best. This will be a great affront to those hearty New Englanders who shout the praises of their lobsters and refer to California lobsters as crawdads. I hate to go against science and zoology and Frank Scali but take a California lobster and a Maine lobster and put them side by side and decide for yourself which one looks like a crawdad.

Here comes the resipee. First, catch a bull lobster. It may seem a bit of a contradiction but even big lady lobsters are called bull lobsters. Just like some women are called bulls. For the record a bull lobster is one that weighs ten pounds or over.

Anyway, after you boil the lobster, rip off the legs, crack the shell, and remove the meat. (Don't ignore the meat in the joints at the base of the antennae. It has a slightly different taste and texture but is equally delicious.) Cut the meat into chunks about an inch long and stab each one with a toothpick. Dip the chunks into melted butter and you will experience the thrill of devouring the ultimate delicacy of the sea.

I got this resipee or procedure from Al and Norma Hanson, the famous hard-hat diving couple from Catalina. They call it "Lobster Bon-Bons" and they have shared the treat with visiting dignitaries from around the world. I'll tell you one thing, it's a hell of a lot better than fox.

BAKED NEW ENGLAND LOBSTER "O'CRONIN"

From John Cronin, President of U.S. Divers Co.

John Cronin is one who deeply appreciates all the finer things of life and this trait in him is especially emphasized by his reputation as a gourmet. When it comes to *Lobster O'Cronin,* John says "No 'crawdad' substitute for 'real lobster' should be used!":

Take a three- to four-pound New England lobster, live, and rinse the lobster thoroughly.

Turn the lobster on its back with the top of the shell on a hard board. Grasp the two claws in the left hand, pulling them together. With a very sharp knife, insert the knife into the center of the under part of the lobster's head. *Do not let the knife go all the way through to the top shell.*

Now very carefully (it will require quite a bit of force) split the bottom half of the shell that is facing you all the way from the head to the tail — again being careful not to cut through the top shell which is on the board. With your left hand, reach into the lobster's head and on the right side (as you look down) you'll feel a medium-sized sac. Very carefully pull out the sac. It is attached to the intestinal tract, and you should continue to lift this out all the way down to the tail. When this is removed, discard it and wash the lobster very briefly.

In the inside you will note a light green "tomally." This should be removed and set aside in a pan. Discard the rest of the entrails. The lobster is now ready for stuffing.

Recipe For Dressing

Take the tomally and mix it with an equal part of well crushed Ritz crackers, ½ cup freshly grated Parmesan cheese, 3 bunches of finely minced parsley, 1 or 2 finely minced chives (if desired), a little bit of salt, and some freshly ground peppers.

Mix this with 1 stick of butter. Put in a pan and heat the butter and mix with the dressing.

Devein eight green (uncooked) shrimp for each lobster shell. Take some of the dressing and, while the lobster is still on its back, put a layer of the stuffing all through the lobster, completely filling the upper half of the shell. Now place the eight shrimp along the lower half of the stomach, one below the other in line. Cover the shrimp with the balance of the stuffing. The lobsters are now ready for cooking.

Using a pan or the grates from the stove, tie the lobster at the claws and tail to prevent curling while cooking. Preheat the oven to 375°. Bake the lobster from 50 to 55 minutes until it's red. Take out and serve — with drawn butter only.

Crabs

Crabs are clawed crustaceans that, except for the horseshoe crab, are closely related to lobsters. The horseshoe crab is in the same class as the sea spider (Archnoidea.) All true crabs (Brachyura) have eight legs, two claws, movable eye stalks, a carapace (shell) of various shapes and colors, and a reduced abdomen that is folded under the thorax. The three major kinds of crabs taken from North American waters are the blue crab from Atlantic and Gulf coasts; cancer crabs, which include the edible or dungeness crab (*Cancer magister*) from the Pacific coast and rock crabs from both coasts; and the king crab from Alaska. There are, of course, many other edible species of local and international importance.

The important consideration in crab grabbing is not so much the type of crab as the size. Large crabs with big, heavy legs and claws provide the most meat. Crabs with thin, short legs and small claws usually render so little meat that they are hardly worth the effort. There is no point in grabbing a crab that is built like a pile of sticks and expect to get a meal from him. Some species of crabs, however, are so small (as the pea crab) that the whole crab is edible without any cleaning, but it takes several handfuls to make one good meal. Pea crabs, for instance, can be fried whole and made into a sandwich.

Horseshoe Crabs

The large mass of green, unlaid eggs of the horseshoe crab, sometimes

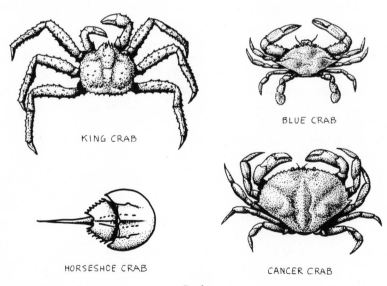

KING CRAB

BLUE CRAB

HORSESHOE CRAB

CANCER CRAB

Crabs.

Rock Crab—California. COURTESY ROBERT B. EVANS.

called the king crab (not to be confused with the Alaskan king crab),
are highly esteemed by Asiatic peoples and are eaten over a widespread
area in those places.

*   Three Asiatic horseshoe crabs have caused human poisoning from eating the unlaid green eggs, flesh, or viscera during the reproductive season
of the year. The mortality rate is high. Death usually occurs within six-
teen hours. Species involved include some from India to Vietnam
(*Tachypleus gigas*), India to the Philippines (*Carcinoscorpius rotundi-
cauda*), and Japan to Vietnam (*Tachypleus tridentatus*). The species
from Maine to Yucatan (*Limulus polyphemus*) has not been involved,
probably because easterners of the United States do not consider the
horseshoe crab palatable.

*   The coconut crab has been found toxic at times on Palau east of the
Philippines and some islands south of Japan. Several other crabs have
been involved in human intoxications on the islands of Rykukyu and
Amami south of Japan.

Crab Meat

A four-pound crab yields about two cups, or one pound, of meat,
depending somewhat on the species of crab. The smaller the crab, the
less meat you get in proportion to its size. A two-pound dungeness yields

about ¾ pound meat. Crabs are boiled in the same manner as lobsters —that is, live.

Use of Crab Meat

Crab meat can be used in salads, seafood cocktails, in creamed crab dishes, or mixed with egg, minced onion, and cracker crumbs to make into balls or patties for fried crab cakes.

Considering its exvellent flavor, crab meat lends itself to your own recipe inventions with little chance for failure. Some hints, however, may aid you in devising your own concoctions:

1. Crab meat is very good with cheddar or jack cheese.
2. Nuts of any kind are very chummy with crab meat and crushed nuts can be added to deviled crab, sprinkled on crab salads, or used as a coating for fried softshells.
3. Since crab must be cooked once to remove the meat from the shell, it is wise to be wary of overcooking the meat in the final recipe. Put meat in last and cook just long enough to heat through.
4. A four-pound crab yields about two cups of meat, depending somewhat on the species of crab. (The smaller the crab the less meat you get in proportion.)
5. Dampening your hands will prevent crab cakes or patties mixtures from sticking to them during the shaping process.

The female crab (left), whose meat is considered richer by some, can be distinguished from the male crab by her much wider tail. Drop crabs into boiling water, cover, and boil twenty minutes.

Separate by lifting shell from body, then remove entrails.

Break legs from body, remove the gills, and break body in half.

Use a pick or knife to remove meat from the body. Crack legs and claws with a mallet and remove meat. Crab "butter" is found in the shell of some crabs. The bowl on the left has crab meat from the body, the center bowl contains the leg meat, and the bowl on the right contains the crab roe.

BOILED CRAB DINNER

(Serves 6)

You Will Need
24 live, hard shelled crabs
6 quarts boiling, salted water or seawater
A beach, patio (or big kitchen!)

Make this a very informal dinner. Guests will make a fun mess, so make it easy on yourself! Have the big pot of water boiling when the crabs are brought in live, washed, and ready for cooking. Drop the crabs into the pot, cover, and let the water return to a boil, then simmer for 15 minutes. Drain and serve heaped on a large platter. Supply each guest with a large bib, nutcracker, and nut picks. Offer Scrumptedelicious Sauce (refer to Lobster recipes) for dipping, or plain melted butter. Corn on the cob, french fries, baked potatoes, and a good green salad are all great accompaniments.

Special Note: Sus Yasada, of the famous Meiji's Market in Gardena, California taught us a special way of eating boiled crab. Instead of cracking a boiled crab, cut it crosswise in several places along the body and at intervals along the legs. After cutting, put the crab back together on the guest's plate; a presentable dish that affords easy removal of crab meat. May not be as romantic as wrestling with an uncut crab, but is a lot less trouble for the guest and leaves no huge chunks of shell to be disposed of later.

BOILED, SPICED BLUE CRAB

Cook and serve as for boiled crab dinner, except that you add vinegar and spices to the water. To the boiling water add 1 quart vinegar, 3 tablespoons cayenne pepper, ¼ cup celery salt, ¼ cup dry mustard, ¼ cup cloves, 2 tablespoons ginger, and 2 tablespoons mace. Simmer water for 5 minutes; add crabs and simmer another 15 minutes. Serve hot or cold.

Note: The above spices can be substituted with a large box of crab and shrimp boil spice. This can be purchased at major markets, usually in the spices section or gourmet section. If you're on the beach, throw in a small sprig of each variety of seaweed found there. Adds a good sea flavor to the dish.

BOILED DUNGENESS CRABS

(Serves 6)

You Will Need
3 live dungeness crabs
8 quarts salted, boiling water or seawater

Large crabs should be dressed before boiling. Dress by inserting knife under rear of top shell and prying it off. Remove spongy parts and wash body cavity. Leave legs and claws attached. Place in boiling water, cover, and let return to boiling. Simmer 15 minutes and drain. Crack claws and legs. Serve hot with butter or chill and serve with mayonnaise.

BROILED KING CRAB LEGS

If you're lucky enough to come up with a king crab or another species of very large crab, remove the legs and slit the backs of them. Spread the shell apart to expose the meat. Spread the meat with lots of dairy butter and place the legs on a preheated broiler about 6 inches from the heat source. Broil 10 minutes or until meat is thoroughly heated. Again, Scrumptedelicious Sauce (lobster recipes) is a fantastic substitute for plain butter in this recipe.

CRAB CAKES

4 cups crab meat, chopped
1 egg
¼ cup minced fresh onion
Cracker crumbs (finely crumbled)

Mix together first three ingredients and form into patties. Chill patties, then roll in fine cracker crumbs. Fry for 3 minutes at moderate temperature. Serve plain or with a favorite sauce. *Note*: These can also be formed into 1½-inch balls and deep-fat fried at 375° until golden.

CRABURGERS

You Will Need

1 cup flaked crab meat
¼ cup finely diced celery
1 teaspoon prepared mustard
Salt and pepper to taste
3 tablespoons mayonnaise

6 onion hamburger buns
(unless plain preferred)
6 slices cheddar cheese

Heat broiler and mix first five ingredients. Split buns and place on a cookie sheet, cut sides up. Spread bottom half of buns with crab mixture and place a slice of cheese on the top halves. Place all bun halves under broiler and broil until cheese bubbles. Turn top (cheese-covered) halves over and onto bottom halves, or serve the two halves open on the guests' plates.

CRAB-STUFFED BELL PEPPERS

(Serves 4)

You Will Need

4 green (bell) peppers
1 medium onion, minced
½ cup chopped celery
2 slices bacon, diced
1 cup bread crumbs or cubes

3 tablespoons butter
1 cup cooked crab meat
2 eggs, slightly beaten
Salt and pepper to taste

Heat oven to 375°. Slice top off peppers and clean out sponge (center portion and seeds). Parboil peppers 5 minutes in salted water. While peppers boil, sauté onion, celery, bacon, and bread crumbs or cubes in butter until the onion is transparent. Mix crab meat with eggs, then with onion mixture, salt, and pepper. Remove peppers from water and drain. Set upright in baking pan and fill with crab mixture. Bake 20 minutes. Neptune never had it so good.

CRAB CURRY

(Serves 6)

You Will Need

1 pound cooked crab   1 teaspoon lemon juice
3 tablespoons butter   Cooked rice for 6
3 tablespoons flour
1 teaspoon salt
½ cup coconut powder (bought in cans)
1 medium onion, chopped
1 tablespoon curry powder
¼ teaspoon ginger
3 cups milk
½ teaspoon grated lemon rind

Melt butter and sauté chopped onion until transparent. Add flour, curry powder, and seasonings, stirring constantly until the mixture is smooth. Gradually add milk to coconut powder in top of double boiler. Add onion mixture and cook until thick. Add lemon rind and lemon juice, then add crab meat. Continue cooking until crab meat is hot. Serve over hot rice.

BAKED CRAB IMPERIAL

The state of Maryland claims this one as its own and it's really the "queen" of crab dishes. Though the famous Chesapeake blue crab is used in Maryland for this recipe, we have found it to be just as effective made with any kind of crab meat.

You Will Need

1 pound crab meat (approximately)
2 tablespoons chopped onion
2 tablespoons chopped green (bell) pepper
2 tablespoons flour
½ cup milk
Salt and pepper to taste
¼ teaspoon Worcestershire sauce
2 chopped, hard cooked eggs

Sauté the onion and green pepper in butter until tender. Blend in the flour, then add the milk gradually and cook until thick, stirring constantly. Add salt and pepper to taste and the crab meat. Bake in 6 well-greased crab shells, clam or scallop shells, or use large individual baking cups. Bake 20 minutes at 350° until brown. These may also be baked, then placed into baked pastry shells as convenient, edible containers.

CRAB AND SHRIMP GUMBO

From "Chilly" Childers

This delicious recipe was given to us by Houston ("Chilly") Childers of Underwater Mechanics International, Houston, Texas. It takes a little work but is so good that Chilly advises you to double the recipe and freeze the unused portion for later. In following his suggestion of doubling the recipe, we *still* finished off the whole lot over a Saturday and Sunday—it's that good.

You Will Need

2 lbs. shrimp peeled and deveined
½ pound crab meat
4 slices bacon
2 tablespoons flour
1 pound onions, finely chopped
¾ cup finely chopped celery
¾ cup diced smoked ham
½ cup finely chopped bell pepper
½ teaspoon grated lemon rind (from fresh lemon)
1 pod garlic, finely chopped
3 to 6 dashes each Worcestershire & Tabasco sauce
Pinch of thyme
1 bay leaf
Salt and pepper to taste
3 cups water
1 pound fresh okra, or one 10-ounce package frozen okra
2 tablespoons bacon fat
¼ cup chopped parsley
¼ cup sliced green onion tops

Drain shrimp on paper towel (thaw if frozen). Remove all shell or cartilage left in the crab meat. Cook bacon in a large sauce pan or kettle, then drain on paper towel. Add ham to bacon fat in pan and cook until brown. Remove ham. Add flour to fat and cook over low heat, stirring constantly to make a scorchy-tasting brown roux. Gradually add onions until well browned and reduced to a pulp, then add celery, bell pepper, and grated lemon rind. Trim white membrane from half a lemon, chop lemon and add to onion mixture. Add garlic, Worcestershire sauce, Tabasco sauce, thyme, bay leaf, salt, pepper, and water. Crumble bacon and add ham. Cook slowly about 45 minutes, meanwhile cleaning and trimming okra if fresh okra is being used. Slice okra and cook in bacon fat, stirring to prevent scorching, until okra is no longer ropey. After sauce mixture has cooked about 45 minutes, add okra to vegetable mixture and continue cooking for 20 minutes. Add shrimp and crab meat.

Bring mixture to a boil and cook for 5 minutes or just long enough to cook shrimp. Add chopped parsley and green onion tops.

Serve with cooked rice in soup plates. Makes 8 servings. As Chilly suggests, this is delicious sprinkled with croutons and served with plenty of French bread.

CRAB-STUFFED ZUCCHINI (OR EGGPLANT)

You Will Need

6 zucchini squash, or 1 eggplant
  Butter for sautéing
1 green (bell) pepper, diced
1 medium onion, diced
½ pound fresh mushrooms, cut up
1 stalk celery, diced
  Chablis wine
1 cup crab meat

For Sauce:
Sour cream (dairy)
Reserved vegetable liquor
Fresh scallops (optional)

Cut zucchini squash or eggplant in half lengthwise. Scoop out center portion and save. In frying pan place butter and heat. In this sauté the green pepper, onion, mushrooms, celery, and center portion of zucchini or eggplant. When onion is tender, pour over a little water and some chablis wine, then simmer 10 minutes—don't let it go dry; add more liquid, preferably chablis, to keep liquid at about 1 cup. While vegetables cook, place halves of squash or eggplant in oven at 350° with a dot of butter in the center of each half. Bake 15 minutes for small zucchini or ½ hour for larger eggplant.

Drain the vegetable in frying pan and reserve the liquor for the sauce. Cut up the crab meat and mix with the vegetables. Fill the cavities of the squash or eggplant with the mixture. Place back in oven and bake 20 minutes, or until squash is tender.

    Sauce: Mix into the reserved vegetable liquor enough sour cream to make it gravy-thick. Heat and stir to smooth. Add a little more chablis if you wish, but don't get the sauce too thin. If you have the fresh, raw scallops on hand, cut them into ½-inch pieces and add to the sauce; as many as you wish.

Remove zucchini from the oven and pour the sauce over each half, distributing the scallops as evenly as possible. Serve good and hot.

Crab Salads

CRAB LOUIS

(Serves 4)

Cook 4 eggs hard-boiled. Cut 4 small fresh tomatoes into wedges.

Use 1 pound crab meat (preferably king crab). Arrange crab meat, some ripe olives, the hard-cocked eggs cut into wedges, some lemon wedges, and the tomato wedges on lettuce placed on four salad plates. Serve with dressing given below:

Crab Louis Dressing

Combine together: ½-cup chile sauce, 1 cup mayonnaise, 2 teaspoons horseradish, ¼ cup sweet pickle relish, 2 tablespoons chopped green onion, 2 tablespoons lemon juice, and salt and pepper to taste. Chill. Serve with, or pour over, Crab Louis Salad. Sprinkle with chopped or crushed nuts if desired.

CHILI CRAB SALAD

You Will Need
- 1 cup combined chile sauce, sour cream, and mayonnaise (equal portions)
- 1¼ teaspoon dijon mustard
- ½ teaspoon lemon juice
- 4 teaspoons chopped capers
- 1 pound crab meat
- ½ cup sliced celery
- ¼ cup sliced green onion
- 3 cups finely shredded cabbage
- 2 hard cooked eggs, sliced.

Combine the chile sauce-sour cream-mayonnaise mixture with the horseradish, mustard, lemon juice, and capers. Place in dressing bowl and chill. Mix together the crab meat, celery, and green onion slices. Arrange the cabbage on four salad plates and pile crab mixture on top. Garnish with the egg slices. Pass the dressing to guests. Serves 4.

CRAB COCKTAIL

Made with *Seafood Cocktail Sauce Supreme*, which follows:

2 tablespoons wine vinegar
1 teaspoon dry mustard
2 egg yolks
1 teaspoon minced celery
1 tablespoon horseradish
3 teaspoons chopped-chives
3 teaspoons chopped parsley
1½ tablespoons chopped green onions
Salt and pepper to taste
½ teaspoon crushed tarragon
3 tablespoons olive oil
4 tablespoons cognac
2 tablespoons chili sauce
Juice of ½ lemon

Beat first 10 ingredients until smooth. Beat in the olive oil and mix well. Add the cognac and chili sauce. Mix thoroughly, then add the lemon juice and blend well. Chill and mix with crab meat, lobster, or fish flakes for cocktail. (Note: California sheep-head fish makes a de-lightful substitute for crab!)

Soft-shelled Crabs

Soft-shelled crabs are those that have been caught just after shedding their shells while molting. These are considered a real delicacy, and while a sport diver can't always plan on coming across them, any that he does find should be treated with the greatest respect, for they are delicious fried in butter and made into a sandwich, sans the trouble of getting the meat out of the shell! The only cleaning necessary before cooking soft-shelled crabs is to slice off the tip of the head to remove the eyes, then cut out the stomach—a soft pouch just behind the eyes and a little below them. Cut along the carapace on each side, fold back the top skin and remove the spongy "devils fingers" under the back. Fry in butter and place whole crab on buttered bread, letting the legs "all hang out" if the crab doesn't quite fit the bread. Place lettuce on top, another slice of buttered bread, and enjoy! (Use any spread you like with this.)

Soft shells are also coated with a mixture of egg and Worcestershire sauce, then rolled in fine cracker crumbs and fried (or deep fat fried) until golden and served for "fork" eating pleasure.

Shrimp and Crayfish

Crayfish tails (from fresh water) make excellent substitutes for shrimp in any shrimp recipe. Either shrimp or crayfish can be boiled, cleaned, and used for shellfish cocktails or cleaned raw by removing the meat and sand tract, then used in fondues, deep-fat fried, or pan fried in butter. Crayfish tails may also be substituted for shrimp in the popular scampi dishes. (For marine "crayfish" refer to Spiny Lobster.)

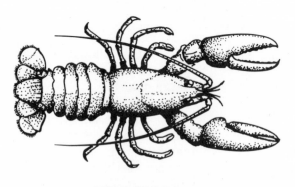

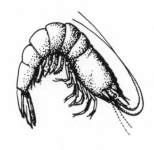

SHRIMP

CRAYFISH

Shrimp and crayfish.

Shrimp

Shrimp are found from salty estuaries to almost fresh water. They migrate to the sea for the winter, the males being the first to move on. They live on sandy bottoms in shallow seas, and by day the common shrimp buries himself in sand or mud. After dark, shrimp come out into the open.

Crayfish (Crawfish, Crawdad)

Various species of crayfish are found all over the world in lakes, rivers, creeks, and fresh-water ponds, and some of the tastiest are found in the western United States. Most of the time they are found in quiet waters between one and ten feet deep and can be caught by hand (if you're quick enough!—grab from the rear, just behind the claws), with bait such as bacon or liver on the end of a line (as with crabbing), or with a net. Warm months are best for crayfish grabbing.

BOILED SHRIMP OR CRAYFISH

Boiling is the basic method of cooking shrimp or crayfish for serving cold. Peeled and deveined shrimp should be cooked in just enough boiling, salted water to cover them: about 1 quart of water and 2 teaspoons of salt per pound. Place shrimp in boiling water, cover, and return to boiling point. Remove from heat and let stand 2 to 5 minutes, depending on size of shrimp. Drain and chill. They cook quickly and will shrink if overcooked.

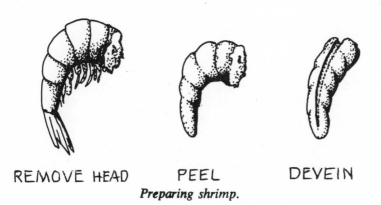

REMOVE HEAD   PEEL   DEVEIN

Preparing shrimp.

CRAYFISH COOKOUT

It takes from one to two dozen crayfish to feed one hungry crayfish hunter (it takes time to extract each tiny morsel of meat). About a dozen crayfish yield ¼ pound of crayfish tails.

After gathering your crayfish, fill a large kettle (about 2 gallons worth) with water and add a pint of white wine. Bring this to a boil and add sliced onions, 3 or 4 sliced or chunked carrots, some parsley sprigs, a dozen peppercorns, a couple of bay leaves, a little salt, and a sliced lemon. Simmer 15 minutes. Meanwhile wash the crayfish well and, if desired, remove the sand vein by cracking the shell at the thorax and tail joining and gently pulling out the dark vein along the under side of the tail. Now drop the crayfish into the boiling mixture, return it to a full boil and cook 5 minutes. They should be bright red. Eat 'em like a lobster—it's more tedious, but worth the effort, especially if you've helped track down the little critters. Serve with plenty of French bread, a green salad, and corn on the cob if you wish.

SHRIMP CREOLE

This specialty is borrowed from New Orleans and is nicely flavored with rosé or white wine, chicken broth, and traditional tomatoes.

Though Shrimp Creole is not a budget item, copy the Chinese and stretch it out with rice!

You Will Need

⅓ cup-celery	1 cup rosé or dry white wine
⅓ cup chopped onion	2 10½-ounce cans chicken broth
⅓ cup chopped green pepper	1 can (1 pound) tomatoes
1 clove garlic, minced	Few drops bottled hot-pepper
1½ cups long grain rice	sauce
1 teaspoon salt	¾ cup parmesan cheese
	3 to 4 cups cleaned, cooked
	shrimp

Cook celery, onion, green pepper, and garlic in butter till onion is tender. Stir in rice; sauté about 5 minutes, stirring occasionally. Add salt, wine, broth, tomatoes, and pepper sauce; stir to blend.

Cover and simmer till rice is tender and has absorbed most of the liquid: 20 to 25 minutes, stirring now and then. When rice is tender, stir in cheese and shrimp; heat about 5 minutes or till hot through. Makes 6 to 8 servings.

SCAMPI

One of the more romantic chafing dish recipes, scampi should be served by candlelight with antipasto, plenty of Italian bread, a tossed green salad, and your favorite wine. This recipe will serve a cozy party of four.

> *You Will Need*
>   2 pounds jumbo shrimp
>   3 cloves garlic, mashed and separated into bits
>   ¼ cup finely chopped parsley
>   ⅓ cup olive oil
>   Salt and freshly ground pepper to taste

Shell and devein shrimp. In the blazer pan of your chafing dish heat about ¼ inch olive oil—be sure it's good and hot. Sauté the shrimp in this for 8 minutes, turning to cook evenly. Add salt and pepper, stir slightly, then place shrimp on heated platter. Add the garlic and parsley to the blazer pan and sauté for about a minute and a half. Pour over shrimp and serve everything very hot.

SHRIMP N' EGG LATE-NIGHT SNACK FOR TWO

(For Curry Fans)

Best to have the shrimp all cleaned before the "late night" arrives as cleaning ½ pound shrimp will take about 20 minutes to a half-hour.

You Will Need

1 green pepper, diced	½ pound deveined shrimp
½ large onion, diced	4 eggs
1 teaspoon tarragon leaves	1 teaspoon curry powder

Brown and sauté onion and green pepper until transparent. Add tarragon and shrimp. Sauté until shrimp takes on a pinkish color on the outside, turning once. Beat eggs with salt and pepper to taste and curry powder. Pour eggs into pan with vegetables and shrimp and scramble to desired doneness. Serves two.

SHRIMP 'N SOUR CREAM

> *You Will Need*
>   1 pound shelled green shrimp
>   ½ cup butter
>   ½ pound fresh mushrooms
>   1½ cups dairy sour cream
>   3 teaspoons teriyaki sauce
>   ⅓ cup parmesan or Monterey Jack cheese, grated

Sauté the shrimp in butter 1 minute. Slice mushrooms and add. Continue to sauté until mushrooms are soft—about 5 minutes. Combine the sour cream and teriyaki sauce, then heat but do not boil. Add salt and fresh ground pepper to taste and some crushed tarragon if you wish. Stir this mixture into the shrimp. Place the mixture into six baking shells (scallop, clam, mussel) or individual casseroles, well greased. Sprinkle with cheese and broil until cheese is barely melted. Serves six.

SHRIMP COCKTAIL SAUCE

Combine:
  ¾ cup chili sauce
  4 tablespoons lemon juice
  2 tablespoons prepared horseradish
  2 teaspoons Worcestershire sauce
  1 tablespoon finely minced onion
  1 teaspoon tarragon or thyme
    A few drops bottled hot pepper sauce
    Salt and pepper to taste
Mix the ingredients well and chill, covered. Pour over or serve with shrimp, crab, sheephead, or lobster bits in cocktail dishes.

SHRIMP IN BUTTERED SHERRY

From Doris and Paul J. Tzimoulis,
Publisher of Skin Diver Magazine
Devein shrimp but leave shells on.

Steam the shrimp, adding green onions/scallions, tarragon, dill, garlic, and parsley.

Melt lots 'n lots of margarine or butter, then add generous amount of dry sherry, white wine, and a little water; enough to make a dip. Add some garlic. Strain the liquid used to cook the shrimp and add the ingredients to the above mixture. Add lots of lemon—to taste.

Guests peel and dip shrimp. This can be used as an entree, as appetizers, or hors d'oeuvres, but Doris and Paul Tzimoulis usually use it as the main course. The left over sauce may be frozen to use later for another shrimp dip or to pour over broiled fish, but it's so good you probably won't have any left to freeze!

Barnacles

Many species of barnacles are edible. A huge species of acorn barnacle(*Balanus nubilus*) on the West Coast of the United States grows to five inches high and may weigh three pounds or more when mature. These are steamed in the shell and eaten with cocktail sauce as hors d'oeuvres. The French consider the acorn barnacle the most delicate in taste. They eat this one either raw or prepare it like crab, the flavor of

GOOSE BARNACLES

ACORN BARNACLES

THATCHED BARNACLES

Barnacles.

which it resembles closely. The acorn barnacle is an extremely common animal of the tidal zones of all oceans. Chile probably has the largest edible barnacles (*Balanus psittaeus*). These grow to nine inches and are relished by the Chileans. The gray and pink goose barnacle (*Lepas*) is enjoyed by some Spaniards, and goose barnacles are also eaten along the French coast. These are usually eaten raw with thin slices of buttered rye bread or sometimes with chopped onions. The goose barnacle *Lepadomorpha* are eaten on the coasts of Greece, Spain, and Italy, sometimes raw with a vinaigrette sauce, or steamed or grilled with butter. These resemble steamer clams in flavor but it is the stalk, or "neck" of the goose barnacle that is eaten, instead of the body.

BOILED GOOSE BARNACLES

Drop whole fresh goose barnacles into boiling, salted water. Boil for 5 minutes, rinse in cold water, and drain. Clean barnacles and remove the heavy skin from the necks. Use white meat as you would crab or lobster. These are very good with butter or our favorite butter substitute, Scrumptedelicious Sauce. (Refer to "Lobster," chapter 2, for "Scrump" sauce recipe.)

Equipment Tips

For lobster, carry a big bag with the handle attached to a snap hook on the weight belt (keep your hands free for bug grabbing!). Use a big light to see in caves and holes; also for night diving. Wear a pair of gloves, especially when after spiny lobster. A pole spear or gig is acceptable in some parts of the world where lobsters are plentiful but outlawed in other areas. Don't, however, take "shorts" (under legal size) or producing females. Carry a lobster scale for measuring lobster in areas

Equipment for catching lobsters. A good lobster or "goodie" bag, strong underwater light, and a lobster scale (gauge for measuring bugs).

where they are controlled. Use a compass and depth gauge to cover a lot of territory effectively.

When diving for the deep bugs, don't forget to use your watch and depth gauge and figure your time on the repetitive dive tables. A decom meter is also helpful. Your regulator should be equipped with a submersible gauge to help you plan your dive.

When taking crabs, you'll need a bag as for lobster. Tempt the crab to clamp down on your diving knife so his claws will be otherwise occupied while you drop him into your bag.

A hoop or ring net may be used when fishing for lobster or crab Bait is tied to the center of the net, lowered to the bottom for a few minutes, then pulled up full of crabs. A simple baited line with lead sinkers and a long handled dip net can also be used to catch crabs. The latter methods can also be utilized in catching crayfish in freshwater lakes and streams.

Commercial fishermen use boxlike baited lobster traps and crab traps.

3
Mollusks

The shellfish of the Mollusca phylum include such animals as abalones, conchs, clams, oysters, octopus, limpets, periwinkles, sea hare,
and whelks. All of these are edible and very nourishing because they
are the closest animals, of edible size, to the bottom of the food chain,
eating algae, plankton, and each other. A few of these animals, such as
abalones, clams, oysters, and scallops, are the most sought after of all
seafoods. The greatest majority, however, are most neglected even
though they contain the most efficient body-building proteins one can
eat. Our forebears of North America, whether intentionally or accidentally, were smart in that they made such exotic foods as whelk, limpets, and tegula (turban) snails part of their daily sustenance. Whether
the early Indians knew the nutritional value of these foods is a moot
question, but they ate tons of the stuff and they were a vigorous, amorous
lot. We divers should be so rugged!

There are five classes of Mollusca. The univalves or snails (Gastropoda) include the flattened abalones and limpets as well as the conchs,
whelks, and other one-shelled animals. The bivalves (Pelecypoda) include clams, scallops, oysters, and all other two-shelled mollusks. The
chitons (Amphineura), have an eight-plated shell but are similar to

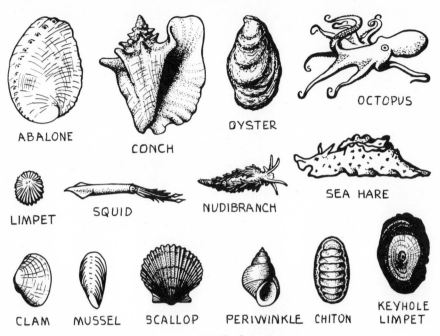

ABALONE

CONCH

OYSTER

OCTOPUS

LIMPET   SQUID   NUDIBRANCH

SEA HARE

CLAM   MUSSEL   SCALLOP   PERIWINKLE   CHITON   KEYHOLE LIMPET

Mollusks.

limpets otherwise. The squids and octopuses (Cephalopoda) are in one class. The squid has a modified inner shell and the octopus has no shell at all. The tooth shells (Scaphopoda) are very small and have a tiny foot that makes edibility impractical.

Both the sea hare and nudibranch families fall under the class Gastropoda and, like the squid, tenaciously cling to a token inner shell. Perhaps this bit of shell serves as a type of "security blanket" for them— a small, atavistic link with the ancient past!

Abalone and conch meat in any form are delicacies. It is the foot, or tough part used for locomotion, of these animals that is used as a food. This portion is separated from the viscera and sliced into steaks, tenderized, and fried. It also can be ground up and added to other dishes or sliced thin and used raw in salad and as appetizers.

Mussels are excellent fare and contain important minerals, vitamins, and, again, perfect proteins. They are used extensively in Europe and on the East Coast of America. In some areas during the summer months, however, bivalves such as mussels, clams, and oysters can be dangerously poisonous.

Octopus and squid are both very delicious boiled, sautéed, dried, or baked. In some areas, octopus are very tender, but most of them must be tenderized before cooking.

Contrary to common belief, the sea hare is edible, and natives on the

Friendly Islands and Society Islands in the Pacific eat some species raw.

Nudibranchs are related to the sea hare but are much smaller and some are brilliantly colored. A live specimen was eaten by a scientist who remarked that the flavor was pleasant and like that of an oyster. Fish, however, pass this creature up as inedible.

Abalones

The abalone is a univalve (one-shelled animal) of the class Gastropoda and is identified variously as *awabi* (Japan), *mutton fish* in some areas of Australia, *senorinas* in Spain, *Venus' Ear* in Greece, and by the slang expression *ab* in California. It is known as *haliotis* in the marine

BLACK
0 FT

GREEN
10 – 20 FT

RED
15 – 50 FT

PINK
20 – 80 FT

WHITE
80 – 100 FT

California abalones and the depth at which they are most abundant.

science world, and during Aristotle's time abalones were called *wild limpets*.

On the Pacific coast of North America there are four very popular types of abalones: reds, greens, pinks, and whites. Others, such as the black, pinto, flat, and threaded, are also present but not as well known as the former.

The pinto, flat, and threaded varieties are not as popular with commercial fishermen due to their small size.

The red abalone is the largest of all and is easily distinguished by its narrow red, wavy rim. The lumpy outside surface is dull red but is usually covered with marine growth.

The pink abalone is more circular than the red, is highly arched, and easily identified by its sharply scalloped rim.

The green abalone is best identified by its interior, which is brilliantly irridescent with predominant shades of dark green and blue. The interior is considered to be the most beautiful of all abalones.

The black abalone is identified by its small size and dark smoky blue to black outside color.

The white abalone, also known as the sorenson (*Haliotis sorensoni*), is oval, highly arched, reddish-brown exterior, and usually covered by lush marine growth and tube dwelling worms. The body, or muscle, is yellow or orange.

Abalone Jingle

The abalone sometimes houses a small rock oyster called the abalone jingle, which attaches itself to the outside of the abalone's shell. The abalone jingle is more commonly found on the red abalone than on others and has a very good flavor not unlike that of the prized Olympic oyster. Many divers miss this delicacy and it should be utilized by those who find it on the shell of a freshly caught abalone. These abalone jingles usually are less than three inches across but have a maximum size of around five inches on the West Coast of North America.

Distribution

Abalones occur in temperate and tropical seas with the greatest number off the coast of Australia. They are distributed along the West Coast of North America from southernmost Baja California north into Alaska. Abs are also found off Japan, China, the Canary Islands, and the English Channel Islands, the West Coast of France, and the Mediterranean Sea.

Habits

Most abalones are found on algae-covered rocks and in kelp beds from which they feed. The strong suction created by the abalone's foot permits him to attach himself to the sides and underside of rocks and ledges even in strong currents and heavy surf. During mild water conditions the shell is raised and the abalone attaches himself only lightly, allowing his tentacles to protrude from beneath the perimeter of his shell.

Abalone Tenderness Scale

Tender abalones are usually found in deep water where light currents and plenty of kelp are prevalent. Tough abalone generally are located in shallow water that is lacking in seaweed and has strong surf action. In relation to this observation, we have come up with a "Tenderness Scale" that seems to be reliable in the majority of cases. "Grade 1" on the scale would be the tenderest and would be the white abalone. The scale grades down to 5, to the black abalone, the toughest. Depths shown on the scale indicate where the greatest numbers of that particular type of abalone are found. You will find that the pink and the red abalones sometimes deviate from the chart as given and do not always conform to the depth/tenderness concept.

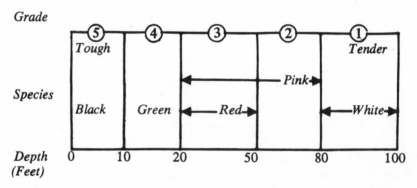

Abalone Tenderness Scale.

Catching Techniques

Approach the abalone slowly so as not to make any sudden, unusual, strong water movements near the animal. Be sure not to touch his shell or the rock on which he lies. The slightest sign of a foe will make an abalone clamp down on his rock with such frantic tenacity that removal of him will be very difficult and sometimes impossible, short of taking his rock along also. When you're in a good position over the ab, take good aim and slide the ab iron quickly between the ab shell and his rock, at the same time pulling the handle up and away from the rock to release the suction of his foot against his resting place.

One way to grab an ab! Diver Henry Evers tries to grab abs the lazy way from Carryl Deck.

Shell Removal and Cleaning the Meat

Remove the abalone from its shell with an ab iron, wooden wedge, or bamboo rice paddle. Insert the tool between the meat and the shell at the end where the shell is the thinnest and flattest. Move the tool around until the muscle is detached from the shell.

Now cut off the entrails and mouth, then wash the meat (foot of the abalone) in cool water. To remove the mouth, cut a V into the meat. Do not remove the fringe or trim the ab any further if you intend to freeze the meat. This way, if your ab develops freezer burn, the burn will effect only the part that you will later trim off.

Preparation for Cooking

With the abalone meat removed from the shell, cut off the outer, dark portions of the foot that are around the perimeter. Use a sharp knife for this operation. Now slice a thin layer off the bottom of the foot; also a

Bamboo rice paddle: an excellent tool for removing abalone meat from the shell. COURTESY AQUA-CRAFT, SAN DIEGO, CALIFORNIA.

Detaching abalone from the shell. Insert ab iron at the thinnest edge of the shell.

thin layer from the top if you want top quality meat. This top portion next to the shell is a little tough and tends to split when pounded. Save the trimmings as they may be minced or ground and used in stew, chowder, or broth. A delicious treat may be made from these trimmings by cutting them into small pieces and boiling them in salted water for five minutes. Garlic salt may be sprinkled on the drained pieces of abalone for a delicious (if tough) serving of appetizers.

The cleaned, whole abalone can now be sliced for steaks (use a sharp knife) or ground up in a meat grinder for use as "ab-urgers" or chowder. The green and black abs, being the toughest, are best suited for ground abalone dishes; others are better as steaks. The cleaned ab meat may also be sliced vertically and each piece dipped into teriyaki sauce, hot mustard, or a miso (Japanese bean curd) mixture for hors d'oeuvres. It is not necessary to pound these vertical slices when used in this manner.

ABALONE STEAKS

For steaks, the abalone is cut horizontally into ¼-inch-thick slices, then pounded with an ab hammer or tenderizer very lightly, but thoroughly, to tenderize. When properly pounded, the steaks should resemble satiny, limp pancakes. Each steak is then dipped in egg beaten with water or teriyaki sauce and coated with cracker crumbs, or better, Dixiefry (the latter gives the steaks an exciting "down South" flavor). Steaks should then be fried in butter and oil, very hot, and very fast. We actually count seconds to 24, *no longer than 30*, then flip them to the other side. If tenderized properly, a tender abalone species cooked in this manner will give you a steak tender enough to be cut easily with a fork.

Cut off the dark portions of the foot and tentacles, slice and pound.

Pounding for tenderizing should be light but thorough.

Slicing abalone meat for hors d'oeuvres. Slice ab meat vertically in thin slices.

Hors d'oeuvres of sliced abalone, scallops, and sea urchin roe with teriyaki sauce.

ABALONE RELLENO

The most popular recipe by far for abalone is one we got down in Mexico. Since 1968 we have demonstrated cooking this exciting concoction for a number of dive clubs and we have never experienced anything but jubilation from the many divers and others who have sampled it. The recipe as given to us originally titled "Abalone Bruha" and was the brainchild of Chef Wayne Bruha.

You Will Need

> 1 large abalone, sliced and pounded as for steaks
> 1 medium can of whole Ortega chilis
> ½ to ¾ pound Monterey jack cheese grated
> 2 eggs, beaten with 2 tablespoons teriyaki sauce
> 1 small bag Fritos, crushed to fine crumbs
> 1 small box Ritz crackers, crushed to fine crumbs
> Salt, pepper
> Butter and oil (equal parts) for frying

Mix together Fritos and Ritz cracker crumbs, salt, and pepper. Set aside. Cut each Ortega chili down one side and scrape out seeds (leave the seeds in if you want it a little hot). Lay one opened chili over each abalone steak, then sprinkle each generously with cheese. Now roll the steak up with the chili and cheese inside and fasten with a toothpick or two. Dip each roll in the egg mixture, then roll in the crumb mixture, coating each roll well. Heat about ¼-inch deep oil and butter in large frying pan until very hot and fry the rolls 30 seconds on each side. DON'T overcook. Drain on absorbent paper and serve. Depending on its size, one whole abalone usually serves two to four people, but make plenty because few people can stop at two of these!

TORTILLA-ABALON SANDWICHES

From René Villacencios,
Punta Abreojos, Baja California

A little over halfway down the peninsula on the Pacific side of Baja California, lies the small but colorful little fishing village of Punta Abreojos. There a beaming benevolent, father-figure for the village, René Villacencios, greets flying gringos at the airstrip and drives them into town—a row of freshly painted, colorful abodes built right on the beach. This recipe is the result of a charming midday repast at René's own home one day when Bud and Josie Smith, of *Dive Magazine*, flew us in and introduced us to their friends in the village. The children are very friendly at Punta Abreojos and showed us how to get dozens of (pismo) clams in about 15 minutes by dancing in the surf and feeling the sand with our toes—but the luncheon we had was Tortilla Abalón:

Prepare abalone as you would for steaks, dipping the slices in fine cracker crumbs and frying quickly on both sides. Keep these hot while you fry as many tortillas as you'll need in hot oil, turning the tortillas once and frying them quickly before they get too crisp. Drain tortillas a little, place an abalone slice on each tortilla, fold over, and tuck into a napkin. Serve with hot chili sauce, potato chips, and plenty of ice cold cerveza!

AB-BURGERS

You Will Need
  1 abalone
  ¼ of an onion, chopped fine
  ½ cup cornflake crumbs
  1 egg yolk
  1½ teaspoon bacon bits
  Salt and pepper to taste

Grind abalone meat with onion. Mix this with the cornflake crumbs, egg yolk, bacon bits, and seasonings. Mix well, preferably with dampened hands to keep the meat from sticking to them. Make flat patties of the mixture (should yield about four patties for a medium-sized abalone) about ¼ inch thick. Coat patties with more crumbs. The patties will be very limp and hard to handle but if placed in the refrigerator for a few minutes they will firm up for easier frying. Fry 30 seconds on each side in clarified butter or half butter, half oil. Eat as is, or build a sandwich!

LARRY CANFIELD'S ABALONE TACOS

Use the biggest abalone steaks you have for this one. Chop some onions and ham and grate some cheddar cheese. Place a portion of each on one half of each abalone round, fold the abalone steak over, and pin with turkey pins. Fry in deep fat at 350°, using your deep-fryer basket, until brown.

BAKED ABALONE EN COQUILLE

From Dick Mondor & Al Schwartz

Beach or patio party, this is a winner. Succulently buttered bite-sized chunks of tender abalone meat are baked right in the abalone shell over a beach fire or grill.

When fire or barbecue coals are burned down and glowing, pile bite-sized chunks of abalone meat into abalone shells. Place a lump of butter over each and sprinkle with a little lemon juice. Set the shells right on the coals and cook until the shells crack (about 15 minutes). Serve right in the shell.

ABALONE HAMBURGER

Jim Stewart, Chief Diving Officer at Scripp's Institution of Oceanography in La Jolla, California, ought to know—he's been diving California waters for many years and we knew we'd get a corker of an abalone recipe from him. You'll need an abalone, sliced and pounded, an equal amount of hamburger, some onions, green peppers, and any other ingredients you care to add. Run abalone and hamburger meat through the meat grinder, add chopped onions and green peppers, et al. Fry quickly on both sides and eat as is or make hamburger sandwiches. This is also delicious as meat loaf, stuffed green peppers, or patties.

ABALONE ROAST

This one will surprise you in that the finished product tastes much like roast beef! This is a Japanese method of preparing abalone and is easy and different.

Remove abalone from its shell and trim off fringe and bottom of the foot. Simmer in brine (below) for one hour with the pan lid on. Drain, then place in a baking pan and bake for 20 minutes at 250°. Refrigerate to chill. Slice thin to serve and eat like beef jerky.

Brine for Abalone Roast: Use 1 cup salt to each quart of water and mix well.

SMOKED ABALONE

Slice abs and tenderize as for steak. Soak in brine 2 hours. Dry on paper towel or smoker racks for 1 hour. Smoke 2 hours. (Refer to "Smoke Cooking," chapter 1, for brine recipe and general smoking directions.) Abalone slices then are cut into 1-inch squares or strips and served as hors d'oeuvres. It tastes like bacon. These will keep in the refrigerator for more than three weeks. If you wish to keep your smoked ab up to two months, you may smoke it for 8 hours. As with any smoked meat, this will make it somewhat drier and tougher, of course.

ABALONE FONDUE

This recipe was contributed by Bruce and Anita Bassett, who live

*Smoked abalone. Cut smoked abalone meat into one-inch squares and serve
as hors d'oeuvres.*

and work on Santa Catalina Island in California. Snuggling around
a fondue pot to enjoy your abalone in a different way is a great way to
end a good day of diving!

> *You Will Need*
>
> 1 16-ounce bottle of peanut oil
> 4 large abalone
> 4 large mushrooms, sliced
> 8 cherry tomatoes
> 2 large bell peppers, sliced in bite-sized pieces
> 4 whole lemons, halved
> *Breading Mixture:*
> 1 cup fresh bread crumbs (preferably wheat)
> 1 cup fresh cornflake crumbs
> 3 teaspoons Lawry's garlic salt
> 2 teaspoons purslane
> 2 eggs, beaten with 1 tablespoon water

Slice abs in ¼-inch slices. Pound until flat and tender. Cut into bite-
sized strips. Dip ab, mushroom, and bell pepper pieces first in beaten egg
mixture, then drop into paper bag containing breading mixture. Toss
until all pieces are well coated.

Heat peanut oil in fondue pot. Guests should cook the ab and mushroom pieces about 30 seconds, tomatoes 45 seconds, and bell peppers

60 seconds. Squeeze fresh lemon on the cooked abalone and dip other items in assorted sauces of your choice. Serves about 4.

ABALONE APPETIZERS

From Ted Martin

You Will Need

2 abalones, prepared as for steaks and using 4 largest slices from each abalone, then cut into strips two inches wide

1 pound bar Monterey jack cheese, cut into 1½ inches long by ½ inch thick

8 strips bacon, cut in half crosswise and fried just until partially transparent

4 10-inch wooden barbecue skewers

Roll each abalone strip around a hunk of cheese, then roll a piece of the partially cooked bacon around the abalone and pin with a tooth-pick. Spear four of these on each of the wooden skewers. Place each skewer on rack over barbecue coals and cook, turning frequently, until bacon is just done. Serves 4 for four appetizers apiece.

SEA SABRES' ABALONE CHOWDER

You Will Need

½ pound bacon slices

4 abalone, ground up

1 pound diced potatoes

1 pound diced onions

¼ pound butter

1 quart Half 'n Half

1 pint salt or sea water

Place the salt water in your chowder pot and start it boiling. Toss in the potato and onions. In an iron skillet, brown the bacon until crisp, then remove the bacon and toss it into the chowder pot. Fry the ground abalone meat in the bacon drippings for one minute and toss everything that is left into the chowder pot. Add the Half 'n Half very slowly, stir-ring constantly, then add the butter. *Don't* let it boil, just *simmer*. When butter has melted add salt and pepper to taste. Serve good and hot.

ABALONE CHOWDER
A LA TELCO DIVE CLUB, CALIFORNIA

Submitted by Tom Brooks, President

You Will Need

4 or 5 abalones
1 can cream of potato soup
1 large can tomato sauce

1 package Lipton Tomato-
Vegetable Soup
1 package Lipton Cream of
Onion Soup
1 small can evaporated milk
½ to 1 cup water

Clean and trim abalone and grind to almost medium-fine texture. In large kettle, sauté the abalone, stirring often for 1 to 3 minutes. Add tomato sauce, potato soup, and mix well, then add tomato-vegetable soup and cream of onion soups. Slowly add evaporated milk and water. Blend all ingredients well. Season to taste with lemon juice, garlic salt, pepper, salt, parsley, and a little wine. (For a thinner chowder add more water or wine.)

Simmer for 30 minutes. Ladle into big soup bowls or mugs. Serve with tossed green salad and crispy crackers. Serves 10 to 15 generously.

Conchs

Clean conchs by first cutting through the spiral tip of the shell (apex of the shell) at about 4 or 5 spirals from the tip. This will release the animal and the meat can be pulled out easily. If you wish to save the shell in perfect condition, it can be cleaned Mexican style by piercing the foot with a hook, then suspending the animal from a tree until the shell drops off. This takes time, however and is not our idea of the most humane method of removing meat from a conch.

GRAND CAYMAN MARINATED CONCH

This recipe is a real winner and was served to us by Dave and Pat Nicholson on Grand Cayman Island. This is the Nicholson's own recipe and is a wonderful appetizer with drinks before dinner.

Slice a raw green conch in thin slices, bite-sized lengths. Combine some fresh lime juice, Pick-A-Pepper or other hot sauce, salt, and pep-

Immature conch (left) with thin lip edge is too young to take. Adult conch has a thick, flaring lip.

per. Place conch meat in a flat dish and pour the mixture over, adding thinly sliced onions at the same time. Cover the dish and allow to marinate 4 to 5 hours. Keep chilled and remove from the refrigerator approximately 1 hour before serving.

SCUNGELLI (CONCH) SALAD

Jeannette Kilczer, an avid and adventurous diver from New York, let us have this recipe that has been handed down through the generations to her from the women in her family.

Use live conch and make sure the animal is alive by pressing its foot to see if the conch will withdraw it. Cook whole conch ¾ hour in salted, boiling water for medium-sized conch or one hour for a large one. Drain and pull out the snail with a fork. Wash well and cut off skin. Remove soft viscera and cut foot into cube-sized pieces. Add olive oil, chopped parsley, salt, pepper, and lemon juice. Mix well and marinate an hour or so in the refrigerator before serving on bed of lettuce.

TULIP COCKTAIL

This is an easy, quick suggestion for eating conch meat and was given to us by Twila Bratcher, a diver and author whose work appears in diving magazines and other publications frequently. Twila ate the tulip conch, *Fasciolaria princeps,* in this manner when she was visiting the Galapagos Islands. This conch is related to the horse conch, which has a peppery taste, but any type of edible conch can be eaten this way. Simply put, Twila says she peeled off the red and blue layer after boiling the tulip shell, then cut the white meat into cubes, which she ate with seafood cocktail sauce as one would prepare crab cocktail.

CONCH FRITTERS

From Bettey Tomasi,
PADI Master Instructor

This recipe is an official recipe from the Admiral's Arms hotel on South Caicos in the Turks and Caicos Islands, West Indies. The Admiral's Arms is known for its succulent food and excellent service to divers. Though we have never tried substituting crab meat for conch in this concoction, Bettey Tomasi says it works beautifully.

You Will Need

5 or 6 conchs	Salt
1 sweet pepper	Flour
1 large onion	2 heaping teaspoons baking
¼ cup finely chopped celery	powder
3 medium tomatoes	1 tablespoon hot sauce
3 eggs	Cooking oil

Grind conch meat, bell pepper, onion, tomatoes through meat grinder. Add finely chopped celery and 3 beaten eggs. Next add baking powder, salt and hot sauce, and enough flour to make mixture of the right consistency to drop by spoon into hot deep fat. (One teaspoon makes a nice size conch fritter.) Fry in deep fat until golden brown. Serve with barbecue sauce; your own special sauce; or a mixture of catsup, hot sauce, Worcestershire sauce, and a few drops of lemon juice.

KEYS CONCH CHOWDER

From Key Largo Diving Headquarters

This is one of the favorites made and enjoyed by Bill and Charlotte Crawford, of the Key Largo Diving Headquarters in Key Largo, Florida. It's bonafide Florida Keys style.

You Will Need

½ pound salt pork	1 green pepper, diced
3 large potatoes (peeled and diced)	2 cloves garlic, chopped
1 cup celery, chopped	1 can tomato paste
2 #303 cans tomatoes	1 teaspoon thyme
2 quarts boiling water	Salt and pepper
4 bay leaves	4 cups ground conch meat

Brown salt pork, add potatoes and brown also. Add remaining ingredients except the conch meat. Cook 30 minutes. Add ground conch and simmer slowly for 20 minutes. Is *that good* after an open air trip!

The giant horse conch of Florida should not be used in this recipe because it has a very peppery-hot flavor.

CONCH STEAKS

Clean conchs by cutting spiral tip of shell and removing meat. Discard soft viscera and slice the foot into ¼-inch steaks. Pound the steaks thoroughly as for abalone and sprinkle with meat tenderizer. Place each steak between sheets of waxed paper and let age in the refrigerator for 24 hours. When ready to cook, dip each steak in beaten egg mixed with a little Worcestershire sauce, then into cracker crumbs or cornflake crumbs. Fry quickly on each side until golden brown.

Raw Conch

Raw conch meat is seasoned with lime, hot peppers, and salt, then garnished with onions, sweet peppers, and a number of other vegetables and transformed into salads, chowders, appetizers, and entrees. It can also be ground up and used as a sandwich or cracker spread when mixed with sour cream or cream cheese.

Scallops

The scallop has one central adductor muscle that is a gourmet's delight—a cream colored, delicately tender, succulent marshmallow-shaped morsel from one inch to two inches or more in diameter and from one-half to two-and-a-half inches thick. The entire scallop is edible, however, and can be ground up for "scalloped" scallop dishes. The muscles themselves are considered one of the most exciting foods of the sea and are often devoured raw by hungry divers coming aboard the boat or back to the beach. A little lemon juice taken aboard the dive boat will make a tasty dip for raw scallops, but will usually preclude any possibility of the scallop getting to the diver's kitchen!

Scallops are easy to open, since every scallop has a small indent near

The meat of a giant rock scallop is very large in comparison to the size of the shell

SCALLOP

ROCK SCALLOP

Scallops.

COCKLE
(NOT A
SCALLOP)

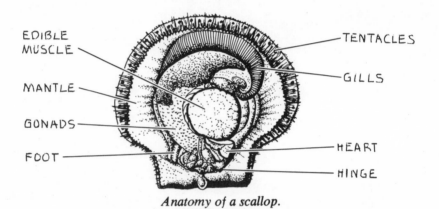

EDIBLE
MUSCLE

MANTLE

GONADS

FOOT

TENTACLES

GILLS

HEART

HINGE

Anatomy of a scallop.

the hinge on one side. Use a thin-bladed, sharp, pointed knife to shove into this indent, then insert the knife with the cutting edge toward the hinge. Cut the muscle to open the scallop, then open the shell and cut the muscle from the shell.

The most important thing to remember when preparing scallop muscles is that they are at their most tender when raw, and the longer they are cooked, the tougher they will become. Up to five minutes on the heat is all the chance you want to take with them.

SCALLOPS N' BUTTER

Pop scallop muscles whole into a pan of hot butter and fry very quickly just until they are shiny and slightly browned. A little celery seed added to the skillet enhances the flavor of these even more.

SCALLOPS-K-BOB

Place several scallop muscles on skewers alternately with button mushrooms, cherry tomatoes, and pearl onions. Brush with oil and sprinkle with crushed anise seed. Broil or barbecue.

These K-Bobs can also be made by first marinating the scallops and mushrooms in a mixture of teriyaki sauce, lemon juice, and oil and seasoned to please you, then placing them on skewers with other vegetables.

SAUCED RAW SCALLOPS

Make sure your scallops are very fresh, and take note that the aphrodisiac qualities of this dish will be more effective if the scallops are still alive when you begin to prepare them! For best flavor, use rock scallops.

Prepare Tangy California Sauce (recipe in chapter 8) and dice the scallops. The sauce is served hot and poured over individual servings of raw,diced scallops. Yummy and exciting.

BAKED SCALLOPS

Mix following ingredients well and fill four scallop shells or individual baking dishes:

    1 pint scallop meat (with or without muscles) chopped coarsely.
    ½ cup dairy cream
    Salt and pepper to taste
    1 cup Frito crumbs, finely crushed
    Dash nutmeg

Mix 2 cups fine breadcrumbs with as much melted butter as they will absorb and cover each serving with this mixture. Bake at 350° for about 20 minutes or until top crumbs are browned.

SCALLOP-SPINACH PIE

(Serves four)

You Will Need

    Pastry for a 1-crust, 9-inch pie
    1 pound spinach, cooked and chopped (use frozen spinach if you wish)
    4 eggs
    1 cup dairy cream
    ½ pound scallop muscles, cut into ½-inch pieces
    Bake the pie shell for five minutes in preheated 450° oven.

Spread the spinach on the bottom of the pie shell. Beat eggs, add cream, and beat some more. Add seasoning and scallops. Reduce heat to 350°. Pour scallop mixture over spinach and place the pie in the oven. Bake until a knife inserted comes out clean, 15 to 25 minutes.

SCALLOPS CHABLIS

You Will Need

½ pound mushrooms, sliced	1 teaspoon minced parsley
2 pounds scallops	Dash cayenne
½ cup water ⎫ combined	Salt and pepper to taste
½ cup chablis wine ⎭	4 egg yolks, well beaten
1 medium-sized onion, finely chopped	1 cup cream
1 tablespoon flour	1 tablespoon butter
	2 teaspoons lemon juice
	Baked patty shells (4 to 6)

Utilize your chafing dish or use a double boiler. Wash and slice mushrooms. Wash scallops. Cut scallops in halves if small, quarters if large. Beat egg yolks and combine with the cream. Keep the patty shells warm while you prepare the rest:

Melt the butter in the blazer pan of your chafing dish or in a skillet if you're using a double boiler. Toss in the chopped oinon and sauté until transparent. Add mushrooms and cook 3 minutes more. Blend in the flour and 1 cup of the chablis/water mixture. Cook over low flame, stirring constantly, until smooth, then add parsley and cayenne. Season with salt and pepper to taste. Now add the scallops and bring to a boil and gradually add the cream and egg yolks. Place blazer pan over the water pan in your chafing dish or transfer ingredients from skillet to top of double boiler and cook over hot water, stirring constantly, until mixture thickens. Add the 1 tablespoon of butter and the lemon juice. Stir well and divide into warm patty shells. Delightful and romantic! Dine under candlelight! Serves 4 to 6 people.

INDIVIDUAL SCALLOP/VEGETABLE CASSEROLES

This is another from Bruce and Anita Bassett (an abalone recipe will be found in that chapter from them). This is a true dream mixture that is delicious and versatile.

1 large package fresh asparagus
Several large mushrooms, sliced
6 shallots, diced
5 or 6 scallops, cut into bite-sized pieces
1½ cups white wine

1 cup hot milk
½ cube butter
3 tablespoons flour
1 teaspoon dry mustard
½ teaspoon chicken seasoned stock base
Pinch white pepper
½ teaspoon Bon Appetite
¾ cup diced swiss cheese
¾ cup diced cheddar cheese—sharp

Simmer scallops in white wine for one minute. Drain, saving wine. Sauté shallots and sliced mushrooms in butter, saving butter. Add left over butter and wine to the hot milk, flour, mustard, chicken seasoned stock base, pepper, Bon Appetite, swiss and cheddar cheese. Blend in a blender until smooth and creamy.

Simmer the cheese mixture for about 30 minutes or until the "winey" taste is gone. Stir in scallops, shallots, and mushrooms and pour into individual serving dishes over freshly cooked asparagus. Place under broiler for about 60 seconds. Serve immediately. Serves two or three people. (This can also be served as a filling for artichokes after cleaning out the "feathers" of the cooked artichoke; and you can also substitute lobster tails for scallops.)

SCALLOPS IN CLOUDS

This recipe is a variation of one of Graham Kerr's (better known as "The Galloping Gourmet"). This is one of the most effective and tasty scallop dishes we know of.

You Will Need

¾ cup fish stock
1 cup dry white wine
2 dozen scallops (1 dozen if very very large rock scallops)

4 egg yolks (*well* separated)
½ cup cream
10 green grapes, peeled, *per serving*

Hot mashed potatoes seasoned with leaf tarragon, nutmeg, butter, and salt and pepper to taste
Clarified butter
A "slug" of brandy

4 real scallop shells or, if necessary, individual baking dishes. (Shells are much more effective for this dish!)

Peel the grapes (tedious but necessary for a real gourmet dish!). Place the fish stock and the wine in a saucepan. Boil until syrupy. Meanwhile, decorate the scallop shells with the mashed potatoes, forced through a cake decorator, around the inside edge of each scallop shell. Place a small dollop of mashed potatoes in four spots on a baking sheet to hold shells in place while baking. Cut the scallops in half and put in a skillet with some clarified butter, then add a slug of brandy and light. Burn down, then drain the brandy juice into the same saucepan with the other liquid. Into a small bowl place the 4 egg yolks; mix with the cream. Pour the cream and egg mixture into the scallops in the skillet, mixing and watching carefully, as it "scrambles" awfully fast. Now place equal portions of the scallops into the scallop shells and pour a drizzle of cream mixture over each one. Add some of the reduced liquid over each one from the saucepan. Decorate each serving with the peeled grapes and place under broiler just until heated and browned.

Clams

The word *clam* means different things to different people. In Scotland, *clam* means *scallop*. In other places the freshwater mussels may be called clams and the name may be applied to any mollusk that can "clam up" between its two-piece shell. For our purposes, clams are those bivalves that have two adductor muscles but do not include mussels or pen shells, which can be prepared as clams. Oysters and scallops have one adductor muscle.

Seashores the world over are abundant with clams and many species are widely used as food. The best time to dig clams is during the lowest tides. These animals bury themselves in sand, mud, and even rocks for

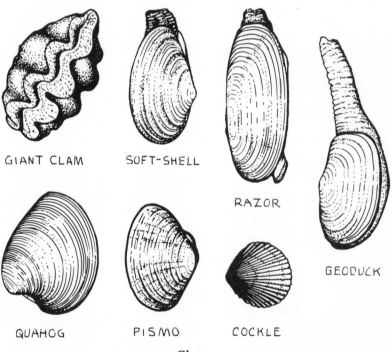

GIANT CLAM   SOFT-SHELL

RAZOR

GEODUCK

QUAHOG   PISMO   COCKLE

Clams.

JACKKNIFE CLAM (ENSIS)

LORIPES

NUT CLAM (NUCULA)

ANGEL WING
PIDDOCK

SOFT-SHELL CLAM (MYA)

QUAHOG, COCKLE

TELLIN

PISMO CLAM
SURF CLAM

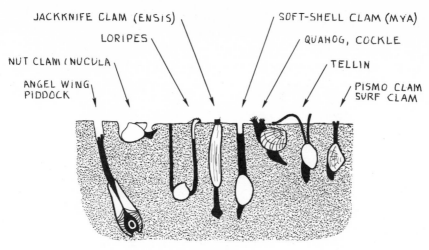

Clam habitat.

Co-author and Arthur Trask digging soft-shell clams near the mouth of the Ipswich River, Massachusetts.

protection and feed by extending their necks, or siphons, up to the water. The giant clam (*Tridacna*) lives on the surface of coral reefs around Australia and the Indian Ocean. These beautiful clams are eaten regularly and get as large as four feet wide, weighing as much as five hundred pounds.

The hard-shell quahog (pronounced co-hawg) and soft-shell clams, or steamers, are popular on the East Coast of The United States. Quahogs (*Venus mercenaria*) up to two inches are called cherrystones; from two to four inches they are called little necks, and the larger ones are called chowders. The quahogs are found near the surface in muddy sand of protected areas and inlets and are gathered with a rake. Soft-shell clams (*Mya arenaria*) are found ten or more inches below the surface in muddy back waters of bays and lagoons and can be dug with a clam hoe or a long narrow shovel with a short handle.

On the Pacific coast of the United States, the razor clam (relative of the jackknife clam) is a favorite and is found at about eighteen inches under surf-pounded beaches. Other favorites are the butter clams, littlenecks, and pismo clams. The geoduck (gooey-duck) is the largest clam in North America and inhabits sandy mud bays and estuaries at depths of four or more feet. Piddocks and angel wings bore into hard clay and even rock. These are the most delicious and beautiful of all clams, and are the most difficult to dig out. Pismo clams and surf clams bury themselves about five inches under the sand of surf pounded beaches and are best hunted during the lowest tides with a hay fork. Pismos are also found in about twenty feet of water and are dug out by divers.

Guide to Eating Clams

Everything under the shell of a clam is edible. During the summer months the black portions should be removed, however (refer to "Shell-fish Poisoning"). The siphons of some clams are too tough to eat and are discarded, but the siphon is the best part of the geoduck, horse clam, and gaper clam. The adductor muscles of the large clams should be removed also as these small muscles are very tough when cooked. *Don't* discard them, however, since they are delicious raw and as tender as fish.

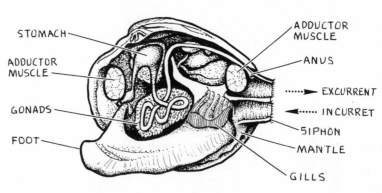

Anatomy of a clam.

The following is a general guide to methods of serving and eating most clams.

1. Little clams from ½ inch to 1 inch. (Coquina, wedge.)
   Used to make broth for chowders and soups. The tiny shells and bits of meat are strained and discarded.
2. Small hard-shell clams up to 2 inches. (Cherrystones, butter clam, Washington clam.)
   These clams are tender and best raw on the half shell or in seafood cocktails.
3. Medium-sized clams up to 3 or 4 inches. (Littlenecks, razor, soft-shell, bent-nose, mud clam, Washington clam, butter clam.)
   These are tougher and best steamed, fried, or used in New England type clam chowders.
4. Large hard-shell clams over 3 inches. (Quahogs, Pismo, surf clam, angelwings, piddocks, gaper, horse clam, geoduck siphon.)
   These tough clams are best ground up for chowders, fritters, etc. Parts of the Pismo can be fried. One 5½-inch Pismo or surf clam weighs 1½ pounds and will render over ¼ pound of meat, with a little under ½ cup juice. The body of the geoduck can be fried. The siphon of the gaper or horse clam can be pounded and fried.

Be sure you don't miss the delicious little pink "buttons" of the larger clams: the two adductor muscles that open and close the clam's shell when he's alive. These, however, should never be cooked, since they are even more sensitive to heat than the scallop muscles and the least amount of heat will render them tough and fibrous. Raw in salads and cocktails or as a snack by themselves, these muscles are as tender as cheese and yield an almost rapturous flavor. Dip them in lemon juice or your favorite sauce, but DON'T cook them!

Purging Clams

Clams should be purged to cleanse themselves of sand if they are to be steamed or eaten from the shell. Cover clams with clean sea water or 2% brine water and let stand from 2 to 8 hours, changing the water every 20 to 30 minutes. Large clams such as Pismo, surf clams, piddock, and angel wings do not need purging. Mud clams (bent-nose Macoma) and other clams found in muddy areas may be purged of mud by hanging them in wire mesh bags in changing sea water for 3 to 4 days. Soft-shell clams of New England and Northern California to Canada should be purged for several days, changing the water two or three times a day. This is the only sea water clam that can be soaked in fresh water.

Opening Clams

Open hard clams by inserting a slender, strong, sharp knife between the halves of the shell at the thickest end and cut one muscle, then cut

Cleaning pismo clams. Insert knife at thick end and cut one muscle.

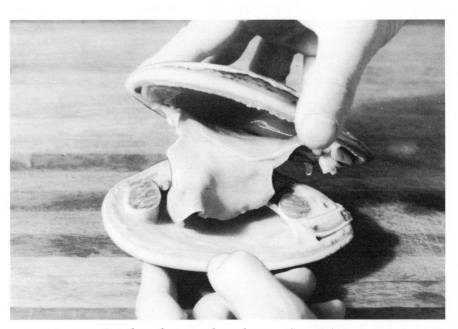

Cut the other muscle and open. Save juices.

Cut off the tough and sandy siphon and discard.

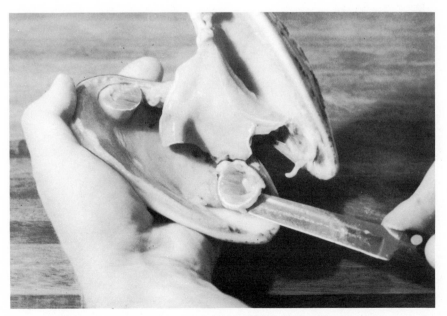

Cut off the adductor muscles. Save this for hors d'oeuvres.

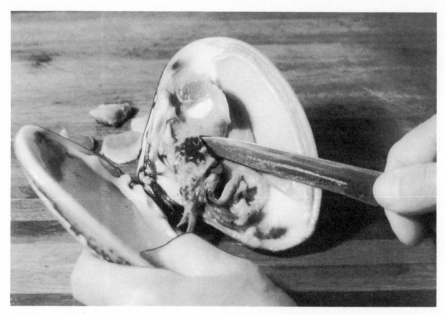

Remove the black portions during the summer months.

The juice, meat, and muscle from one pismo clam.

the other muscle and open. Catch the juices in a pan as you open the clam. If the clams are to be served on the half shell, remove only one shell. For other recipes, remove and rinse the meat.

Soft-shell clams do not have tight-fitting shells and are easier to open. Clams may also be steamed open and this is the most popular method. To steam them open, place the clams in a large container with a little water and cover with a tight-fitting lid. Bring water to a boil and steam about 5 minutes or until clams open. Be sure to save the nectar at the bottom of the pan. Another method is to cover the clams with boiling water and allow them to stand for several seconds. Pour off the hot water and cover the clams with cold water. This will cause the clams to pop open. The most practical method is to place the clams in the freezing compartment of a refrigerator for an hour or so. As soon as the clam freezes, the muscles relax and the shell opens.

STEAMED CLAMS

Small clams such as steamers, cherrystones, and littlenecks (2″) can be steamed. Scrub the clams under running water to remove the sand. Place them in a large kettle with ½-inch water or white wine (or half and half of both). Cover tightly and simmer for about 5 to 10 minutes or until most clams are open. Serve hot in the shell with side dishes of hot clam broth and melted butter. Dip clams in broth, then in butter, and enjoy! Note: Use "Scrump Sauce" instead of butter for a real treat. (Refer to chapter 2 under lobster recipes for Scrumptedelicious Sauce recipe.)

CLAMS ON THE HALF SHELL

You Will Need
36 live clams (littlenecks, cherrystone, or Washington clams)
Cocktail sauce (refer to chapter 8 under "Sauces")
Fresh lemon

Open clams and remove only one shell. Arrange a bed of crushed ice in 6 shallow bowls or plates. Place 6 half-shell clams on the ice with a small container of cocktail sauce in the center. Garnish with lemon wedges. Serves 6.

IPSWICH FRIED CLAMS

This great and easy recipe is one that made the little town of Ipswich,

Massachusetts famous. It was given to us by Dottie and Wilbur Trask of Ipswich, who also gave us our first real introduction to authentic New England cooking. Use soft-shell clams. Razor clams or other tender clams may be substituted.

You Will Need
1 quart clams, shelled and drained
1 egg, beaten with:
1 tablespoon milk
1 teaspoon salt
Dash pepper
1 cup dry bread crumbs

Cut off dark neck of soft-shell clams. Dip in egg mixture and roll in bread crumbs, coating evenly. Fry in basket in deep fat at 375° for 3 minutes or until golden brown. Drain on absorbent paper and sprinkle lightly with salt. Serves 6.

STUFFED CLAMS BAKED IN SHELLS

Grind the meat of four pismo or surf clams with ¼ of an onion, 1 whole green pepper, and one stalk of celery. Mound on four pismo or surf clam shells or large scallop shells. Top each with a slice of bacon. Bake at 350° until bacon is crisp.

CLAM FRITTERS

If soft-shelled clams are used in this recipe, the results are just as good as the deep-fat-fried clams served in some family and drive-in restaurants of New England. Razor clams or other tender clams may be used.

You Will Need
1 pint clams, drained
1 cup flour
1 teaspoon baking powder
1 teaspoons salt
1 teaspoon sugar
⅛ teaspoon pepper
½ cup clam juice or milk
2 eggs, slightly beaten

Sift together flour, baking powder, salt, sugar, and pepper. Stir in clam juice and eggs to make a thick batter. Cut off dark colored neck of soft-shell clams and dip into batter. Drop into hot fat (375°) and fry for 3 minutes or until golden brown and drain on paper towels. Serves 4.

CLAM PUFFS

Use Clam Fritter batter recipe and substitute ½ teaspoon nutmeg for the sugar. Add 2 teaspoons grated onion and increase baking powder to 2 teaspoons. Grind clams and stir into the batter. Drop by tablespoonfuls into hot fat, 350°. Fry about 3 minutes or until golden brown. Drain on absorbent paper. Makes about 2 dozen fritters.

FRIED PISMO CLAMS

The success of frying a whole clam the size of a Pismo or surf clam is in first pounding the outside flange of the meat to tenderize it. Leave the clam whole after removing it from the shell, then pound the flange well and cut the meat in half. Dip each half in flour, then egg beaten with a little milk and roll them in fine cracker meal. Deep fat fry or pan fry in about ¼-inch oil. Cook on each side until golden.

COLD CLAM SANDWICHES

A topper for hungry divers, whether at the beach, on the boat, or home after game cleaning chores. Steam open clams and grind the meat in a meat grinder. Mix the meat with enough sour cream or cream cheese to make a spread. Add garlic salt and minced onion to taste, mix well and spread on bread or buns for sandwiches or on toast or crackers for open-faced treats. The latter may be placed under the broiler for a few minutes if you prefer hot snacks.

PISMO CLAM CHOWDER

This is the official Sea Sabre Dive Club recipe and is used on the Sea Sabre clam dives where from 80 to 150 people are fed. Larry Canfield, who concocted this recipe, has broken it down to feed 4 to 6 people at home:

You Will Need
    About 8 Pismo clams
 1 pound potatoes, diced (use frozen diced potatoes if you wish)
 1 pound onions, chopped (ditto above)
 ¼ pound bacon, cut in ½-inch squares
 1 cup frozen whole kernel corn (optional)
    Clam juice from cleaned clams
 1 pint Half 'n Half
 ¼ pound butter (1 cube)

Clean and grind clams in meat grinder, saving juice.

Sauté onions in a pat of butter. Drain and place with the potatoes in a large kettle with just enough sea water or salt water to cover. (If using salt water, use 1 teaspoon of salt to 1 cup of water.)

In frying pan, fry bacon until crisp, drain, and add to the kettle, then add corn. Brown about half the ground clam meat in the bacon fat, then add this along with the raw clam meat to the chowder. Add the clam juice and cook 20 minutes. Now add the 1 pint of Half 'n Half and cube of butter. Heat until the butter is melted and serve with crackers or big hunks of French bread.

MANHATTAN CLAM CHOWDER

You Will Need

1 pint clams	1 cup diced potatoes
¼ cup chopped bacon	¼ teaspoon thyme
½ cup chopped onion	1 teaspoon salt
½ cup chopped green pepper	Dash cayenne
1 cup chopped celery	2 cups tomato juice
1 cup clam liquor and water	

Drain clams and save the liquor. Chop clam meat. Fry bacon until lightly browned then add the onion, green pepper, and celery; cook until tender. Now add the clam liquor, potatoes, seasonings, and clams. Cook about 15 minutes or until the potatoes are tender. Add the tomato juice and heat again.

NEW ENGLAND CLAM CHOWDER

This is the real McCoy—straight from Ipswich, Massachusetts. This is Sally Trask's favorite recipe.

1 pint chopped clam meat	
4 large potatoes, cubed	1 pint milk
1 large onion, chopped small	½ cube butter
½ pound salt pork, cubed	

Place clams, potatoes, and onions in water to cover. Boil until potatoes are done, then add salt and pepper.

Fry salt pork and add to mixture in kettle, adding 3 tablespoons of the fat also.

Warm the milk and add butter. Reheat and serve with crackers.

SCALLOPED CLAMS

The topping alone on these individual servings are enough to make you shiver with delight!

You Will Need

1 pint chopped clams	Dash nutmeg
½ cup cream	Fine bread crumbs
salt and pepper to taste	½ cup (or more) melted butter
1 cup cracker-crumbs	½ cup finely chopped nuts
	Your choice!)

Mix clams with the cream, salt and pepper, cracker crumbs, and nut-meg. Fill clam shell with this mixture and cover with bread crumbs that have been stirred with all the melted butter they'll absorb and the ½ cup nuts. Bake at 350° for about 25 minutes or until the bread crumbs are nicely browned. (Use this recipe also with scallops, mussels, or abalone.)

CURRIED CLAMS

(Use your chafing dish for this!)

You Will Need

25 small or 5 large clams, chopped fine

2 tablespoons butter	Dash Tabasco, salt and pepper
3 tablespoons flour	3 tablespoons sherry wine
½ cup clam juice	½ teaspoon minced parsley
½ cup cream or sour cream	Cooked rice for 4
½ teaspoon curry powder	

Mix cream with curry powder. Melt butter in blazer pan of chafing dish (or top of double boiler, if you must!) directly over flame. Blend in flour and add clam juice, then stir until creamy. Add minced clams and heat well. Add the cream and curry powder mixture and cook until thoroughly heated, stirring constantly. Just before serving, add the sherry wine and pile over mounds of boiled rice. Add a sprinkle of minced pars-ley for color.

Mussels

Mussels are the most abundant of all mollusks and are used extensively for food in most areas of the world. Some rocky coasts have a veritable carpet of these oval bivalves for miles at a stretch where mussels grow thickly, up against one another and sometimes on top of each other, on rocks below the low-tide line to the outer reaches of the spray area. They are held to their rock or other solid surface by means of the byssus, a pod of strong threads at one end of the shell. They are easy to gather and can be twisted from the rock by hand, though sometimes a knife comes in very handy. All mussels are edible, but some are toxic during certain periods of the year. Be sure to refer to "Shellfish Poisoning" at the end of this chapter before gathering mussels.

The most preferred mussel for eating is the common blue mussel (*Mytilus edulis*). But others, such as the California sea mussel (*Mytilus californianus*) and various species of horse mussels, are every bit as

Three favorite methods of preparing mussels: mussel chowder, deep fried, and steamed. COURTESY CORBETT PHIBBS.

wholesome as the common blue mussel. The ribbed or striated mussel has a disagreeable taste. Mussels are easy to prepare and one of the most delectable seafood dishes known.

STEAMED MUSSELS

Wash and scrub with a stiff brush to remove outer shells that may be clinging to the shells of live mussels—NEVER use mussels that do not respond to your touch by bringing their shells tightly closed. A mussel that stays open during handling is dead and may be spoiled. Place the mussels, still in their (tightly closed) shells, into a large kettle that has a well-fitting lid, then pour in enough white wine to cover the bottom of the pot to about ½-inch. Place the lid on the kettle and steam for about 15 minutes. This will steam open the shells and cook the meat inside just right. Save the juice and use it as a dip and hot nectar drink along with the mussel meat. Place the mussels, still in their shells, in a tempting

A plate full of tasty steamed mussels. COURTESY CORBETT PHIBBS.

stack on a large platter in the center of the table. Provide plenty of melted butter for dipping, and lots of napkins! Dip the mussel meat in the mussel nectar and the melted butter, and drink the nectar along with their meal. Serve plenty of French bread and a big green salad.

FRIED MUSSELS

Easy and delicious for breakfast, late night snack, or after a hunger-inducing mussel hunt. Steam mussels open as for plain steamed mussels and remove the meat from the shells. Cut off the "beard" (inside portion of the byssus) from each piece of meat and stir mussels into egg that has been beaten with a little teriyaki or soy sauce. Drain in a strainer about 3 minutes, then toss in a bag of fine cracker crumbs. Fry in deep fat until well browned, or use ¼-inch fat in frying pan, browning both sides of the mussels. Drain on paper towel and serve with lemon wedges.

STUFFED MUSSELS WITH PINE NUTS

(For 6 mussel lovers)

You Will Need

36 mussels	½ teaspoon tarragon
1 cup chopped onion	¼ cup chopped pine nuts
¼ pound butter (1 stick)	½ cup melted butter
4 cups bread crumbs	1 cup bread crumbs
½ teaspoon thyme	Chopped parsley

Steam mussels open (save nectar). Remove meat and cut into ½-inch chunks. Sauté onion in butter until clear, then add mussel meat, bread crumbs, seasonings, and ¼ cup of the nectar from the mussel kettle. Mix and stuff into mussel halves, then sprinkle with the pine nuts. Mix the ½ cup melted butter, 1 cup bread crumbs, and chopped parsley. Cover each serving with this mixture and brown on cookie sheets in a 350° oven until golden.

FRENCH-ITALIAN MOULES MARINIERE

(Fancy Steamed Mussels)

The fancy,French steamed mussels are merely a dressed up version of plain steamed mussels, but are utterly delicious with the added spices.

You Will Need

Enough live mussels for about 10 per person
1 cup chopped onion
10 green onions or shallots
3 cloves garlic, mashed lightly
2 tablespoons chopped parsley
1 tablespoon crushed dried thyme
2 bay leaves
1 cup white wine
½ teaspoon coarse ground pepper
Melted butter

Steam the mussels as for plain steamed mussels in water that contains all the above ingredients except the melted butter. Divide the mussels either with one shell removed or with both attached into diners' soup bowls and pour over the steaming broth. Sprinkle chopped parsley over each serving and serve the melted butter in individual cups to each guest for dipping. Serve lots of French or Italian bread alongside.

MUSSELS AU GRATIN

This recipe will serve 2 as a main dinner course or several as hors d'oeuvres. Do you love cheese? Ahhhhhh.

You Will Need

24 mussels, washed	¼ cup flour (approx.)
1 onion, finely sliced	½ cube butter
1 cup dry wine	1 cup milk
Thyme leaves	2 ounces grated cheddar cheese
1 bay leaf	Salt, pepper, nutmeg

Cook onion, wine, thyme, and bay leaf about 5 minutes to infuse flavor. Add mussels and cook until mussels open, about 5 minutes more.

Make a roux of the butter and flour, melting butter in a sauce pan, then mixing in the flour a little at a time and stirring until smooth. Add milk slowly and stir to make a thick sauce. Add a little white wine and stir in for added flavor.

Remove mussels from kettle and add the nectar to the roux, stirring in slowly to keep smooth. Add grated cheese and heat to melt. Add salt, pepper, and nutmeg to taste.

Remove meat from the mussels saving the bottom shell of each mussel and cutting off the byssus ("beard"). Place each piece of mussel meat on a half shell, cover with some of the sauce, and sprinkle with more grated cheese. Place under the broiler until brown.

BAKED MUSSELS À LA BARESE

This recipe originated with Jennie Taylor, wife of Herb Taylor, underwater photographer from New York. Baked Mussels à la Barese are just great whether you eat them piping hot or cold for a quick snack.

You Will Need

4 dozen scrubbed mussels	½ teaspoon fresh black
½ cup grated cheese (romano, etc.)	pepper
¾ cup bread crumbs	½ teaspoon salt
4 tablespoons parsley	Olive oil
½ teaspoon fresh minced garlic	2 eggs
	2 tablespoons water

Steam open mussels and reserve any juice. Arrange each mussel on a half shell and place them all on a large, shallow baking pan. In a bowl mix the mussel juices with all the dry ingredients and sprinkle the mixture onto the mussels. Now dribble the olive oil onto the mussels and bake in a 400° oven for about 15 minutes. While the mussels are cooking, beat the eggs with the water and another sprinkle of cheese. Spoon this mixture over the mussels just before they're done, removing from the oven when the egg is set. Serves 4 to 6.

Oysters

If you're a real oyster connoisseur, you'll follow the example of the "masters" of seafood culinary art and eat your oysters at once from the

CN THE HALF SHELL

Oysters.

sea, so fresh that the oyster contracts visibly when a drop of lemon juice is deposited upon it just before you pop the live little animal into your mouth. Once you've gotten rid of the mental block of eating raw seafood, you will find raw oysters to be one of the most exciting flavors of the sea, so give it a try!

For the "tenderfoot," oysters are delicious broiled in their shells after being sprinkled with bread crumbs and a drop or two of lemon juice. Oysters are also made into scalloped dishes and are especially delicious dipped in batter and deep-fat fried.

The Olympia oyster on the Northwest coast of the United States is considered the most desirable of all for flavor, but these are very small and difficult to gather even for a diver. They are grown commercially in some areas, however, and are available at the marketplace. On the East Coast, divers and others gather large Chesapeake oysters in great quantities, up to the limit allowed daily by the conservation laws in that area. Stu Stinchfield, who has the Divers World dive shop in Silver Spring, Maryland, can show you where and how to gather these great oysters.

OYSTERS ON THE HALF SHELL

(Oysters should be eaten raw for maximum potency as an aphrodisiac!)

Former astronaut Dr. Edwin E. "Buzz" Aldrin, Jr., who traveled to the moon in 1969 on that very first and most famous trip, is now President of Research and Engineering Consultants, Inc. in Hidden Hills, California. Buzz is also an avid diver, and one of his favorite seafood dishes is Oysters On The Half Shell.

The oysters are served raw on the rounded half shell over a bed of cracked ice. Oyster forks are provided and a lemon wedge is given each guest. The oyster is sprinkled with lemon juice, then eaten plain or dipped into a choice of sauces. Some people like wine vinegar or cracked pepper on raw oysters, but some gourmets frown upon pepper. "To be at their best," agreed Buzz, "oysters for this appetizer must be very *alive*—and should quiver when the lemon juice hits them." He went on to say "My test of a really good seafood restaurant is that the lemon wedge is served wrapped in a small piece of cheesecloth so that when the lemon is squeezed over the oyster, the lemon seeds don't escape onto your oyster. Tabasco sauce and horseradish are both good dips on the side."

Oysters on the Half Shell can be served dressed up with green sprigs of watercress and bright red wedges of tomato, if desired.

DEEP-FAT-FRIED OYSTERS

Stu Stinchfield, Silver Spring, Md.

Remove oysters from their shells by placing them on a flat surface and knock off the outside tip of the outer shell edge so that you have made an opening big enough to insert your knife tip. Slip the knife into the hole you've made and run it around the flat side of the shell to sever the adductor muscle. Now lift off the flat shell and cut the oyster meat free from the rounded shell. Save the oyster juice. Cut the meat into coarse pieces and drain.

Batter

2 cups flour	2 eggs
1 tablespoon baking powder	¾ cup milk
1½ teaspoons salt	1 tablespoon melted shortening
Paprika (dash)	½ cup oyster juice

Mix together the flour, baking powder, salt, and paprika. Beat into the dry ingredients the eggs, milk, melted shortening, and oyster juice. Fold the oyster pieces into the batter. Drop the mixture by scant ¼-cupfulls into deep fat heated to 350° and fry until golden brown. Drain on paper towels.

BACON BABIES

Cover the bottom of a cookie sheet with rock salt. This will hold the rounded half of the oyster shell upright. Place oyster shell (rounded half) containing the oyster meat on this bed of salt, and sprinkle each with some fine bread crumbs and just a touch of lemon juice. Cover each one with a piece of sliced bacon and sprinkle with paprika. Broil 3 inches from the heat about 15 minutes or until bacon is done to your taste.

PLAIN FRIED OYSTERS

You Will Need

  1 egg, beaten together with a pinch of monosodium glutamate and a dash of fresh ground pepper

Soda crackers, crushed (use two crackers per large oyster)
Shelled oysters
Dip oysters first in the egg mixture, then roll in the cracker crumbs.
Repeat the whole process. Fry in hot oil, turning once after 2 minutes
and frying 1 minute only on the second side.

BARBECUED OYSTERS

A great appetizer to precede a steak or seafood barbecue. Place un-
opened, fresh oysters on the coals of a fired-up barbecue pit or fireplace.
When the shells pop open, retrieve the oysters, remove the flat side of
the shell, and serve the oysters on the half shell over a bed of lettuce in
a large platter. Supply a favorite sauce for dipping. More fun when the
guests help!

Octopus and Squid

The octopus and squid are just as edible and delicious as their rela-
tives, the clams, abalones, and oysters, and several foreign cuisines have
revered the octopus and squid as delicacies for centuries. The octopus
and squid are members of the class Cephalopoda, which also includes
the nautilus, argonaut, spirula, and cuttlefish. In all cephalopods the
tentacles circle the mouth, which has a parrotlike beak. The bites of
some cephalopods are poisonous; bites from these shy creatures, however,
are very rare. The small blue-ringed octopus of Australia secretes a
poisonous venom with its bite, and this is the only octopus that has been
incriminated in several reported deaths. Also, it is difficult for an octopus
to position itself so that its beak can come in close contact with the skin
to execute a bite. On the other hand, the cuttlefish uses its beak to attack
its prey and can produce a serious bite.

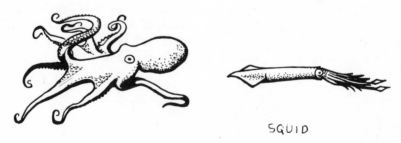

SQUID

OCTOPUS

Octopus and squid.

Willard Manus, of Greece, lifts an octopus from the Mediterranean Sea near Lindos, Rhodes.

Catching Octopus

Octopuses can be gathered by the tide-pool hunter during extreme low tides. Look into crevices and under rocks. Sometimes just a quick grab will get the job done, but other methods, such as shoving spears or gaff hooks into holes and crevices will snare an octopus.

Divers should look for a pile of shells in a rocky area under water. Many of these spots will house an octopus. The octopus dines on shellfish fare and pitches the shells out his front door as he consumes his meal, which makes him a pretty untidy housekeeper but makes it easier for you to find his lair.

The huge Pacific octopus of Washington state is caught differently than the many small ones throughout the world. Big ones such as those in Washington must be forced out of their lairs and away from rocks before grabbing them. The small ones can be taken with a hand spear or with a quick grab around the neck. To maintain control, keep the octopus's tentacles away from bottom rocks, your arms, and your legs. Bob Scoles, a diving instructor friend of ours in the Los Angeles area, has a rather unorthodox method of catching an octopus. After Bob grabs the octopus, he smooths the tentacles down away from the head to keep the octopus under control, then subdues it by one barbaric but effective maneuver: Take your regulator out of your mouth, bare your teeth, and bite the octopus—hard—right between his eyes. (This can also be done after you're topside with him, but never try it without your face mask in place—a tentacle in your nostril can be a very sticky problem!) Between the octopus's eyes there is a nerve nodule about the size of his eye. By biting hard on this nerve you will render him limp and helpless by paralyzation. It won't kill him but he will be very easy to handle from this point to your freezer or kettle.

Tenderizing and Cleaning Octopus

The Greeks tenderize an octopus by beating it against the rocks at least 50 times. Tenderizing can also be accomplished by beating the octopus with a mallet. Our favorite method is to freeze a fresh octopus for a few days after slitting open the head and eviscerating it, then drop-

Willard Manus demonstrates the Greek method of tenderizing octopus by beating it against rocks.

To prepare octopus, remove tentacles, peel off the skin, and cut into bite-sized pieces.

ping it into a plastic bag as is. When we are ready to use the meat, the octopus is thawed out, then dropped in boiling wine or water for 2 minutes (with lid on the pot). Then it is cooled in the cooking liquid, the tentacles (arms) are separated from the body, and the skin peeled off down to the white meat. No pounding is necessary with this method and the octopus is now ready to cook.

Cleaning Squid

This little fellow mollusk still has a remnant of a shell inside his body which must be removed. Hold the tubelike body in one hand and twist off the head with the other. This will pull the innards right out with the head. Now remove the long, clear shell. Grasp one of the winglike fins and pull downward—the skin will come off with the fin, though you may want to scrape off the remainder with a knife. Clean out the tube or cut it open and lay it flat to scrape it out. A little tenderizing may be necessary and for this the squid should be pounded lightly with a mallet until it is limp and satiny, as for abalone.

BOB SCOLES' OCTOPUS HORS D'OEUVRES

Utilize octopus or squid meat that has been cooked just enough to

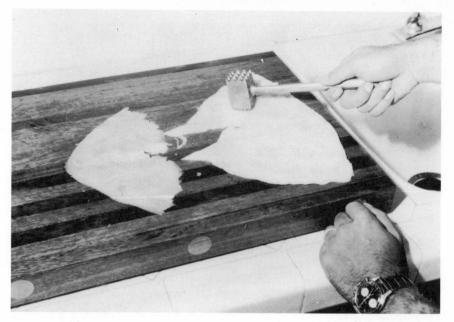

Squid should be pounded lightly until the meat is limp and satiny.

remove the skin. (Refer to paragraph on tenderizing octopus.) The dip for this calls for the oriental soybean paste, *miso*.

You Will Need

1 carton of miso (found in the Oriental foods section at markets)
Rice vinegar
Ground ginger
Soy sauce
Sugar
Chopped onion

Start with a glob of miso, then mix in a little rice vinegar, some soy sauce, ground ginger, a little sugar, and some chopped onion—all to your taste and to desired consistency. Mix well and use as a dip for lightly cooked octopus or squid.

OCTO-MAKI

(Variation of Rumaki)

Wrap a piece of bacon around a ½-inch piece of octopus meat and a small piece of pineapple. Spear the ball with two toothpicks to keep it together. Dip in the batter given below and deep fat fry at 375° until brown. Drain on paper towels and serve as appetizers or hors d'oeuvres.

Octo-Maki Batter: Mix 1 cup flour with ¼ ounce yeast that has been softened with water. Mix in 3 ounces beer and 1 tablespoon oil. Thin with a little water if necessary. Set aside and let the yeast work until the mixture is bubbly. Add ½ of a beaten egg white and stir.

OCTOPUS SALAD

Sus Yasuda, at Meijis Market, Gardena, California, taught us that, except under special recipes, boiling an octopus in water toughens it. For this recipe you first clean the fresh octopus by slitting the head of the animal and turning it inside out, then cleaning and washing. Drop the whole thing into an ungreased, very hot pan. Put the lid on and let it cook for about 5 minutes, then add some wine— NO WATER. Slice the meat thin and toss in a salad. This is especially great, we have found, if your salad is your entree. Octopus meat is delicious with vegetables and you get lots of good protein with your meal.

OCTOPUS PILAFI (GREEK)

Willard Manus, whose diving articles and several books on other subjects are enjoyed throughout the world, is originally from the United States but has lived with his wife and children in Greece for the past several years. Willard and his wife, Mavis Manus, are connoisseurs of Grecian cookery and this recipe of theirs is one of the finest.

You Will Need
   2 pounds octopus cooked with 2 tablespoons vinegar and 1 bay leaf
   ½ cup olive oil   1 teaspoon (each) salt and pepper
   1 finely chopped, large onion   ¼ cup vinegar
   3 peeled, chopped tomatoes   2 cups rice

Cook octopus with vinegar and bay leaf, covered, over low heat until tender, about 35 minutes. Cool slightly and cut into 1-inch pieces. Heat the olive oil and, in this, cook the chopped onion and peeled tomatoes until they are soft. Add the salt and pepper. Add the ¼ cup vinegar and let the dish sizzle. Add 5 cups water (include the liquid from the octopus cooking) and bring to a boil. Now add the rice. About 10 minutes before the rice is done throw in the octopus and shake the pot. Continue cooking until the rice is tender. Serve as part of a buffet dinner or an entree with a mixed lettuce salad. Cheese and fruit are nice at the end of the meal. Willard and Mavis Manus served white bordeau and a chilled, lightly resinated Greek white wine with the meal, both of which are very good with octopus dishes.

OCTOPUS STEW

William L. High is well known as an instructor and for his work with the Tectite II project in the Virgin Islands. He also has a file he calls "Personal Recipes for Fun Food." His octopus stew is one of the best—given to you here just as he wrote it down for us. (Bill lives in Seattle where the octopus grows pretty big!)

"Take one octopus—not too large or it may throw you into the pot. With a sharp knife and patience cut arms and body flesh into manageable pieces. Place in continually boiling salted water for 5 minutes. Remove, cool, and place in freezer until freezing just begins. Peel away and discard skin. Process one pound through a hamburger grinder. Set aside.

"Cut 4 bacon slices into small pieces and fry over moderate heat. Add one chopped onion and sauté. Boil 3 peeled medium diced potatoes about 10 minutes until not quite done. Drain and add 5 cups milk to potatoes, add bacon, grease, and onion, 1 bay leaf, and ground octopus. Salt and pepper to taste. Cook below boiling for 45 minutes.

"More milk may be added to provide a thinner soup.

"Make a double batch because it improves each time you warm up leftovers."

SQUIDICIOUS

(Quick N' Delicious)

You Will Need

2 pounds cleaned squid
6 tablespoons butter
1 onion, diced
2 cloves garlic, minced
½ pound sliced mushrooms

4 small peeled tomatoes sprinkled with ⅛ teaspoon rosemary.
½ cup dry sherry wine
Salt and pepper
⅛ teaspoon crushed tarragon
Chopped parsley

Heat half the butter in a saucepan and add the onion, garlic, and sliced mushrooms. Sauté until brown. Add sherry and seasonings. If tomatoes are used, add them at this point. Simmer 7 minutes, adding more wine if tomatoes are not used.

While the sauce cooks, cut cleaned squid into cubes or strips about 1-inch wide. Brown and then sauté these pieces in hot butter until tender, adding a drop or two of wine for moisture during braising if necessary. Mix the squid and sauce and cook over low flame for 10 minutes. Sprinkle with chopped, fresh parsley and serve hot either plain or over cooked white rice.

SQUID NEAPOLIAN

You Will Need

1½ pounds small squid
3 tablespoons olive oil
1 clove garlic, minced
1 #1 can peeled tomatoes
½ teaspoon salt and pepper
1 tablespoon pine nuts

1 tablespoon seedless raisins
½ cup water
12 black olives, chopped
4 thin slices Italian bread,
  toasted lightly

Clean squid, cut off heads, and wash well. Brown garlic in olive oil, then remove from the pan and add the tomatoes, salt, pepper, and squid to the oil. Cook 10 minutes or until the squid are tender. Place a slice of the bread, toasted, into each plate and pour squid and sauce over. Serve hot. Serves 4.

INSALATA DI CALAMARI

This is an Italian squid dish and was given to us by Dr. William L. Orris, an avid diver and staff physician at Scripps Institution of Oceanography in La Jolla, California. Bill said it originated with Al Petrie, of the Cen-Cal Diving Council. At any rate, it is delicious.

You Will Need

12 squid, cut into two-inch pieces
  Salt and freshly ground pepper
¼ cup olive oil
  Juice of one lime
1 clove garlic, minced

Oregano
Angostura Bitters
Lettuce, sliced lemon,
and tomato wedges

Drop the squid into a pot of boiling, salted water and simmer about half an hour or until they are tender. Drain on a kitchen towel and sprinkle them with salt and pepper. In a dish large enough to marinate the squid, place the olive oil, lime juice, garlic, a sprinkle of oregano, and a dash of the Bitters. Add the squid and chill overnight in the "ica boxa." Serve on a bed of lettuce along with the lemon slices and tomato wedges.

CALAMARY PIQUANT

Jack Chappell is not only a great diver but a seafood connoisseur. Jack's favorite seafood dish is squid and one of his favorite recipes is "Calamary Piquant."

You Will Need

1½ pounds very small squid	2 tablespoons bread crumbs
½ cup olive oil	2 tablespoons butter
2 cloves garlic	2 tablespoons chopped parsley
½ teaspoon salt	2 lemons, cut into wedges
1 very small hot pepper	

Use raw, cleaned squid. Brown the garlic in olive oil and add the squid, salt, and red pepper. Cook over high heat until the squid are tender. Remove the garlic and red pepper, then add the bread crumbs. Add the butter and the parsley, stir, and keep on the fire 2 minutes longer. Stir again well. Serve hot with French bread and lemon wedges. A mixed green salad is nice to serve on the side.

STUFFED SQUID

Leave the squid body in its tube form for this one so you can stuff it before baking. Serve the dish with baked or boiled potatoes and plenty of garlic butter on the potatoes for a gourmet flavor and appearance.

You Will Need

Chopped onion	Honey
Cooked rice	Cinnamon
Bread crumbs	1 egg, beaten
Grated parmesan cheese	Two small squids apiece
Finely minced garlic	
Chopped fresh parsley	
Salt and pepper	

The stuffing is made to your own taste, so use amounts of each ingredient that suit you and that will make enough to stuff the number of squid you have.

Sauté the onion in oil until it's transparent. Stir in the cooked rice. Mix in the breadcrumbs, grated cheese, garlic, parsley, and seasonings, using about ¼ teaspoon honey only. Now mix in the beaten egg. Stuff squid tubes.

Make a sauce: Use tomato sauce with a little Tabasco or buy the tomato hot sauce. Stir in some water to make a medium consistency and add some chopped onion and minced garlic. Simmer about five minutes.

Place stuffed squid in a greased casserole dish and pour the sauce over all and sprinkle with more parmesan cheese. Bake, covered, for 1 hour 15 minutes at 350°. Uncover and bake another 15 minutes or until cheese is browned a little.

KEYHOLE LIMPET

LIMPET

CHITON

Limpets and chitons.

Limpets and Chitons

The world is literally peppered with limpets and chitons on just about every seashore where there are rocks to be found. Limpets are very like abalones in that they are simply a tough, muscular "foot" covered by a single, dome-shaped shell. Some are more peaked than others and they grow in a variety of colors, mostly drab but some speckled, others a smooth gray or brown and some a delicate pink. The main difference in their appearance from the abalone is their very small size, ranging from one quarter-inch adults to about four inches (owl limpets).

Chitons, too, have a muscular foot but their shell, instead of being one dome, is a segmented construction made up of eight sections, or plates, so that they are capable of rolling themselves up, like a pill bug, when removed from their rocky homes. Chitons range in size from one-half-inch or so to the very large "gum boot" giant Pacific chiton. Both these species can be gathered at any time of the year and we, among other people, sometimes pluck very small species from rocks and eat them from the shell raw while scrounging around the seashore. Again, once you have rid yourself of the mental block about raw seafood, these can provide a very pleasing, nutritious, and entertaining way to beach comb!

Giant Chiton/Gum Boot

This sea cradle, called also the giant chiton and gum boot, is the largest chiton in the world. It gets to be as much as thirteen inches long. This chiton was used as food and eaten raw by the Indians and was eaten also by the Russian settlers in Alaska. The sea cradle is a dull, brick red and appears to be nothing more than a tough, leathery, oval blob, but contains good meat and, incidentally, eight butterfly-shaped, snow-white shell plates worth gluing back together after you cook the

The giant chiton or "gum boot" of the Pacific is the largest chiton in the world, growing to thirteen inches.

animal. They make interesting and conversation-provoking displays. These animals live in deep water and presumably come in to the rocky beaches to spawn. They range from San Nicolas Island off Southern California to Alaska and westward to Japan. They are not abundant south of Monterey Bay, California. If kept cool, they will stay alive for several days. The meat is used as a filler for bouillabaisse, stews, chowders, or in sea cucumber stew recipes.

To prepare the gum boot for cooking, boil the whole animal twenty minutes, then slit open the back and remove the eight shell plates. Remove the intestines under the shells and cut out the mouth. Cut off the leathery foot and cut off the intestinal lining. Now scrape the meat off the outside skin. This light yellow or tannish meat is the part that is eaten.

Cooking Limpets and Chitons

Smaller varieties of limpets and chitons can be removed from the shell and used as "Penny Steaks," or put through a meat grinder to use as additions to scrambled eggs, casseroles, or chowders. Small, whole limpets (with shell still attached) can be used as hors d'oeuvres after broiling.

BROILED LIMPET APPETIZERS

This is a variation of naturalist Euell Gibbons's method of cooking small limpets in Hawaii; a method he utilized on the *Acmaea* species, which Hawaiians call *opihis*. Gibbons writes that he has not as yet tried this with West Coast limpets. We have, however, and find that all small limpets lend themselves beautifully to this treatment. We prepare these often and they are a "natural" for beach cookouts. In the wilds (without a broiler), cover the limpets with foil so heat will surround them evenly. These delectable little tidbits resemble smoked oysters in flavor and make a great hit served neatly arranged, still in their shells, on an appetizer or hors d'oeuvres platter.

All you will need are the limpets, some butter (or better still, "Scrump Sauce"—found in chapter 2, "Lobsters") garlic salt, and lemon juice, plus a cookie sheet and plenty of table salt or rock salt. Place the live limpets upsidedown on a ¼-inch bed of salt in a cookie sheet. The salt bed holds the limpets in position. Sprinkle each limpet with a drop of lemon juice, Scrumptedelicious Sauce or butter and garlic salt. Broil about 4 inches from the heat for 10 minutes. Be careful when you're arranging the limpets on a tray after they're cooked—the meat drops out of the shell easily.

PENNY STEAKS

You'll need about a dozen "Penny Steaks" per serving. Actually, limpet steaks from the larger, small limpets are much like abalone steaks and are cooked in much the same way. However, where you will get several steaks from one abalone, it takes several four-inch owl limpets to make one good mouthful of meat! Gather the largest owl limpets you can find in the littoral zone of a rocky area. These limpets are of a drab, grayish color and moderately rounded to the apex. Most will be around two to two-and-a-half inches long but a few larger ones are not uncommon in good areas.

Clean the limpets as you would abalones, then place the little meat disks between two layers of muslin and pound lightly to tenderize. Dip them in egg beaten with teriyaki sauce or milk, then coat the steaks with cracker crumbs. Fry as abalone—quickly in hot butter and oil— about seven seconds to a side. Make into sandwiches, serve as appetizers or hors d'oeuvres, or serve a pile of them on each plate as an entree.

Boiled Keyhole Limpet

The giant keyhole limpet becomes very tender and palatable when boiled and can be used for making broth, chowders, stews, or bouillabaisse. This limpet is prepared by cutting off the top shell, re-

Preparing the keyhole limpet. Cut off the shell, remove the viscera, cut the meat into slices, and boil in salted water for fifteen minutes.

moving the viscera, and cutting the meat into thin slices. The meat will be almost fatty tender after it is boiled in salted water for about 15 minutes. (No amount of pounding the raw meat, however, will alter its leatherlike toughness.) Eating this limpet raw will cause a pucker in your mouth that will take a case of beer to get rid of.

Periwinkles, Moon Snails, Whelks

Periwinkles, moon snails, and small whelks are all closely related as far as cleaning and preparing for the table are concerned. They are all

PERIWINKLE   KELLET WHELK

Periwinkle and whelk.

Combination plate of steak and lobster is a favorite for divers aboard the dive boat.

Baked fish is delicious, simple to prepare, and very effective on the platter when dressed up with a stuffed olive sliver on its eye and surrounded by glazed carrots and small potatoes.

Crackers in the middle of this hors d'oeuvres plate are spread with delicious sea urchin butter. Circling these are owl limpet hors d'oeuvres (foreground) and kellet whelk with baby onions on picks (around top).

Sea anemones boast a wide variety of species and colors. Most are good to eat when prepared properly.

spiral-shaped gastropods that can be found in littoral zones down to some depths, and beach combers as well as divers can enjoy the gastronomical delights of these nutritious little animals.

These can also be removed from the shell, ground up and used in various egg dishes, sandwich spreads, and mixed with raw egg and crumbs to shape and fry into patties, or "burgers."

WINKELBURGERS

Drop the live periwinkles in boiling water to which a handful of salt has been added. Boil about 5 minutes, or until you can see the foot of the animal emerged from the shell a little. This shrinks the meat and makes it easy to "unscrew" it from the shell with your fingers or a pick. Remove the meat from the shell in this manner, then remove the operculum, or hard, thin "trap door" from the outer end of the foot. Grind these little pieces in a meat grinder or leave whole, depending on the size of the meat. Mix with a little beaten egg and enough fine bread or cracker crumbs to make them workable, season, and form into patties. (Dampening your hands will help to keep the meat from sticking to them.) Fry quickly on each side.

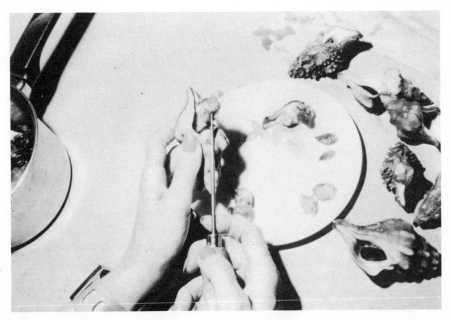

Removing meat from small whelk shells. "Unscrew" the meat with a pick or similar tool.

PERIWINKLE APPETIZERS

Boil live periwinkles in water to which some oil has been added, about 10 minutes. Serve as is, in the shells, on an appetizer plate. Provide picks so guests may remove the meat themselves.

MOON STEAKS

This recipe can be used for large moon shells, conchs, or whelks. Remove the meat raw by breaking the shell with a hammer (this will be a painful process if the shell is particularly unique or beautiful for shell collectors!). Clean away any bits of shell that adhere to the meat and cut away the viscera and operculum. Slice the meat (foot) into ¼-inch slices.

Sprinkle with a little commercial tenderizer and pound as for abalone. If possible, place the slices between pieces of waxed paper and leave in the refrigerator overnight before cooking them, since this will make them even more tender and flavorful. Dip in flour, then egg beaten with Worcestershire sauce, milk, or water, and fry quickly on both sides.

PICKLED WHELK

Boil whelks in their shells 10 minutes. Unscrew the meat from the shells and discard soft viscera. Remove the operculum. Cut the meat into small, bite-sized rounds, then alternate with slices of lemon and onion in the bottom of a sterilized canning jar. Add a small fistful of pickling spice or crab boil spice. Fill jar to top with boiling vinegar. Seal the jar and let it age 24 hours before serving. Alternate pieces of pickled whelk with pickled cocktail onions on picks.

The vinegar may be substituted with left-over pickle juice.

Sea Hares

The sea hare (class Gastropoda, family Aphysiidae) is a large, slug-like animal that resembles his tiny cousin, the nudibranch. Sea hares are found in rocky areas and some species grow to fifteen inches long. The name *sea hare* is very old and was used by the Roman naturalist Pliny, because of this animal's resemblance to both the mollusk and a crouching hare. There are two pairs of tentacles, the upper pair somewhat resembling the ears of a hare. The mating process of this animal is interesting in that as many as eight sea hares at a time have been seen mating in a circle and the mating process may last for many hours up to several days. After laying their eggs, the adults soon die and most

SEA HARE   NUDIBRANCH

Sea hare and nudibranch.

species have a life span of only about a year, the longest lived surviving no more than two years.

SEA HARE

The following recipe for sea hare is from Mr. Makato Irie and Mr. Toyo Tamamura of Japan and was contributed by Donna and Dr. Glen Egstrom. Glen is a scuba instructor from California, working at the University of California at Los Angeles.

When sea hare is boiled it shrinks to half its size and the shell is exposed.

Wash the live sea hare, then soak it at least 3 hours in sea or salt water. Boil the animal from 3 to 5 minutes. It will shrink to about one half its size and resemble a small, firm, auburn-black football (with tiny ears!). Cut the sea hare open down the back from head to tail and remove the entrails so that all that is left is the muscle wall. Slice this into strips about ¼-inch wide. Slice some unpeeled cucumbers and sauté the sea hare slices and cucumber in hot sesame oil with some chopped jalapeno peppers. Salt to taste and sprinkle with toasted sesame seeds for additional flavor.

Turkey Wings

Most turkey wings (Arca) are tropical and many are gathered commercially for food. They have no siphons and are anchored by hairlike threads, or byssus, as a mussel and are prepared like mussels.

TURKEY WING   CONE SHELL
Turkey wing and cone shell.

Cone Shells

Some cone shells are considered the most valuable shells in the world to some collectors, yet are of no value as food as far as we have been able to determine. Some are also the most venomous of shells and have caused death. All of them are venomous to some degree but only a few from the Indian and Pacific Oceans can inflict serious stings.

* Shellfish Poisoning

Octopus and Squid Poisoning

Although the common Japanese squid has been incriminated in intoxications involving several thousands of people in Japan, poisoning from the ingestion of octopus and squid is extremely rare. There is a definite seasonal incidence that occurs during the months of June through September in the Japanese poisonings, but the nature of the poison itself is unknown. During this period also some intoxications have been caused by the octopus *dofleini*. The problem squid is *O. sloani pacificus*.

Abalone Poisoning

Poisonings from abalone have been the results of eating the viscera and the poisonings have been mostly in oriental countries where the custom of eating the entire mollusk is practiced. Two species, the *Haliotis discus* and *H. sieboldi*, have been involved and both of these inhabit Japanese waters. The toxin originates from the abalone's diet of *Desmarestia* seaweed and concentrates in the abalone's liver. The musculature, or foot, of the animal is not affected and is safe to eat.

Sea Hare Poisoning

The toxic effects of sea hare poisoning upon humans has not been confirmed and any toxic substances have been isolated in three glands of the sea hare but not in its musculature. One scientist found the toxin to be very sensitive to heat. Sea anemones eat sea hares without ill effects and the natives of the Society and Friendly Islands also use sea hare as a regular dietary item without any trouble.

Tridacna Clam Poisoning

Giant clams of the Indo-Pacific area are eaten regularly, and the *Tridacna maxima* species eaten in French Polynesia may sometimes cause digestive disorders and serious disturbances of the nervous system. At Bora Bora in the Society Islands about thirty persons were affected in 1964 and two died (Bagnis, 1967). Toxicological studies of specimens taken at the time have not isolated the cause but the poison was concentrated in the mantle and viscera of the clam (Banner, 1967).

Whelk Poisoning

Whelk poisoning has occurred in Japan from eating whole whelks, a mollusk of the genus *Neptunea*. The poison is in the salivary glands and consists of tetramine. No deaths have been reported to date, however. This is another poison that ordinary cooking procedures do not destroy.

Callistin Shellfish Poisoning

As its name implies, this poisoning is caused by the ingestion of the Japanese callista clam (*Callista brevisiphonata*). The ovary of this clam contains a high concentration of choline during its spawning season between May and September. Victims usually recover within two days. Cooking does not destroy the toxic properties.

Venerupin Shellfish Poisoning

Two species of shellfish cause this poisoning in Japan—the Japanese oyster (*Crassostrea gigas*) and the asari (*Tapes [Venerupis] semi-decussata*). The poison is believed to be derived from shellfish that have been feeding on toxic dinoflagellates during the months from December to April. Death results in about thirty-three percent of the poisoning cases. Ordinary cooking procedures do not destroy the poison.

Mussel and Clam Poisoning

Though winter months from November through April are safe for mussel gathering, the summer months invite poisonous plankton that is ingested by, and contaminate, the mussels. Mussels are delicious, nutritious, and provide wonderful fun and great eating in many parts of the world, so we feel, in order to encourage those who have heard disillusioning and discouraging tales about the safety of indulging in these bivalves, that it is important to cover mussel poisoning to some extent here. By fully understanding the principal poison involved and how to avoid mussels that have been contaminated, seafood lovers can approach this universally delicious repast with confidence.

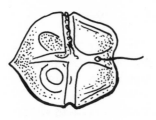 

GYMNODINIUM   GONYAULAX

Dinoflagellates.

The poison in question is caused by a unicellular, microscopic organism of the ocean, a dinoflagellate. Some of the dinoflagellates reported toxic to man are *Gonyaulax catenella* on the Pacific coast of North America, *Gymnodinium brevis* and *Gonyaulax tamarensis* on the East Coast, and *Pyrodinium phoneus* in Belgium. Others also are suspected of being toxic. This planktonic organism grows profusely during warm summer months when conditions are right. On the Pacific Coast, the upwelling of cold, nutrient waters, coupled with the strong radiation of the sun in summer forms a perfect hothouse for the growth of dinoflagellates, some nontoxic, but including the deadly *Gonyaulax*. The plankton thus formed and ingested by mussels and clams during these times, though harmless to the shellfish themselves, may be very toxic to humans who eat them. The poison is a paralyzing type and belongs to the alkaloid class along with strychnine, among others. Eventually, over a period of several weeks after the organisms have disappeared from the water due to changing conditions, the poison is slowly excreted by the mussel and the shellfish are safe to eat once more. These changing water conditions, as well as the mussels and clams themselves, are closely watched and tested both in the field and in the laboratory by the Department of Fish and Game. Mussel quarantine notices are posted along the shoreline during dangerous periods to inform the public of the hazards of eating mussels.

The digestive glands usually contain the greatest concentration of poison in contaminated shellfish. During the late fall months, the poison concentrates in the gills of the soft-shell clam *Mya* and the bar clam *Mactra*. Butter clams also have a high concentration of poison in their siphons when this clam is affected. Mussels and clams that inhabit the open coast or in inlets directly adjacent to ocean shores may develop poison from dinoflagellates. A few of those reported toxic other than those previous mentioned are the Atlantic Coast surf clam, Pacific Coast pismo clam, gaper clam, Atlantic and Pacific razor clam, bent-nose clam, quahog, smooth and common Washington clam. Other mollusks reported poisonous from dinoflagellates are Pacific Coast chitons and shield limpets, murex on the West Coast of Africa and the Mediterranean Sea, European edible cockle, giant Pacific oyster, and scallops. The adductor muscle of the scallop and foot of the single shell mollusks, the parts usually eaten, have never been found to be toxic and are perfectly safe to eat year round. Areas incriminated thus far in human intoxications are Alaska to California, New Brunswick, Nova Scotia, Maine, Gulf of California, Vera Cruz, Mexico, Scotland, England, Ireland, France, Belgium, Germany, Denmark, Norway, Japan, Admiralty Islands and New Zealand.

It should be noted and considered that though virtually every area in the world has been involved at one time or another with cases of shellfish poisoning, yet with the tremendous tonnage of shellfish that are consumed each year, the fact is that an infinitely small number of poisonings have occurred in comparison. Under the right conditions, anything we eat can become deadly poisonous, and by following a few simple rules and inquiring of local people when you are not absolutely sure, you can avoid the dangers of being subjected to shellfish poisoning.

To prevent shellfish poisoning, certain precautions should be applied. Do not eat the viscera (dark meat), gills, or siphons or drink the juice from clams or similar shellfish from the open coast between May 1st and October 31st. Wash the white meat thoroughly before cooking. When in areas away from home, ask the local people about the shellfish in their area. It has been said that the addition of baking soda in cooking shellfish helps to reduce the possible toxicity of thoroughly cleaned shellfish meat, but this is no safeguard against poisoning if highly toxic whole shellfish are prepared. Further, shellfish poisoning is deadly and there is no cure for it as yet; only the symptoms can be treated. Last, it is urged that strict adherence to shellfish quarantines be practiced.

Equipment Tips

Abalone

Abalones are usually taken with a heavy ab iron and stored in a diver's goody bag that is attached to the weight belt with a snap hook for quick release. To prevent problems when diving for deep abalones, be sure you are well equipped with such items as a watch, depth gauge, and submersible tank pressure guage. An abalone scale is helpful to prevent taking "shorts."

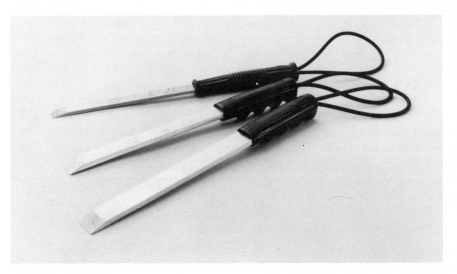

Different types of ab irons. COURTESY AQUA-CRAFT, SAN DIEGO, CALIFORNIA.

Rock Scallops

Rock scallops require a large, heavy knife with a hammer head on the end of the handle for momentum when prying and for tapping the scallop loose from the rock. A goody bag of some kind is also necessary and a lift bag or a buoyancy compensator may be necessary if you have a heavy load of scallops.

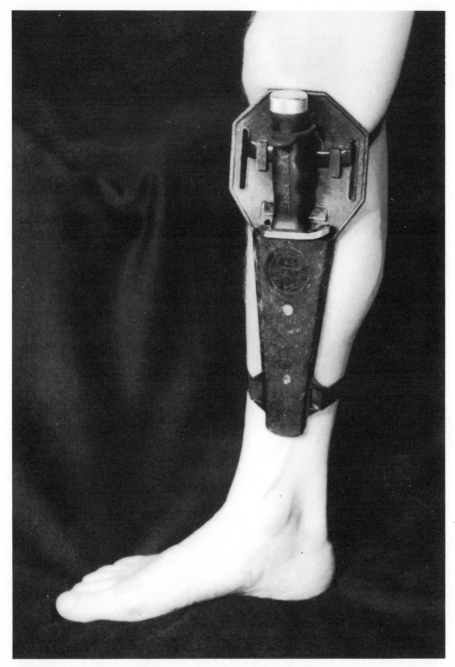

The diver's knife is usually strapped to the inside calf of the leg for convenience and to preclude entanglement in seaweed.

Buoyancy compensators are important pieces of equipment to safe diving and one of the seafood collector's most important tools. COURTESY *Skin Diver Magazine.*

Clams

Many types of implements are utilized in taking the various species of clams. Diving for clams requires a heavy knife for probing and digging and large clams are heavy, so you will need a lift bag or buoyancy compensator to safely haul back your heavy load. When digging for clams, use a long-handled shovel for the burrowing clams; for probing, a hay fork, potato fork, or commercial clamming fork is used; in soft mud use a three-foot rod with a right angle hook to slip under the clam and pull

SHOVEL

CLAM RAKE FOR
SHALLOW CLAMS

COMMON CLAM
HOE OR FORK

CLAM HOE FOR
HARD OR ROCKY
BOTTOMS

Clamming implements.

him out. Small shallow clams may be taken with a clam hoe, garden trowel, or hand cultivator. In some areas, such as down Mexico way, surf and Pismo clams are located merely by doing the "twist" in the surf, feeling the clams with the toes, then reaching down and digging them out with the hands!

Oysters

Take a big goody bag along on the dive and a lift bag or buoyancy compensator. Oysters are taken by hand easily unless they are in a natural bed and attached to other hard objects. In natural beds a knife may be necessary to pry them off rocks.

Limpets and Chitons

Limpets, chitons, and other univalves are pried off rocks with a sharp, strong knife (for the very tiny ones that you may want to sample right at the shore, a fingernail may do!).

Octopus

A quick hand grab for some octopuses is effective. Others won't be obtainable any other way than by utilizing a hand spear with a slip tip.

4

Fishes

The abundance of fish on our planet is almost unbelievable, their number in species alone totaling over twenty five thousand. Fish are the dominant animals of the sea and the most complex of all sea life. It is not surprising that these great numbers have fed man and nourished him with the highest quality protein since he first discovered them as a life sustenance. Man eventually took advantage of most species and in time, through trial (and sometimes disastrous error!), discarded from his fare those that proved distasteful or toxic. The toxic fish proved to be in the minority and, though most fishes of the sea are edible and nourishing, some are more palatable than others and a few can cause anything from upset stomach to death. Most poisonous fishes of this type, however, occur in the greatest numbers in tropical waters—particularly in the tropical Pacific—and North America is relatively free of poisonous species.

Most fish are never toxic, but there are some that are always toxic or certain parts of a certain fish will be toxic. It should be well noted, furthermore, that an edible species in one locality may be poisonous in another, and that an edible species may become toxic during certain periods of time in the same locality.

Due to the great number of edible fishes, we have grouped them by characteristics so as to present a clear discussion of the subject without giving an overwhelming mass of detail. Each group is discussed first in general, then this general discussion is followed by the toxic properties (if any), and finally, equipment tips.

Because most recipes for specific fish can be utilized with other species, this chapter has been treated a little differently in relation to the recipes. Most recipes are found after fish identification and are categorized according to cooking methods; i.e., frying, baking, etc. Exceptions are a few special recipes that appear immediately following certain types of fish where the recipe can be used for that fish only. For easy location of recipes such as these, refer to the index at the back of the book.

Toxic properties are covered for each group of fishes and a general discussion of poisonous fishes is included near the end of the chapter. Likewise, a general coverage of equipment is included at the very end of the chapter.

All classifications in this chapter are from the American Fisheries Society, special publication number 6, "A List of Common and Scientific Names of Fishes from the United States and Canada."

The perchlike fishes (order Perciformes) are the largest group of fishes, containing an estimated eight thousand species. It was the freshwater perch (*Perca fluviatilis*) that gave its name to this order. The yellow perch east of the Rockies is the counterpart of this European perch. Among the many ocean fishes listed as Perciformes that are covered here are the sea basses, groupers, snappers, grunts, porgies, croakers, surfperches, mackerel-like fishes, rockfishes, sculpins, lingcod, wrasses, parrotfishes, barracuda, damselfishes, and scaly-fin fishes.

Sea Basses

This family (Serranidea) includes basses, groupers, and jewfishes. There are a large number of these important food fishes in all seas. The basses are often called the typical fishes and are recognized by a lower projecting jaw, large head, and solitary inshore habits. The original name was *barse* (Old English meaning *spiny* or *bristly*) but they are now called freshwater perch. Early emigrants from Britain took the word *bass* to the United States and applied it to a number of spiny-finned marine and freshwater fishes. The common bass (*Morone labrax*), or marine perch, that extends from the Mediterranean to the British Isles is very popular as a sport fish and is good cooked by any method. Kelp bass (or calico) of California, as well as most other cold water basses are excellent when cooked by most any method. The white seabass along the Pacific coast of North America is in the croaker family and described there. The striped bass is the king of game fishes among United States fishermen. This bass is usually taken near the surf line of

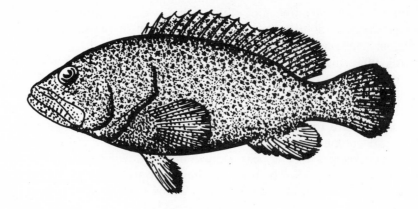

GROUPER

Sea bass.

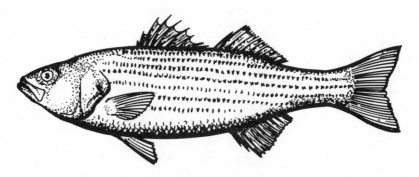

STRIPED BASS

the Pacific and Atlantic coasts and has a delicious flavor.

The largest bass is the giant black seabass, also called the California jewfish. They grow up to six feet in length and weigh more than seven hundred pounds. Spawning takes place between June and September. During this period, large adults aggregate in relatively shallow water.

* The liver of the black seabass is said to be toxic during certain seasons although the liver of most other fish is edible and highly nutritious. At any rate it would seem that the fortunate captor of the "big black" has enough problems filleting this monster to be concerned about salvaging its liver!

* More than eighteen species of sea bass classified as grouper develop ciguatera poisoning in the Indo-Pacific area. Some groupers in the tropical Atlantic also have ciguatera problems.

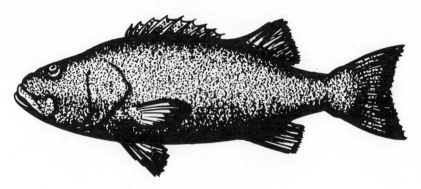

Black seabass.

*   Sea basses around some reefs in the tropical Pacific and Indian Ocean have caused ichthyoallyeinotoxism. (Harder to pronounce than it is on the body!) For more information on these two poisonings, refer to "Poisonous Fishes" at the end of this chapter.

Equipment Tips—Black Seabass and Large Groupers
Use a long powerful gun with breakaway gear and a large tri-cut slip tip. The reel or line pack should contain two hundred to three hundred feet of line. The shooting line and the tip line should be stainless steel cable to prevent breaking when the big fish holes up. When hunting large groupers, the breakaway line can be attached to a surface float to prevent losing the gun. Several guns may be necessary to get the big ones. Some experts advocate the use of power heads for deep penetration.

Equipment Tips—Striped Bass
Use a medium gun, about forty eight inches (best for poor visibility waters), with three powerful slings. A three-barbed detachable head is recommended along with twenty to thirty feet of strong nylon line, and a shock cord would complete the outfit.

Equipment Tips—Small Bass
Use an intermediate gun that is quick and easy to load, with a twin barb fixed head or a multitined spear tip. A detachable head may be used for fish over twenty pounds. A 7-foot pole spear equipped with a slip tip or a three-pronged paralyzer tip will get everything up to twenty five pounds.

Snappers
Second only to the basses in abundance, diversity, and importance are the snappers (family Lutjanidae). There are about 250 species of these fishes in the world and most are delicious as food fishes. The greatest

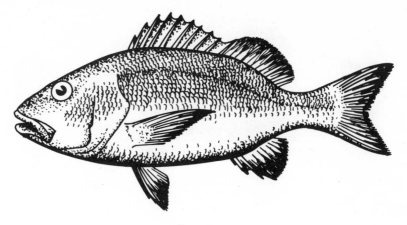

Snapper.

numbers of species are found in the Indo-Australian area, and fewer in tropical Atlantic America.

The gray snapper or mangrove snapper is reputed to be one of the best tasting snappers in the Florida Keys. The yellowtail snapper also has a fine reputation in this regard and the red snapper is a famous food fish along the Atlantic coast, Gulf of Mexico, and the Caribbean. The snapper earned its name from the way it snaps its jaws open and shut after it is landed, a performance that can cause bad wounds to the fingers of a careless handler.

*   Some snappers in tropical waters and around Australia can cause ciguatera poisoning.

For equipment tips, refer to sea basses.

Grunts

Grunts (Pomadasyiidae) are closely related to snappers but are smaller and are very plentiful in tropical waters. The sargo of California has a slight iodine taste and is best fried crisp. The white grunt, bluestripe grunt, and pigfish are good food fishes in southern United States waters.

*   Several grunts in the Gulf of California to northern Peru and one in the Galapagos Islands develop ciguatera poisoning.

Grunts may be taken with a hand spear.

Porgies

Porgies (Sparidae) are closely related to grunts and the larger ones are sport and food fish. Most are tropical and are common over sandy or grassy bottoms. Several species are found in temperate waters such as the sheephead porgy, which extends from Cape Cod, Massachusetts into the Gulf of Mexico. It is not related to the Pacific sheep-head, which is a wrasse.

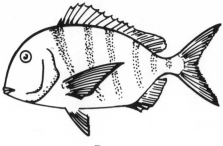

Porgy.

*   Some tropical porgies develop ciguatera poisoning including the scup and saucereye (now there's a pair!) of Florida and West Indies. The northern scup is safe.

Croakers

Croakers (family Sciaenidae) are numerous and extremely variable in form and include the weakfish, sea trout, totuava, white seabass, drum, corbina, and whiting. Most inhabit warm water, usually over sandy or muddy bottoms. Most make a noise by vibrating their air bladders and

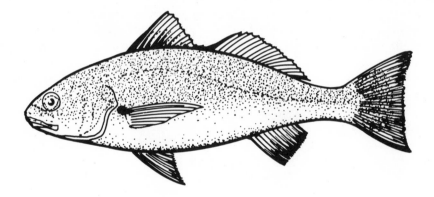

TOMMY CROAKER

Tommy croaker and Tom cod.

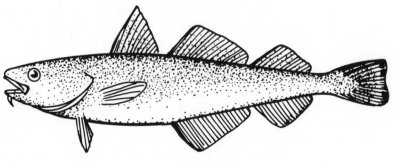

TOM COD (PACIFIC)

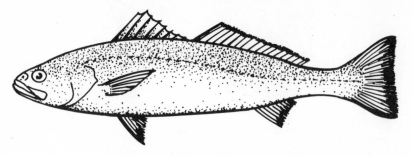

White seabass.

this is described variously as croaking, drumming, grunting, or snoring. Weakfish or sea trout are important food and game fishes and are the best known of the croakers. The white seabass, a large Pacific croaker, is the most challenging and most difficult fish a Southern California diver can hunt. Drums are the largest and noisiest and are good to eat. The corbina is most highly esteemed by surf fishermen in Southern California, while whitings are highly prized for their food qualities in all areas. The tommy croaker (*Genyonimus lineatus*) is erroneously termed *tomcod* in California. It is a desirable food fish and caught by commercial fishermen for market. The real tomcod (*Microgadus proximus*) must be kept cool and damp after catching (as any fish should) or the flesh will soften, making it undesirable. Some croakers are white, soft, and mild and good when fried crisp.

* The black drum (*Pogonias cromis*) of the East Coast of the United States usually carries a parasite infiltrating the flesh near the tail. This is the larval stage of a tape worm and the fish should be cooked thoroughly before eating. Very few croakers develop ciguatera poison—one in the Mediterranean, one in Indo-Pacific (Nibea sina), and one in the Galapagos Islands.

For equipment tips refer to sea basses.

Surfperches

This group (family Embiotocidae) is viviparous and gives birth to live young. They are found only off the Pacific coast of North America except for three species in Japan. Those that prefer the sandy surf are surfperches and those that prefer rocky areas or deeper water are called seaperches. They are recognized by a distinct furrow on each side of the base of the continuous dorsal fin. The body is compressed, deep, and elliptical in shape. Most come into surf to drop their young in the spring and summer months. Mating takes place within two days of birth. Males mature at birth and females mature soon after. Breeding goes on throughout the summer. The opaleye (Girellidae), zebraperch (Kyphosidae), and halfmoon (Scorpididae) are not of this group. The flesh is white, fine grained, and mild in flavor. They are tasty fried, either filleted or as panfish, and deep-fat fried.

* This group is free of poisons although there are two so-called sea perches in Australia of the family Arripidae that may develop ciguatera poisoning. One is also called the "tommy rough."

Equipment Tips
Medium pole spear or gun with a multi-tined spearhead.

Mackerel-like Game Fishes

These are fast, pelagic game fishes found in all seas. This group (sub-order Scombroidei) includes all mackerels, bonito, albacore, tuna, spear-fish, jacks, wahoo, roosterfish, and dolphin fish. All of these are characteristics of the group with sleek, streamlined, symmetrical bodies, like torpedoes that taper off to thin tails and V-shaped tail fins. Usually, they are a metallic bluish or greenish color with a silver belly.

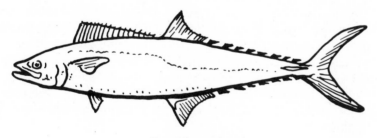

Spanish mackerel.

Most mackerel type fishes are of high commercial value. Spanish mackerel (*Scomberomorus*) is considered among the finest. The Pacific mackerel, though oily and with a strong fish flavor, is delicious when smoked, broiled, or barbecued. Bonito is good when prepared as mackerel.

Scombrotoxism
* Any fish in the Scombridae family can cause scombroid poisoning after being left in the sun or exposed to warm room temperatures for more than two hours after being caught. The Scombridae family includes mackerel, bonito, albacore, tuna, skipjack, sierra, wahoo, cero, and kingfish. The culprit is a bacteria (*Proteus morganii*) which causes decomposition of histidine into a highly toxic saurine (Kimata, 1961), a histamine-like substance—for all practical purposes, spoiled fish! The

symptoms of this type of poison resemble those of a severe allergy, and deaths have been reported. Antihistamines are recommended.

Discard any scombroid that has been left in the sun more than two hours or has pallor of the gills or off-odor. A toxic scombroid fish can frequently be detected by the taste test; it may have a sharp, peppery flavor. To prevent scombroid poisoning, eviscerate fish soon after they are caught and keep them cool, preferably on ice or in a wet burlap sack. It should then be eaten, refrigerated, or frozen as soon as possible after catching.

Escolars

The escolars or pelagic mackerel (family Gempylidae) are long, skinny relations of the mackerel-like fishes and include snake mackerel, castor-oil fish, and snoek. Most live in moderately deep water and have oily flesh. The snoek is an important food fish in the southern hemisphere. It is eaten fresh, salted, or smoked.

Snoek is a Dutch word for *pike;* and in Australia it is also called *barracouta,* and sometimes *pike.*

Gempylid Poisoning

* Some escolars such as pelagic snake mackerel (*Lepidocybium flayobrunneur*), which range from the South Pacific Ocean to Africa, and castor-oil fish (*Ruvettus praetiosus*), from the South Atlantic Ocean to the Indo-Pacific area, contain an oil that produces a pronounced purgative effect. This oil is also present in the fish's bones. Eating these escolars will cause rapidly developing diarrhea and cramps. The poisoning is usually not a serious matter—it only seems so while you are struggling through it!

Special Preparation for Cooking Mackerellike Fishes

A few of these fishes have a thick layer of dark, oily meat along each side just under the skin. This dark meat has a strong, fishy flavor and should be removed to improve the quality of the rest of the meat. It is necessary, therefore, to fillet and skin these fishes to get to the dark meat. If the fish, such as the Pacific mackerel, has a large percentage of dark meat, it should be left in, however, and the fish smoked, barbecued, or broiled, as this dark meat is very good when cooked by any of these three methods.

FRENCH FRIED BONITA

From Larry and Sharon Canfield

Bonita is very easily bruised, as an apple. As soon as you bag bonita, bleed it and then keep it moist until you get it home. Skin the fish as soon as possible after catching. When the bonita is filleted, the strip of dark, reddish meat should be removed from each fillet. This removes the strip of bones in there also and will leave you with four strips of fillets. Cut these strips into 3-inch lengths, then dip them into "Beer Batter" (recipe for Beer Batter follows the Deep Fried Fish recipes further on in this chapter) and deep fry until golden brown. Fried this way your bonita will taste more like chicken breasts than fish and your reputation as a fish gourmet will benefit greatly!

Equipment Tips

Use a long, powerful gun with breakaway gear and a detachable star head for holding in soft flesh. Use nylon line from the head to the shaft slide ring to prevent flesh damage. The safety should be noiseless. Try for a solid meat shot and don't hold the line back or the tip may pull out. (Refer to Spearfishing Equipment at the end of this chapter.)

Scorpionfishes and Rockfishes

These fishes (family Scorpaenidae) dwell near the bottom and are typical mailed-cheeked fishes that bear live young (viviparous), grow spines on the head, have winglike pectoral fins, and have all spiny fins. The black rockfish (also called black seabass) of the North Pacific coast of America is the only free-swimming schooling rockfish. All of the rockfish (sometimes called rockcod) are valuable food fish and have been California's leading market fish. The flesh is usually white, fine in texture, and mild in flavor. They are best filleted, skinned, and deep fried.

The scorpionfish of the rockfish family is marketed as a "sculpin" in California but is not a true sculpin.

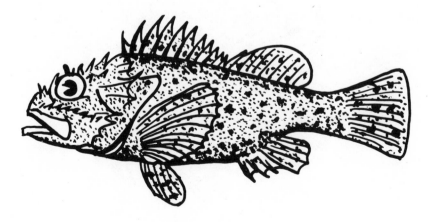

Scorpionfish.

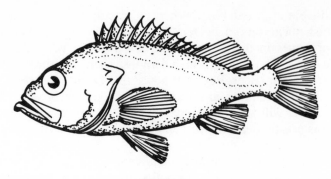

Rockfish.

*   Scorpionfish develop ciguatera poisoning in tropical seas. Use caution when handling a live one; its sharp spines are venomous and a spine accidentally puncturing the skin will cause instantaneous and excruciating pain that lasts for several days, diminishing with time. The pain can be reduced by immediate immersion of the part in hot water. The stonefish and the lionfish, two rockfish of tropical waters, can inflict dangerous stings. The stonefish (*Synanceja verrucosa*) packs the most poisonous venom of any fish.

Equipment Tips
Use a short gun or pole spear with multi-tined head.

Lionfish, zebrafish, or turkeyfish.

Sculpin

The sculpins (family Cottidae) are good food fishes and some look like the scorpionfishes. The cabezon is of the sculpin family and is considered by many the best food fish of all. But there are some divers in the Puget Sound area who consider the cabezon undesirable. The flesh is usually a beautiful light bluish-green but turns white when cooked. Cabezon is best filleted, skinned, and deep fried.

* Do not eat the roe (eggs) of the cabezon—it is toxic and capable of causing violent illness.

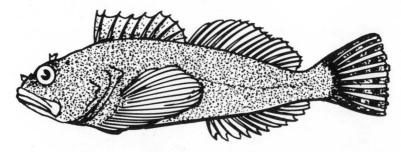

Cabezon.

Lingcod

The lingcod (Ophiodontidae) is recognized by its long body, long dorsal fin, large mouth full of sharp teeth, and blotched and spotted coloring. The lingcod is found in the North Pacific around rocky areas and kelp beds, especially where there is a strong current. The flesh is sometimes greenish, becoming white when cooked. It is one of the richest sources of insulin among fish and the liver is extremely rich in vitamins A and D.

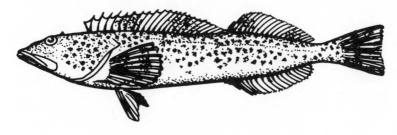

Lingcod.

Equipment Tips

Use a medium pole spear or gun with a single tip or multi-tined spear-head for sculpins or lingcods up to twenty five pounds, and a double-barbed fixed head for larger fish. Use an underwater light for the deep holes.

Wrasses and Parrotfish

This group of fishes (suborder Pharyngognathi) have heavy pharyn-geal teeth with which they crush their food. The wrasses (family Labri-dae) have a bucktoothed profile with projecting canine-like teeth and thick lips. The parrotfishes (family Scaridae) have a parrot-like beak of fused teeth. Wrasses include the tautog, hogfish, California sheep-head,

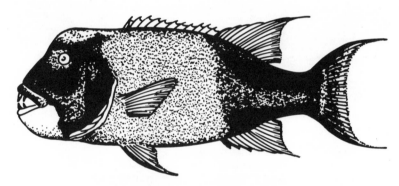

CALIF. MALE SHEEP-HEAD

California sheep-head and parrot fish.

PARROT FISH

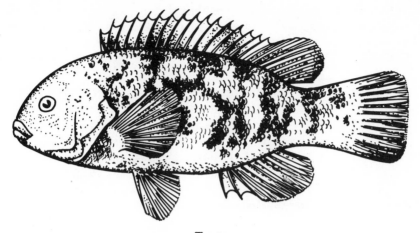

Tautog.

and senorita. More tautogs have been speared in the southeastern waters of the United States than any other species in that area. The male sheep-head is a favorite in Southern California. All are good food fishes except for the little cleaner fish, which usually are too small to eat. The flesh is white, firm, and mild in flavor. Chunks of boiled California sheep-head are often used to complement lobster or crab meat in a salad or seafood cocktail. These fishes should be filleted and skinned to make them more palatable due to the oily skin that imparts a strong, gamey flavor to the meat.

Wrasses and parrotfish sometimes develop ciguatera poisoning in tropical waters.

Equipment Tips
Use a pole spear or short gun with a twin barb tip for small ones and a detachable head for the big ones.

Barracuda

The barracuda has a slim, pikelike, silvery body with a huge tail. Its long pointed jaws are well supplied with large, heavy teeth. They are

Barracuda.

beautiful, extremely fast, sleek, and though they can be observed often at a dead stop in the water, display great power during thrusts of speed when they decide to make a run. At other times they will be seen slowly and gracefully inching their way about, gliding in curious observation or in search of food. Small barracudas are good food fishes but it is the large roe, abundant with vitamins, that is highly prized. The flesh of the barracuda is rather soft and the flavor is mild. Used primarily in steak form, barracuda meat is good fried, broiled, baked, or barbecued.

*   The great barracuda of tropical and subtropical seas, including Florida, can be dangerous to eat. Eating an occasional large one (thirty pounds) may cause ciguatera poisoning. The small Pacific barracuda caught off the coast of California and Baja California grows to twelve pounds and is harmless and safe to eat.

Equipment Tips

Use a long-range, hard-hitting gun and a strong nylon line. Use a fixed head rather than a detachable head so the weight of the shaft will slow down this fast fish. Aim for the head. The body flesh is soft and the shaft may tear out if a body shot is made.

Damselfish and Scaly-fin Fishes

These are mostly small, colorful tropical fishes not popular as food. The damselfishes, or demoiselles (family Pomacentridae), are jewellike in color and include the sergeant major, clown fish, blue chromis, blacksmith, and garibaldi. The garibaldi is the largest damselfish, is edible, and ranges from Southern California (where it is protected by law) to the tropics.

The scaly-fin fishes are the most beautiful in color, form, and movement and include butterflyfishes, angelfishes, tangs, surgeonfishes, unicornfishes, and spadefishes. The spadefish is the largest (to three feet) and is a fine food fish.

*   All of these fishes sometimes develop ciguatera poisoning in the Indo-Pacific area. The Pacific coast of tropical America has ciguatera problems with the sergeant major, butterflyfish (*C. nigrirostris*), angelfish (*Holocanthus passer*), and surgeonfish (*P. punctatus.*)

Equipment Tips

A good underwater camera is the best equipment to use on this delightful and beautiful group.

Scaly-fin fishes.

SERGEANT
MAJOR

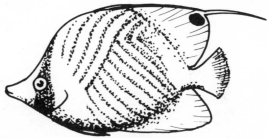

THREADFIN BUTTERFLYFISH

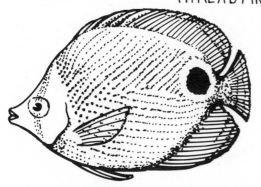

FOUREYE
BUTTERFLYFISH

ANGELFISH

Flatfishes

Emerging from his egg as an enthusiastic, symmetrically formed pelagic fish, the flatfish becomes rebellious early in his youth and decides to become a bottom dweller This necessitates some complicated body modification that nevertheless fails to deter the youngster's decision. After much deliberation over the millennia, baby flatfish merely causes his features to migrate to the top, so that both eyes are positioned close together on the same side of his body—the side which will face upward. Now he can lie on his side and hide on the bottom by flipping sand over his entire body, leaving just his two eyes protruding to watch for food and predators. This all results in a very odd-looking, very flat, fish.

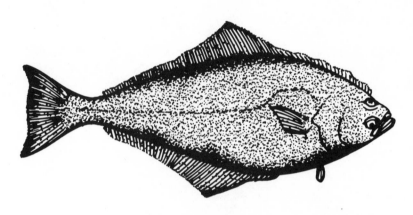

PACIFIC HALIBUT

Flatfishes.

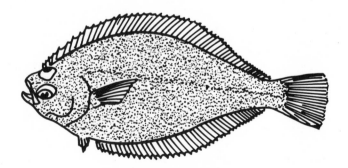

The flatfishes (order Pleuronectiformes) include halibuts, soles, turbots, sandabs, flukes, plaice, and flounders. Large flatfish can be steaked or filleted and are excellent broiled, fried, or baked. Small ones are prepared by removing viscera, and fins. The sole is considered by some to have the best flavor of all fish after it has been dead for several days. The plaice is the best known of flatfishes in Europe and commerically the most important. The flavor of this fish is best when it is fresh. Some turbots have an iodine flavor.

*   Some flounders in Europe, Mexico, and the Indian Ocean occasionally develop ciguatera poisoning.

Equipment Tips
Pole spear or small gun will get the small ones. Large halibuts will take a medium gun with a detachable spearhead. Look for the two eyes protruding from the sand and sometimes a very faint outline of the wide body under the sand.

Herringlike Fishes

This group (Isospondyli) includes herrings, shad, sardines, anchovies, menhaden, tarpons, ten-pounders, and bonefishes (order Clupeiformes); and smelts, salmons, and trouts (order Salmoniformes.) They are characterized by a single dorsal fin in the middle of the back. The tarpons, bonefish, salmons, and trouts are among the gamest of all game fish. The herrings smelts, sardines, anchovies, and related species are vitally important to the economy of man and the sea. The most numerous of all fishes and commercially the most valuable to cold water countries is the common herring, which is prepared in many ways for tasty eating. Bonefish (family Albulidae) must be very fresh to be at their best. The grunion of California, which resembles smelt, is not related to this group. Surf smelt are a delicacy when fried but a squirmy worm of an object when netted. These tasty little fish run the summer surf from icy Alaskan waters to Point Conception of California. They come in to spawn in tidewaters off sandy beaches and are scooped up with dip nets or small seines.

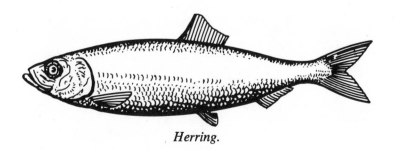

Herring.

FUN WITH HERRING

Herring weren't hatched just for packing into cans for the supermarket.
Here's three ways to prepare your own and save the cost of the middle-
man:

PICKLED HERRING

(Scandinavian)

You Will Need
3 herring   1 cup sugar
1 onion, sliced   6 bay leaves
2½ teaspoons whole allspice, crushed
1 cup vinegar

Clean herring and soak in cold water 24 hours, changing the water
several times. Remove head, skin, and bones. Rinse and drain. Cut into
1-inch pieces. Arrange in covered refrigerator dish in layers with onion;
sprinkle with allspice. Combine vinegar, sugar, and bay leaves; pour
mixture over herring. Store, covered, in refrigerator for at least 24 hours
before serving.

ROLLMOPS

You Will Need
6 herring   1 red pepper, cut up
  Prepared mustard   2 bay leaves
2 small sour pickles, sliced   6 peppercorns
1 tablespoon capers   1½ cups cider vinegar
                                                   1 cup water

Clean herring and soak in cold water for 24 hours, changing water
several times. Remove head and bones. Rinse and drain. Spread herring
with prepared mustard, pickle slices, onion slices, and capers. Roll up
each herring and secure with toothpicks. Place in small container with
red pepper, peppercorns and bay leaves. *Do not* use a metal container.
Boil together vinegar and water. Cool; pour over herring. Cover and let
stand for 3 to 6 days. Drain before serving. Serve with sour cream, if
desired.

HERRING IN SOUR CREAM

You Will Need
5 herring   ½ teaspoon powdered mustard

1 cup dairy sour cream	2 onions, sliced
2 tablespoons cider vinegar	Dash cayenne
1 teaspoon Worcestershire	Chopped parsley

Clean herring and soak in cold water for 24 hours, changing water several times. Remove head, skin, and bones. Rinse and drain. Cut into 1-inch pieces. Combine remaining ingredients; add herring and mix lightly. Place in glass jar; cover. Let stand in refrigerator for about 12 hours before serving.

Clupeotoxism

* Tropical herrings and anchovies, sardines, shad, and sprats (Clupeiformes) have been incriminated in human poisonings around the island areas of the tropical Atlantic, tropical Pacific, and the Caribbean Sea. This form of poisoning is called clupeotoxism, and is a sporadic, unpredictable health problem, but tropical clupeiform fishes are most likely to be toxic during the warm summer months. Those that were toxic have been captured close to shore. Eating affected fish usually leaves a metallic taste in the mouth. Death can occur in less than 15 minutes with this type of poisoning, and the case fatality rate is very high.

Grunion

"The grunion are running!!!" This exciting and tantalizing exclamation belongs to those on California or Gulf of California beaches exclusively, and though there are still some who believe the grunion runs on these beaches are a hoax, these unique fish delight Californians several times annually. Grunion are of the silverside family and are the only fish that spawn and lay their eggs on land. They are small, to about seven inches in length, but are excellent eating. Though they are neither a diver's nor fisherman's game, per se, every seafood lover should be acquainted with some details on the grunion's habits and how to catch and eat them.

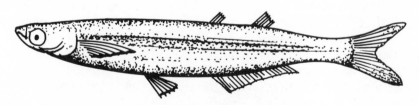

Grunion.

Grunion range in color from ashy grey to the thin blue and silver lateral stripe and the silvery belly. They range from Monterey, California to San Quintin Bay, Baja and on the shores of the Gulf of California.

Their remarkable built-in timing system directs them to their spawning grounds on sandy beaches exactly on the second, third, or fourth nights following the full or new moon at high tide. Also, they have their own discriminating system which dictates that the one-year-olds shall spawn in April and May (the height of the spawning season) and that the two- and three-year-olds only shall perform the spawning ritual during March, June, July, and August. Newspapers usually note the date and time that the grunion are expected to make their runs for several days or weeks before the run. This is for the benefit of beachgoers who wish to try their luck at catching a pailfull of the slippery little fish. A beach party during grunion season often turns into a wild, late night scramble where soaking wet participants laugh and scream in glee as thousands of six- or seven-inch, wriggling fish squirm ankle deep around the hunters' bare feet. Grunion on California beaches make their runs late at night and beach parties are planned around these times. Many times the excitement of the hotdog crowd, however, frightens off the grunion and they will not appear at all that night. On Gulf of California beaches, high tides occur during the daytime (but grunion hunts during daylight hours aren't nearly as much fun!).

During the three or four nights of the "run" the fish appear on intermittent beaches for a half hour to an hour, appearing one hour later with each succeeding night. If they make their run at 11:00 P.M. the first night, the next night they may be expected at around 12:00 midnight and the following night at around 1:00 A.M. and so forth. A few "scouts" will be seen on the wet sand first but these scouts retreat with the next wave. The orgy begins several waves later as thousands of wriggling, silvery fish hit the beach. The female grunion, after succeeding in luring one or more males to chase her around in the surf, waits for the next big swell, then scuttles up on the sandy shore with the breaker. Then the flopping, stranded fish go to work. The female quickly digs tail-first into the wet sand until she is about half buried. While she lays her eggs two or three inches below the surface, the male curls his body around her and releases the milt that will fertilize the eggs below. The fish then let themselves be washed back into the sea with the next wave. The eggs will mature for fourteen days, until the next high tide. When high tide waters finally reach the now mature eggs, sea water mixes with them—a necessary ingredient to the hatching—and the eggs hatch into the ocean. Out of one or two thousand eggs laid by the female grunion, only about two or three baby grunion survive the elements and predators.

The law allows no tools for grunion hunting—all fish must be caught entirely by hand. The only implement seen during a grunion hunt, therefore, is a bucket or pot (or even your pockets!) in which to hold the grunion once you have caught them. No limit is placed on the number that may be taken, but it is unlawful to catch grunion in April and May when the one-year-olds come in. During March, June, July, and August,

The beautiful red syrup that is a by-product of Krazy Kelp Kandy makes a delicious, nutritious ice cream or pudding topping. Kelp Kandy is in the fore-ground on the platter.

Edibles and inedibles of the sea. Tiny blue chromis fish of the tropics accent sea fans and staghorn coral in the Grand Cayman Island waters.

Crayfish cookout with boiled crayfish and dip. COURTESY CORBETT PHIBBS.

however, anyone with the patience and purpose is welcome to try his luck at the game of grunion grabbing.

John Olquin, the curator and director of the Cabrillo Beach Marine Museum at Cabrillo Beach, California, has delighted thousands of adults and children with his lectures and demonstrations on the beach during grunion run seasons. The recipe we used for frying grunion for crowds on the beach during two of Mr. Olquin's lectures one year will be found with the fish recipes in this chapter.

Eels and Eel-like Fishes

Eels, though shunned by the squeamish because of their snakelike appearance, are true fish and are enjoyed by people the world over, the common eel (family Anquillidae) being popular in many parts of the United States. Common eels are actually freshwater fishes that enter salt water to breed. They are of worldwide distribution wherever there are continually flowing rivers to the sea. They are not found in Southern California or Baja because rivers in these areas are sporadic and dry up from time to time, flowing only during the wet seasons.

Moray Eels

Moray eels (family Muraenidae) are strictly ocean fish and lurk worldwide in tropical, subtropical, and some temperate reefs. Morays differ in some respects to freshwater eels in that they are larger and have no pectoral fins or scales. In temperate waters, such as Southern California, morays are usually very timid and live in reef or rock holes and crevices. Tropical morays, however, are more aggressive and may come out of their lairs to look you over. Attacks from eels are rare and it seems possible that unprovoked attacks have occurred during the eel's breeding season.

Moray eel.

Moray eels are usually very timid.

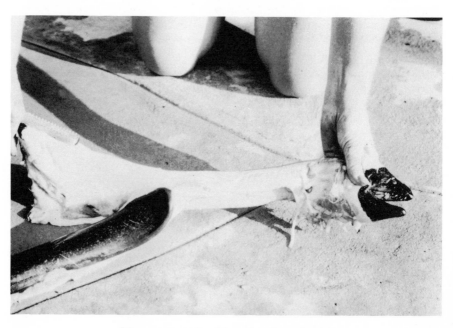

Morays must be skinned to be palatable.

Moray eels have a delicious chicken-like flavor and are one of the few fish that are cooked slowly, much as chicken. The moray must be skinned to make him palatable, because the skin is laden with a strong oil.

* Poisoning from eating morays is also very rare. Morays have been eaten in Mediterranean, tropical, and subtropical countries around the world for hundreds of years. At one banquet given by Caesar, six thousand morays were eaten! Though the morays of California and colder seas are safe to eat, the flesh of some tropical varieties (*Gymnothorax genera*) occasionally develop ciguatera poisoning. The toxins are water soluble, consequently eel soup would be especially dangerous. Moray eels should be avoided as food around the Hawaiian Islands, Polynesia, westward to East Africa, Japan, and south to Australia.

Lampreys

Lampreys differ from eels in many respects and where eels are in the class Osteichthyes, lampreys are of the class Agnatha. Lampreys are minus pectoral and ventral fins and also lack functional jaws. The mouth is an interesting-looking round opening that has great suction power and is used to attach the lamprey to a fish so that it can feed on the fish. Lampreys are not generally popular as food in the United States but are a well-known dish in New England and Europe. Some people feel the flesh of the lamprey is finer and fatter than the common eel and therefore quite tasty. The lamprey must be scalded before the skin can be removed. The meat can be used in most eel recipes.

Lamprey.

* Often, lampreys have toxin in the slime and flesh. Eating toxic lampreys or hagfish can produce gastrointestinal upset known as cyclostome poisoning.

Wolf Eels

These are not true eels but are the largest of the blennoid fishes. They have an unmistakable eel-like appearance but are not as sleek as the moray and have a puffy, almost bulldog-like countenance. The wolf eel is of northern distribution in the Atlantic and Pacific and holes up like the moray. A wolf eel will grow to a length of eight feet or more. Eastern fish markets have sold a half million pounds of wolf eel annually.

Equipment Tips
Use a pole spear or small gun with a slip tip. A noose has been found most practical in taking wolf eels.

MINI-EEL

This is a Japanese recipe that uses small eels. It can be applied, however, to larger eels that have been cut into small 1½- to 2-inch lengths.
You Will Need
      8 small eels or cut up large eels, cut into short lengths
      Salt
      Make a sauce of:
      1 cup Shoyu (soy sauce light)
      ½ tablespoon Meering cooking wine
      ½ tablespoon sake wine
      4 tablespoons sugar
Mix sauce ingredients well and boil for 2 minutes. Allow 2 small eels per person, or 2 strips cut up large eels. Season eels with salt and cook under preheated grill for 7 to 10 minutes, brushing with sauce frequently and turning when first side is browned. Serve hot.

FRIED EEL

This recipe is mainly for moray eel, which has a thick, solid body and must be prepared as one cooks chicken, that is, fried slowly until done clear through.

Cut the cleaned eel meat into 6-inch long slices. Sauté sliced onions and green pepper in oil until limp, then remove from pan. Dip eel meat first in milk, then in seasoned crumbs, coating evenly. Brown on both sides, then turn heat down and simmer in juices until tender when tested with a fork. Serve on a bed of the onion and green pepper mixture.

Pufferlike Fishes and Relatives

This group (order Tetraodontiformes) includes some of the most unusual and interesting fish in the ocean as far as appearance is concerned. Puffers, porcupinefishes, boxfishes, molas, trunkfishes, triggerfishes, and filefishes are all members of this clan. Most of them are in greatest abundance near ocean shores in the tropics.

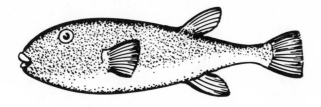

NORMALLY DEFLATED

Puffer fish.

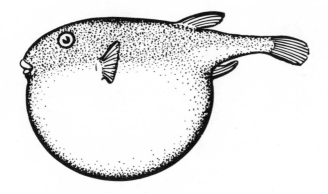

INFLATED PUFFER

Puffer Fish

Puffers (family Tetraodontidae) are also known as swellfish, globefish, swelltoad, blowfish, fugu fish, sea squab, and toadfish, and all are capable of inflating themselves with water or air when frightened or molested. The puffer *Sphaeroides maculatus,* found on the middle Atlantic coast of the United States, is edible and marketed. Skinned fillets of most smooth skinned puffer fish are edible.

Some puffers develop a powerful nerve poison in their gonads, liver, intestines, and skin that is called tetraodon poisoning. The greatest concentrations of poison are usually in the ovaries and liver. The weakest toxins are in the flesh or musculature and has been found not lethal with less than 100 grams, or slightly under one quarter pound. It is well to note that over 60 percent of the victims poisoned by puffers die and it behooves one to be very cautious in determining whether the species at hand is edible or not.

Especially trained fugu cooks in Japan are capable of preparing the puffer so that it is edible, and only government licensed restaurants are

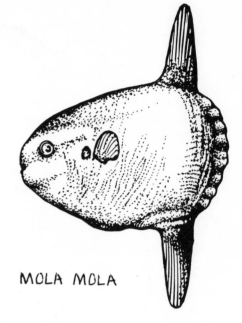

Porcupine fish and mola mola.

allowed to serve fugu; also, cooks in these restaurants must display their fugu cooking training certificates. These cooks are required to know the names and positions of all the puffer fish's organs, and the procedure for preparing fugu is tedious and time consuming. The finished product, however, is a beautiful arrangement of finger lickin' good fugu ready to eat. Naturally, it all results in very high prices for this fare, but the Japanese consider the dish a great delicacy. Fugu enthusiasts in Japan generally consume about three pounds of the meat at one sitting, and the after effects are notable, leaving a slight tingling in the extremities—which the diners seem to enjoy—though this seems a rather expensive method of acquiring a high!

The maki-maki, or "deadly death," and the black-spotted puffer are among the many poisonous species. These range from the tropical Pacific and Japan and to Africa and the Red Sea. The poisonous white-spotted puffer ranges from the West Coast of Central America to Indonesia. The gulf puffer is also poisonous and ranges from California to Peru.

Porcupinefish and Boxfish

These are two derivations of the puffers and are able to inflate themselves as other puffers. Their bodies, however, are covered with sharp spines which give them appearance of a large pincushion when they are inflated.

* The porcupinefish is eaten, however a poison in its liver and skin can contaminate the flesh.

Mola Mola

The mola mola (Molidae), or ocean sunfish is related to the puffer fish but is a very round, flat creature. Its flesh is white, tough, and of a disagreeable odor. It has a thick, leathery skin over a two- to three-inch coat of gristle that is very difficult to pierce, even with a harpoon. These fish grow to tremendous size, their disklike bodies having been found to weigh as much as 4,400 pounds (the record to date). There is probably no fish more infested by parasites, internally and externally, than this
* sluggish creature, and it is considered poisonous to eat in some areas. Many people claim to have eaten mola mola without harm, however, and say that the meat has the flavor and consistency of crab meat. Most are not tempted to sample a taste of this creature, nonetheless, due to its odor and appearance. The mola mola is sometimes called the moonfish by sailors, due to its phosphorescence at night.

Trunkfishes

The trunkfishes (family Ostraciidae) and cowfish have a solid, triangular shell from which the fins and tail protrude. Their distribution is worldwide in tropical seas. Trunkfishes are edible and sometimes baked in their own shells.
* Trunkfishes in the Indo-Pacific area and Atlantic coast of the United States sometimes develop ciguatera poisoning.

Triggerfishes and Filefishes

These fishes are not popular as food fishes and sometimes develop ciguatera poisoning. They are found in all tropical and some warm temperate seas.

The Folly of Fugu

The following recipes are mostly for the readers' interest and education and can be used if you are in an area where puffer fish are not toxic, such as the middle Atlantic coast of the United States. We strongly urge you not to attempt to prepare tropical fugu (puffer fish). Dr. Bruce Halstead, one of the world's leading authorities on sea life toxicology, and who has eaten seafood the world over for many years, told us he has never tasted fugu and doesn't intend to because he "can't afford to play that kind of Russian Roulette!"

FUGU RECIPES

The methods below are those used by the specially trained fugu cooks in Japan in preparing fugu for the table.

1. Fugu Chrysanthemum

Thoroughly clean, fillet, and skin the puffer. Clean puffers very carefully to remove the toxic viscera. Some have very strongly toxic ovaries and liver. Sometimes the skin is toxic. The muscle of most puffers is not toxic. Wrap the meat with clean cloth and keep in a refrigerator one day for dehydration. Boil skin one minute and slice into thin strips for decoration. Cut fillet into small triangular shaped pieces. Deform pieces with thumb into concave, flower-shaped petals. Arrange slices on a plate in the form of chrysanthemum, rose, etc. Season and eat.

FORM INTO FLOWER
SHAPED PETALS,
ARRANGE ON PLATE
INTO FORM OF A
CHRYSANTHEMUM.

Fugu chrysanthemum.

2. Hiresake

Cut off dorsal and pectoral fins and rub with salt. Wash and then dry one week. One of the best ways to eat this dry fin is to roast it over a charcoal fire and then pour hot sake over it. This is called *hiresake* (sake with fin) because after several cups of sake you forget about the fins!

3. Fugu Sake

Place 4 or 5 slices of puffer fish in a cup and pour hot sake over it—eat, drink, enjoy.

4. Sake-Seasoned Dried Fugu

Soak puffer fillets in sweet sake for about an hour. After drying for several days, it will be ready to eat. Dry it in the refrigerator.

5. Sake and Fugu Roe

(These appear to be recipes for sake rather than for puffer!) The most delicious sake of all is prepared by pouring warm sake over braised, coated fugu testes. Testes are used because ovaries are usually toxic in the female puffer.

Equipment Tips

Puffers are so slow that they can be caught by hand, although a short pole spear will make the job easy. For a long and healthy life, we recommend a camera as the best equipment to use for this fish. This will keep you *and* the puffer out of trouble.

Lancelets

The lancelet (Amphioxus) is not a true fish because it has no backbone but it does have some other internal characteristics similar to the fish families. For this reason it is considered an evolutionary link between the invertebrates and the vertebrates. The lancelet is fish shaped, has a narrow body that is pointed at both ends, is colorless and almost transparent, and grows to three or four inches long. It lives buried upright with its mouth protruding from clean sand in shallow waters of most coasts of semitropical and tropical regions. In North America lancelets appear as far north as Southern California and Virginia. On Amoy Island, South China, they are gathered for food daily with an average catch of a ton a day. Lancelets are considered a great delicacy in China and are eaten there either fresh or dried. They can be cooked as any small fish. To catch, shovel sand through a coarse box screen, wash away the sand, and pick out the lancelets.

Lancelet.

LANCELET TERIYAKI

Wash lancelets (no cleaning is necessary). Sauté in butter in a frying pan, then cover with teriyaki sauce and cook from 5 to 10 minutes. Serve as an entree and use the sauce to pour over vegetables or rice.

Seahorses

Seahorses and pipefish (order Gasterosteiformes) are usually found

Seahorse.

around seaweeds and though the common small species aren't really worth the bother, the large ones are good cooked in their shells. The seahorse (family Syngnathidae) has remarkable features, its head resembling that of a horse and its tail resembling, and put to somewhat the same use as, that of a monkey. Adding to this one-bodied menagerie is the seahorse's pouch like that of a kangaroo, the hard outer skeleton of an insect, and independently moving eyes like those of a chameleon. The giant seahorse (*Hippocampus igens*) of Magdalena Bay in Baja California grows from twelve to fifteen inches in length and is used as food.

*   The seahorse of Western Europe, Africa, and the Mediterranean develop ciguatera poisoning occasionally.

BARBECUED SEAHORSE

Wrap the whole seahorse in foil. Cook on a rack about four inches from hot coals, cooking 10 minutes on each side for a 12-inch seahorse.

Equipment Tips
Most seahorses can be caught easily with a net.

Sharks, Skates, and Rays

Sharks
Most sharks on the East and West Coasts of the United States and other temperate waters are good food fishes when prepared properly, with the consideration that *baked* shark meat can be disappointing.

Sharks.

LEOPARD SHARK

SPINY DOGFISH

GREENLAND SHARK

TOXIC SWELL SHARK

ANGEL SHARK

Their meat vies for flavor with many popular fishes sold at markets. Cowsharks, threshers, bonita sharks, salmon sharks, basking sharks, porbeagles, tiger sharks, mackerel sharks, makos, palomas, sand sharks, dogfish, smoothhounds, mud sharks, grayfish, and dog sharks are all included in this group. The basking shark also boasts a liver valuable for its oil. Smoothhound sharks and dogfish sharks are sold as grayfish in markets. In England, during World War II, spiny dogfish shark meat was used in the traditional "fish-and-chips." The bay grayshark and soupfin are good, also containing livers very high in vitamin A. Shark fins are a delicacy in the Orient. Blue sharks have poor quality flesh that nevertheless is good when smoked. Angel sharks are delicious, the "wings," or pectoral fins, being the most edible part and good fried as fish. The California horn shark and the similar Port Jackson shark have a delicate and excellent flavor when cooked. Use care when catching these; their spines are grooved and give out a mild poison. Their egg capsules look like the business end of a screw.

Although most sharks are edible, the flesh of tropical and arctic sharks should be indulged in only after consulting local inhabitants, and even then with due caution. The flesh in most cases is mildly toxic and seldom will cause more than a mild gastrointestinal upset and diarrhea. The flesh of the Greenland shark (*Somniosus microcephalus*) has been observed to cause intoxication on numerous occasions to man and sled dog. It was found, however, that the Greenland shark was feeding in areas subject to heavy man-made pollution.

*   The California swell shark (*Cephaloscyllium uter*) has toxic flesh. Any amount may cause nausea and diarrhea. Other species reported poisonous are the hammerhead shark, great white shark, black-tipped sand shark, six-gilled shark (*Hexanchus grisseus*), and seven-gilled shark

Dr. William L. Orris, staff physician at Scripps Institution of Oceanography, cuddles a leopard shark, an exceptionally fine food fish. COURTESY UNIVERSITY OF CALIFORNIA, SAN DIEGO, CALIFORNIA.

(*Heptranchias perlo*). The most severe forms of poisoning usually result from the eating of shark liver. Liver poisoning can cause nausea, diarrhea, muscular paralysis, and death. Avoid eating the liver of any shark unless it is known with certainty to be edible.

One way to make sure your shark meat is fresh is to catch it yourself. This is a tiger shark being handled carefully by Jean Deas, Australia. COURTESY WALTER DEAS.

Handling and Storage

Freshly caught shark is handled the same as other fish to preserve the delicate flavor. Eviscerate as soon after catching as possible and keep it cool. Some sharks have a strong ammonia odor, but after a few days of being frozen, this odor disappears. Shark may be filleted or steaked the same as bony fish. When cutting through the sandpaperlike skin, stab a hole with your knife and cut with the blade at a 90-degree angle to the skin. Otherwise the rough surface of the skin will leave you with a knife about fit for cutting butter. When preparing angel shark, cut the "wings" and tail off as close to the body as possible to obtain a maximum amount of meat. When working on the wings, run your knife between the cartilage and separate the meat from the skin by sliding a sharp knife along the skin. Fillet the tail by running a sharp knife down each side of the back bone. Cut the skin from the meat. Remove the intestines by cutting off the head and cutting the body in half to separate the back from the stomach. Fillet the top piece and remove the skin from the stomach meat. This will give you fillets from the tail, wings, back, and stomach.

SHARK N' CHIPS

Skin and fillet the shark. Cut into serving pieces ½-inch thick. Make a batter of 1 cup flour, ½ teaspoon baking powder, ¼ teaspoon salt, ¼ teaspoon pepper, 2 beaten eggs, and ½ cup water. Dip shark pieces into this batter and deep fry at 375° until golden brown, turning once. Serve with potato chips or french fried potatoes.

MARINATED SHARK FRIES

You Will Need
1 garlic clove, crushed
4 tablespoons Worcestershire sauce } For marinade
1 teaspoon lemon juice
1 cup cornmeal
½ cup flour } For dredging
Leopard, shovelnose, or angel shark, skinned and filleted

Cut the shark meat into ½-inch-thick pieces and wash them in salt or seawater. Wash again in fresh water. Place meat pieces in a flat dish and cover with marinade mixture. Marinate in refrigerator overnight. Drain the meat and dredge in a mixture of the cornmeal and flour and deep-fat fry at 375° until golden, turning once. Delicious served with three-bean (calico) salad and warm slices of French bread and butter.

SHARK AND SAUCE

You Will Need
   3 cups fried blue fin shark fillets, flaked
   2 tablespoons butter
   2 tablespoons flour
   1 cup milk plus ½ cup heavy cream
   ½ teaspoon chili powder
   ⅛ teaspoon cayenne
     Salt, pepper
     Toasted tortilla chips
Melt butter and blend in the flour. Gradually add milk and cream; cook and stir until thickened. Add sauce to the shark meat and season with chili powder, cayenne, salt and pepper to taste. Heat over low heat and serve with toasted tortilla chips. Serves 4.

Shark Fin Soup

Shark fin soup is very good, but processing the fins for cooking is complicated and difficult for the amateur. We suggest, therefore, that you purchase the shark fins for this purpose at a Chinese grocery. There are two kinds of dried shark fins sold—one is an unprocessed fin still containing the skin and bone; the other is boned and skinned and washed. It is better to buy the latter type for purposes of simplicity in cooking. Pick the pieces that look clean and of the palest color. These fins keep for several months. Shark Fin Needles are easy to prepare—easier than the whole shark fin and are sold in ½- and 1-pound packages at the Chinese groceries.

The Chinese treasure shark fin soup as the westerners laud caviar. Chinese gourmet dinners are not complete without it but it requires many hours of preparation.

"NEEDLE" SHARK FIN SOUP

You Will Need
1½ pounds shark fin "needles" (needlelike gelationous protuber-
     ances from the fin itself)
     Water
   8 green onions including green stems
   4 ½-inch pieces fresh ginger, peeled
  16 chicken necks or backs, wings, and bony chicken parts
   1 whole chicken breast, boned and skinned
   ½ egg white, beaten (beat first for ease in dividing)
2½ tablespoons cornstarch
6½ cups chicken broth
  18 thin slices cooked ham

Empty shark fin needles into a bowl and add cold water to cover about 2 inches above the fin needles. Soak 8 hours or overnight. Drain well.

Rinse the fin in warm water, drain, and place in a *large* kettle. Add 4 quarts warm water and add onions that have been tied together in a bunch. Add ginger. Simmer (covered partly) for an hour and cool. Drain the fin again and discard water, onions and ginger. Pick over the shark fin, retaining only the golden needles and other edible matter, discarding any tough or dark portions or foreign particles.

Rinse fin again and wrap in cheesecloth. Put into a kettle and add 10 cups of water and chicken pieces except the chicken breast. Cover and simmer 1½ hours. Remove and discard the chicken. Drain again and discard liquid.

Cut chicken breast into thin slices, then into fine shreds. Place shreds into a bowl and add the egg white and 1½ teaspoons cornstarch. Blend well with fingers and refrigerate 30 minutes. Meanwhile, heat the chicken broth in a kettle and add the shark fin (removed from the cheesecloth). Bring to a boil and stir simultaneously. Take off the heat and stir in the chicken breast pieces, stirring to keep pieces separated. Add the ham and stir again. Bring to a boil and blend in the remaining 2 tablespoons cornstarch which has been combined with ¼ cup water to smooth. Stir in cornstarch mixture slowly and simmer about 5 seconds. Serves 6 to 10.

Skates and Rays

Most skates and rays are edible. The skate is commercially valuable in European fisheries, where it is taken in trawls with long lines and rod and line; and rays up to two hundred pounds have been landed. It is the wings of these animals that are used as food commercially, though the heavy tails of some contain plenty of meat also. As with sharks, tropical skates and rays should be eaten only after asking local people
* and even then with due caution. The liver and other viscera of skates and rays should not be eaten. Use caution when handling a stingray—a powerful poison is secreted along the sides of the barb, which is located on top of the tail. Should injury occur, soak the injured part in hot water or hot epsom salts solution. The electric ray should be left alone due to its ability to produce a powerful, high-voltage shock.

Sharks, skates, and rays have firm muscular fibers that will become more tender by aging in the refrigerator or freezer for several days. Some sharks, skates, and rays have an oily, unpleasant taste when cooked, but are good when smoked. Skates and rays should either be fried as you would any other fish, or smoked.

Equipment Tips

Use a slip tip on a medium-sized spear gun or pole spear for small sharks and rays to twenty pounds. Larger sharks will require an explosive power head. A forty four magnum cartridge is more efficient than a shotgun shell. For some large sharks, breakaway gear with a slip tip is satisfactory. Before hunting sharks, read a good book about them; some species, of course, can be extremely dangerous.

Skates and rays.

MANTA RAY

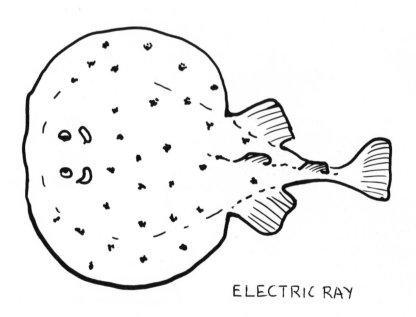

ELECTRIC RAY

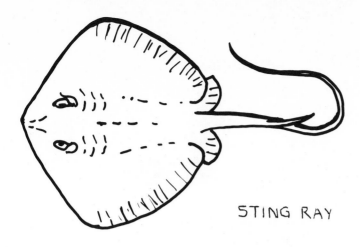

STING RAY

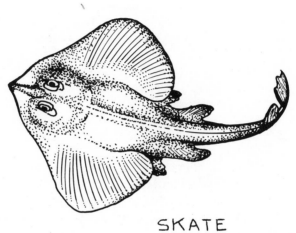

SKATE

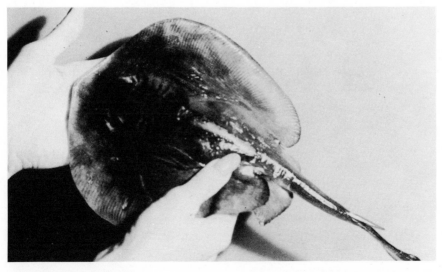

The barb on the tail of a stingray can be seen about halfway between the end of the tail and the anal fin.

FRIED SKATE OR RAY

Dip skate or ray meat strips or cubes into beaten egg and roll in your choice of crumbs. Fry as fish in butter until brown, or french fry by dipping in a batter of 2 cups milk and 3 beaten eggs, then roll in flour and deep fat fry at 375° until brown. Serve with rice.

FRIED GUITAR FISH

Since the pectorals of the guitar fish are quite small, it is the tail we are interested in as food in this fellow. Fillet and slice the tail into ½-inch strips. Dip in egg beaten with a little Worcestershire sauce, then roll in seasoned cracker crumbs, or use Dixiefry if your market has it. Fry in a half-and-half mixture of oil and butter. Cook just until brown, or about 5 minutes on each side, depending on how thick the meat is. Serve with lemon wedges.

Chimaeras

Ratfish, or chimaeras, are more closely related to sharks and rays, since they have a cartilaginous skeleton rather than the hard skeleton of the bony fishes. The flesh, liver, and roe of some of the chimaeras have been found to be toxic. There is also a single dorsal spine as venomous as the scorpionfish.

Ratfish.

Cleaning Fish

Nothing is tastier than a freshly caught fish, and a few simple precautions taken right after the fish is landed will insure the preservation of the delicate, fine flavor.

The first action to take after capturing your fish is to eviscerate it. Slit the stomach open from anus to gills. Leave the head on to help pre-

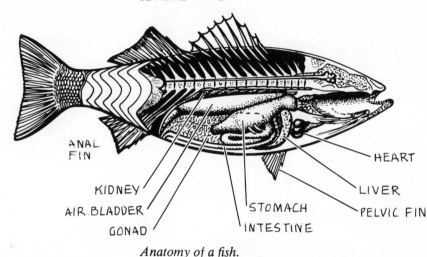

Anatomy of a fish.

serve the fish. Don't forget to remove the kidney along the spine at the very back of the abdominal cavity under the air bladder. This preliminary cleaning will allow the blood to drain and retard deterioration. Later, you can fillet it or scale it if you intend to bake it. Remove the liver from the rest of the innards if you desire to save it too. The liver is low and forward near the gills and is considered to be the most nutritious part of some species of fish. It may be cooked with the fish or separately as with chicken livers.

Keep your fish cool by putting it on ice or in a wet burlap bag. Keeping the fish cool retards decomposition. If you intend to freeze the fish, drop it into a plastic bag and evacuate the air to retard evaporation and dehydration.

Fish may be prepared for cooking in a number of different forms. These are whole, drawn, dressed, steaked, filleted, and sticks. Whole fish must be scaled and eviscerated before frying or baking and are then called "drawn fish." Dressed fish are scaled, eviscerated, usually with the head, tail, and fins removed. Steaks are slices of the larger sizes of dressed fish. Fillets are the sides of fishes cut away from the backbone. Usually the skin is removed. Sticks are cut from fillets or steaks.

Cooking Fish

The Orientals and some Latin nationalities will tell you that the best way to cook fish—is not to. It is true that if prepared properly, raw fish can be delectable, and two or three recipes for preparing fish served raw appear at the beginning of the fish recipe section. Most Westerners pre-

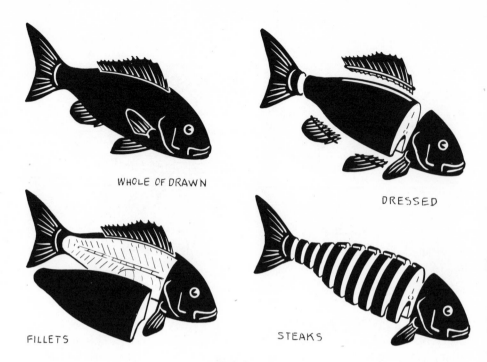

WHOLE OF DRAWN

DRESSED

FILLETS

STEAKS

Fish forms.

fer their fish cooked, however, and most fish can be cooked in any of six basic methods with good results, keeping in mind a few rather obvious points such as size of fish and thickness of fillets. One of our recommendations is to think not in terms of "cooking" fish but merely of heating it together with seasonings and juices to firm the meat somewhat and to enhance the flavor. Unlike most warmblooded animals whose meat becomes more tender the longer it's cooked, fish has flesh that becomes dry and tough with long cooking, much as in the case of an egg. Fish protein is best when cooked only slightly to keep the full flavor and to preserve its naturally moist, tender quality. One of the exceptions to the above rule is the cooking of eel. Eel is a fish, yet the meat is so thick and solid that the best method of cooking it is to braise it, cooking it slowly until the meat is cooked through. Another exception is the garibaldi of California. Though this fish is delicious, we highly recommend that you don't cook it—as a matter of fact, don't even bring this beautiful sea-going "goldfish" home. Garibaldi in California, though becoming abundant enough to be a pest to divers, at this writing are still protected by law and the stiff fine for catching one makes it a very expensive dish!

Make a cut behind the gills and toward the head to get more meat.

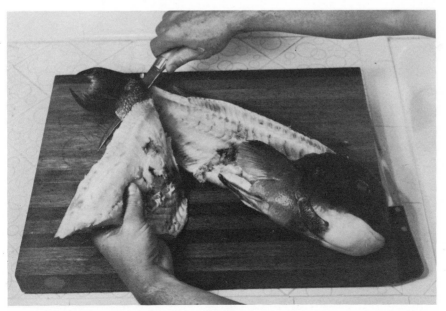

Slice along the backbone to the tail, leaving the skin attached at the tail.

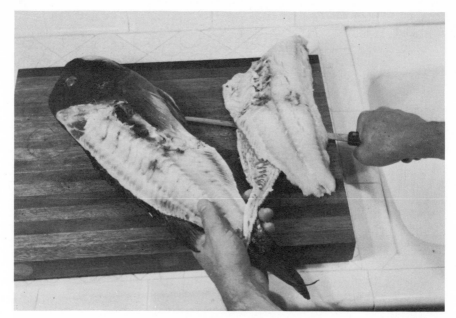

With skin side down, slip the knife along the skin to cut off the meat.

Remove the rib section and all other bones. Now you have a real fillet. Repeat the procedure on the other side of the fish.

By observing two important tips before cooking your fish, you will greatly improve the finished product:

1. Wash the meat of fish as little as possible in cold water right after cleaning. Don't wash it a second time when thawing from the freezer—you'll wash away the zing in the flavor. Wash in cold, salted water or seawater and NEVER use warm water or you'll partially cook your fish on the spot.
2. Blot fresh or thawed fillets with paper towels before cooking—this prevents undue splattering while cooking and helps any crumbs or batter to cling better during cooking.

FIVE BASIC COOKING METHODS

Butter Sauté (Small, whole fish and thin fillets)

Use clarified butter if possible or half butter and half oil. Have oil and/or butter from ⅛ to ¼ inch deep in skillet. Sprinkle fish with salt and fresh ground pepper (freshly ground salt also will add excitement of flavor to any cooking. Buy rock salt and use a regular pepper grinder). Coat fillets if desired and sauté 1 to 3 minutes on each side, depending on thickness of fillets—it's the old thing, "until the fish flakes when probed with a fork."

Deep-fat Frying and Pan Frying (Small, whole fish or thin fillets)

Dip fish in beaten egg and crumbs or coating mix. Fry in salad oil or oil and butter. Or deep fat fry at 375°. Either method, fry 3 minutes on each side—a little longer for thicker pieces, again using a fork to test for doneness.

Broiling and Barbecuing (Any fish cleaned and scaled)

Place large fish directly on grill and small fish in hinged rack. Blot each side of fish with paper towel and season each side with salt and pepper. If you broil in the oven, dust with flour or brush with oil before broiling unless you're cooking salmon, shad, cod, or any fish that has a little more fat. Baste with lemon juice or garlic butter sauce while cooking. Cook 5 to 10 minutes on each side, depending on size of the fish.

Poaching (Cleaned and skinned firm-fleshed fish)

Poaching is used a lot for cold fish dishes such as salads or cocktails (sheep-head is a natural as a crab substitute and some restaurants use it this way). Many recipes can be found, however, for hot poached fish and the variations of sauces and poaching mixtures give this method a top billing. Place enough water to cover fish in pot and add either 2 tablespoons crab boil spice or 1 sliced onion, 2 teaspoons salt, and ⅓ cup white wine; also tie into a piece of double cheesecloth 5 peppercorns, some leaf thyme, a bayleaf,, a short stalk of celery, and a strip of carrot if you like. Drop the cheesecloth package in along with the fish and cook 15 minutes, then remove cheesecloth bag and fish. Slip bones from the fish and strain the broth. The broth itself is so delicious you may want to serve it as a first course soup—or some of it can be used as the base for a fish sauce.

Steaming (Any size firm-fleshed fish)

Steaming fish is done by utilizing the steam generated from boiling water. This method insures that the fish retains its natural juices and flavors. A steam cooker is ideal but any deep pan with a tight cover will work for you in the same manner. If a steaming rack is not available, anything may be used that keeps the fish from touching the water. Water used for steaming may be plain or seasoned with various spices, herbs, or wine. After the water is boiling rapidly, place the fish on the rack and cover the pan tightly, then steam the fish for 5 to 10 minutes or until it flakes easily when tested with a fork. Steamed fish is used in much the same manner as poached fish.

Baking (Large, whole fish or large, thick fillets)

Fish with strong, oily skin such as the sheep-head, some rockfish, and moray eels should always be skinned before cooking due to the strong, gamey flavor that the oily skin imparts to the meat. The same is true of the garibaldi (which, of course, is illegal to take in California).

Bake fish at about 350° from 10 to about 45 minutes—again, how big is your fish—and figure about 15 minutes per pound. Use your imagination for serving and presentation; stuff it, baste it with special sauce, fiillet it, bake it whole or with fins and head on or off. If you leave the head on, a slice of stuffed olive placed over the fish's eye adds to its appeal on the platter.

If you're at a beach cabin, traveling on a boat, or on a safari without proper implements and feel you just have to bake your fish, use an improvised oven or even a trench in the sand. Follow the rule of thumb of moderate heat and baste the fish with butter and lemon juice periodically (if you have them) or wrap the fish in seaweed to add moisture and flavor. Bake until the flesh separates neatly when probed with a fork, stick, or diving knife. A 1-pound perch will bake in about 15 minutes— a 400-pound bass will take about 7 days!

DISHES OF FISHES

In the Beginning (Fish Was Raw!)

Many of the world's healthiest peoples have been eating uncooked fish for hundreds of years, enjoying not only the nutritional aspects but the tender, moist, delicate flavor of "fish in the raw," to say nothing of the benefits they derive from ease in preparation. Tahitians sometimes "cook" the raw fish first by marinating it in lime or lemon juice. The Orientals are famous for constructing beautiful, mosaic-type patterns with their foods, and their raw fish displays are something to behold.

Peter Matthiessen, who wrote the wonderful book *Blue Meridian* when he was a crew member on Peter Gimbel's expedition which resulted in the movie *Blue Water—White Death*, told us he prefers his fish raw or marinated briefly in plain lemon juice. "The Japanese dried algae called 'nori' is marvelous," said Peter, and he is a true seafood lover who could add remarks about several types of shellfish—but those are other subjects in this book.

To begin the recipe section for fish we give you three raw fish dishes; one for the very popular Mexican ceviche, one for Tahitian cru, and one for the Japanese sashimi.

RAY CANNON'S "CIVICHE"

Ray Cannon is well known to everyone who loves the sea. His book *The Sea of Cortez* is the most beautiful and informative compilation about Baja California that has ever been published to date. Another of his works, *How To Fish the Pacific Coast*, is dog-eared by every fisherman and diver who owns it. When we asked him for his favorite recipe or favorite fish, this is what he told us:

"There are several scientific accounts of shipwrecked fishermen of Mexico cast up on one of the barren islands in the Sea of Cortez—and surviving for several weeks. Recently a victim got ashore with nothing but his shorts, but when rescued 5 weeks later he had gained 5 pounds. His secret for water and food was raw sierra, which he speared with a driftwood javelin. But he didn't need to adjust to eating raw fish—the favorite food of most fishing folks around this sea is 'Civiche':

Dice 2 cups of fillet of fresh sierra or other freshly caught fish. Now put the juice of a lemon or lime, along with a sprinkle of salt, into a shallow container with the fish and marinate it for 1½ hours. Then add a cup of diced, very ripe tomatoes, ½ cup onion, ¼ cup Bell pepper, and sprinkle of black pepper and oregano, and serve."

Another recipe given to us by Ray Cannon will be found under "Steamed Fish."

TAHITAN CRU

You Will Need

1½ pounds firm, white fish fillets, cut in ½-inch chunks
2 medium onions, finely diced
1½ cups lime juice (juice from 6 limes or bottled lime juice)
1 cup peeled, diced cucumber (about ½-inch cubes)
1 cup diced celery (about ½-inch cubes)
½ cup shredded coconut

Cut fish into ½-inch pieces and place with onions in a bowl that has a lid. (A partially frozen fillet is much easier to cube than one at room temperature.) Cover with lime juice and secure lid. Place in refrigerator for 12 hours or at room temperature for 6 hours. Now drain off the lime juice and set fish mixture aside. Drop coconut into 1 pint of boiling water. Stir slightly, place the lid on the pan and set off the heat for 20 minutes. Meanwhile add celery and cucumber to fish and onion mixture.

Pour the coconut mixture into a cheesecloth covered colander that has been placed over a pan. Now pull up corners of cheese cloth and squeeze to get as much coconut nectar as possible—it will be hot! Discard coconut meat and pour coconut nectar over the fish and vegetable mixture. Stir, then chill for several hours or overnight. Drain off liquid and serve as a salad for a barbecue or as an appetizer. Very cool and unique in flavor—and straight from Tahiti.

SASHIMI

This is a basic recipe for Sashimi that explains how to cut up the fish and how to arrange and serve it. Usually, several types of fish are used on the platter for color and flavor variation. The delicate color of albacore or tuna, the brilliance of salmon, and the pure white of sea bass make a beautiful arrangement in combination. It is very important that the fish be fresh.

You Will Need

1 pound tuna or other fish, or ⅓ pound each of three types
2 cups shredded lettuce
   Small dishes of grated daikon (Japanese radish), horseradish, ginger; or various miso mixtures.
   Shoyu sauce (soy sauce)

Fillet and skin the fish. Remove any dark portions of the flesh. With a large, thin, sharp knife, slice the fish across the grain into thin slices, about ⅛ to ¼ inches thick. This gives the pattern of the grain and color to the fish. Line a platter with shredded lettuce and arrange the sliced fish over this, overlapping the pieces and creating an attractive pattern, keeping each type of fish separate from the others to create color uniformity. Each guest dips a slice into shoyu sauce and then into the sauce of his choice from the small dishes on the side.

Fried Fish

CURRIED LINGCOD

"If I were to name one particular fish that I enjoy more than any other," said T. F. "Duke" Pawlowicz, "I guess it would have to be ling-cod, though the decision is very difficult because I love all fish and shellfish." Duke is a well-known United States and world spearfishing champion and is among the majority of spearfishermen who practice fish conservation religiously, taking only enough fish at a time to eat.

The recipe below is adaptable also to rockfish, halibut, or sheep-head.

You Will Need
4 fish steaks or fillets (about 1½ to 2 pounds)
2 tablespoons minced onion
1 clove garlic, minced
1 teaspoon curry powder
½ teaspoon salt
Generous dash cayenne

Combine all ingredients except fish. Mix well and rub over both sides of the fillets or steaks. Cover and let stand in refrigerator for three hours. Remove and dust fish with flour to coat. Heat 1½ tablespoons each butter and oil in skillet and brown both sides over moderate heat. Serve with parsley, lemon wedges, and chutney if desired.

THE NUTS IN FILLETS

You Will Need
Thin fillets
2 egg whites
½ cup fine cracker crumbs
¾ cup white flour
1 cup black walnut meats, chopped fine

Beat egg whites until stiff in deep bowl. Mix cracker crumbs and flour in a paper bag. Shake fillets in bag with flour mixture, then hold fillets with a fork and dip into egg whites. Now dip them quickly into nut meats, covering well with the nuts. Melt a good glob of butter in a frying pan and add 2 tablespoons water or melted beef suet to keep the coating from getting too brown. Fry fish slowly until done.

FILLETS AND FRIES

You Will Need
  1 pound fish fillets
  ¾ cup all-purpose flour
  1 teaspoon chili powder
  ½ teaspoon salt
  ¼ teaspoon pepper
  ½ cup milk
  2 onions, peeled and sliced
  ½ cup butter
  1 16-oz. package frozen cottage-fried potatoes

Cut fish into 4 portions and dredge in combined flour chili powder, salt, and pepper. Dip coated fillets in milk, then dredge in flour mixture again; let dry a few minutes on a wire rack. Sauté onion in butter till tender; remove to a platter. Arrange fish in the same pan in single layer and fry 4 minutes on each side.

Prepare potatoes according to directions on carton. Serve fish on the bed of onions, arranging potatoes around the edge of the platter.

FISH CAKE

from Cal Matsuda
You Will Need
  Fish fillets (about 1 lb. or 1 fish)
  Fresh onion
  Salt, pepper, other seasonings you like
  Chopped chives
  1 can shrimp (optional)
  Beaten egg

Grind fish fillets, onions, and shrimp (if used) in meat grinder. Place in bowl and mix with seasonings and chives, adding a little beaten egg to give it body. Shape into patties as for hamburgers and fry quickly on both sides. Serve hot or cold. Makes delicious cold sandwiches.

ROY HAUSER'S CALICO BASS

Roy Hauser is one of the most popular and well-liked divers and dive-boat skippers in Southern California who leave from L.A. to offshore islands. His boat, the *Truth*, is used extensively by dive clubs and others in the area. Roy looks after his passengers like an old mother hen. He knows areas where specific types of sea life are most abundant, the best seasons, and best times of day they are to be found better than anyone we know in that area. Roy frequently takes time out to fry up big batches of calico bass for his passengers—just for the fun of it—after the day's diving is ended. His method is simple and has no secret (unless it's the brand of bread crumbs he uses!) but is delicious, succulent, and aromatic. You can't miss with a calico fresh from the sea, frying oil, and Contadina Seasoned Bread Crumbs.

Simply fillet the fish and coat the fillets with Contadina Seasoned Bread Crumbs—using no predip beforehand. Fry quickly in very hot oil until golden. *Don't overcook.* Better fry plenty of fillets—they'll go fast! If your area doesn't seem to have Contadina Bread Crumbs, inquire of the Carnation Company, who makes them.

BATTERS, COATINGS, AND MARINADES

Larry's Beer Batter (for frying or deep-fat frying)
Mix together: 3 cups flour, 2 teaspoons salt, 2½ teaspoons baking powder, and 5 tablespoons oil. Pour in beer, slowly, and mix as you pour until mixture is smooth and of a "pouring" thin consistency.

Plain Batter
2 eggs	1 teaspoon baking powder
½ to ⅔ cup milk	½ teaspoon salt
1 cup sifted flour	2 tablespoons melted shortening

Put the eggs into a bowl and beat well, then add milk. Sift together flour, baking powder, and salt. Add to milk mixture. Adding shortening and beat at low speed until blended. Dip fish into the batter and let excess drain off.

Coatings
Fish fillets should be dipped first in cold water, seawater, or milk, then dredged in one of the following: Flour seasoned with salt and pepper, seasoned pancake flour, packaged biscuit mix, fine dry bread or cracker crumbs, or Dixiefry.

Fish also can be dipped first in seasoned flour, then in a mixture of 2 eggs beaten slightly with ½ cup milk or Worcestershire sauce, then dipped in fine dry bread or cracker crumbs, or a mixture of ½ cup flour and ½ cup cornmeal.

Marinated Fish
Combine:
¼ cup chopped onion, ¼ cup catsup, 1 tablespoon vinegar, 1 teaspoon Worcestershire sauce, 3 tablespoons lemon juice, ⅓ cup tomato juice, ½ teaspoon celery salt, ⅛ teaspoon pepper. Cook mixture for about 5 minutes. Cool, pour over fish fillets or steaks and let soak several

hours, covered, in refrigerator. Remove fish from the mixture and drain. Dip into fine, dry seasoned or unseasoned bread crumbs or a mixture of corn meal and flour. Fry in preheated shortening at 375° until brown, about 5 minutes. Drain.

DEEP-FRYING FISH

Any firm-fleshed fish can be successfully deep-fat fried; even shark meat, as mentioned earlier, is used as the traditional "Fish n' Chips" in England.

Deep-fried fish can be coated with crumbs or dipped in a batter before frying, using one of the suggested crumb choices or batters given under the heading "Batters, Coatings, and Marinades" immediately preceding.

Cut the fish into serving-sized pieces and blot each piece with a damp towel to remove excess moisture, then sprinkle both sides with salt and pepper. Coat or dip each piece and drop into basket of deep-fat fryer. Lower the basket into salad oil that has been heated to 375° and deep enough to cover fish. Fry 2 or 3 minutes and turn the pieces over. Fry another 2 or 3 minutes and drain on a paper towel. Cooking time varies with thickness of fillet pieces but the fish is ready when the outside is golden. Overcooking will make the fish dry. Serve immediately (with green salad if preferred).

Barbecued and Grilled Fish

BARBECUED HALIBUT

You Will Need
4 halibut steaks about 1 inch thick
Chablis Sauce (Recipe below)

Lightly oil grill and brush fish on both sides with Chablis Sauce. Prepare barbecue with hot coals and place steaks on the greased grill over the coals. Broil about 4 minutes on each side until fish flakes easily when probed with a fork, basting with Chablis Sauce often by brushing it on with pastry brush. Serve with additional sauce.

Chablis Sauce

Mix ¼ cup olive oil, 1 teaspoon rosemary, 1 teaspoon tarragon, ½ cup small dice tomato, 1 tablespoon lemon juice, ¾ cup Chablis wine, and ½ teaspoon each (fresh ground if possible) salt and pepper. Mix well and baste broiled fish of any kind during cooking. Makes about 1½ cups.

GRILLED FISH IN FOIL

You Will Need
5 to 7 pound whole fish
  Butter
1 medium onion, sliced thin
  Salt and pepper
  Fresh leaf tarragon, parsley, thyme, and lemon

Clean fish, leaving head on. Remove eye if desired and place stuffed olive, cut in half, in hole. Butter a large sheet of foil (heavy duty) and place onion slices on the foil, making a pattern about the size of the fish. Salt fish cavity with spices and sprinkle lemon juice over, then dot the cavity with butter. Place fish on foil and sprinkle with more of the seasonings. Bring up foil around fish and fold edges together to seal. Cook on grill over medium hot coals 25 minutes for up to a 5 pound fish or 35 minutes for a bigger fish, turning once or twice during cooking. Finish cooking off by opening up foil and placing another foil "tent" over top so heat can circulate around fish. Cook 10 minutes longer until fish flakes when probed with fork. Slide foil containing fish onto platter, then crimp edges of the foil neatly around bottom of fish. Garnish with baked tomatoes and lemon slices. Foil-baked potatoes can be served with this dish but potatoes must cook about an hour after being buttered and salted and wrapped securely in foil. Begin cooking potatoes about a half hour before putting fish on grill.

SALMON GRILL

You Will Need
  6 fish steaks (salmon, albacore, yellowtail, mackerel, etc.)
½ cup salad oil
¼ cup chopped parsley
¼ cup lemon juice
  4 tablespoons grated or minced onion
½ teaspoon dry mustard
¼ teaspoon salt
¼ teaspoon crushed tarragon

Place fish in shallow dish. Mix together next seven ingredients and pour over fish. Sprinkle with a little coarse ground pepper. Marinate at room temperature for 2 hours, basting with juices or turning from time to time. Now put steaks in a well-greased wire broiler or chicken basket and grill over medium hot coals until lightly browned, just 5 to 10 minutes at most. Baste with marinade, then turn and cook other side, until fish flakes easily when probed with fork, about 6 minutes.

CAYMAN FISH BAKE

From the Caribbean Kitchen of Dr. Mort Walker.

Mort Walker has a beautiful home at Cayman Kai, Grand Cayman Island in the Caribbean, where some of the best seafood recipes in the world are found. If you can get breadfruit in your area, be sure to serve it with this dish for real authentic native flavor to the meal.

Have on Hand

　　3 pounds assorted fish fillets such as grouper, trigger fish, barracuda, parrot fish, jack, snapper, etc.

　　2 whole limes

　　2 ounces Worcestershire sauce

　　8 ounces catsup

　　1 large onion, sliced

　⅛ pound butter

　　Salt and pepper

Place fish fillets in single layer, 3-inch chunks on heavy-duty aluminum foil. Foil should be double thickness. Allow sufficient foil to fold and butcher wrap the package later.

Squeeze limes over the fish and pour catsup and Worcestershire sauce evenly over all. Sprinkle with salt and pepper. Drop slices of onion rings in a sporadic spread and dot with butter. Bring the ends of the foil together to fold butcher wrap style, then flatten the package and fold in short sides securely.

Place the flat foil package on glowing hot driftwood or briquet coals and place several embers on top of the package. Bake for 20 minutes. The foil will puff up when the fish is cooked. Eat and savor every morsel, for this is food for the Gods!

MAHI MAHI

Dr. Bruce W. Halstead, of World Life Research, is one of the world's foremost authorities on sea life. Dolphin fish, and especially mahi mahi, is one of his favorite seafood dishes. This recipe for mahi mahi can be used for halibut or sole also and is an authentic Hawaiian dish.

You Will Need

　1½ to 2 pounds halibut, dolphin fish, or sole steaks

　1½ sticks butter or margarine

　　2 teaspoons salad oil

　　¼ teaspoon garlic salt

　　1 teaspoon minced garlic

　　1 teaspoon teriyaki sauce

　　1 teaspoon lemon juice

Melt butter and mix with other ingredients (except fish). Pour over the fish steaks and marinate at least 30 minutes. Now grill over hot coals until fish flakes with fork probing.

Note: Dr. Halstead's studies take him on extensive travels; therefore he has eaten seafood all over the globe. During discussions with us about toxic sea life, he revealed that the best seafood in the world is to be found on the island of Mauritius in the Mascarene Islands off Madagascar. "While you're there," he said, "be sure to 'drop in' at Kenya, Africa, my second favorite for fantastic restaurants and seafood dishes."

LINGCOD SAN JUAN

From William L. High's *Personal Recipes for Fun Food**
As Bill suggested, this recipe of his is "ideal for after-diving beach parties!"

"Begin with one successful lingcod spearing trip (poor hunters may substitute a large rockfish). Fillet fish and remove skin if using rockfish. Lay 2 small (or 1 large) fillets on a single heavy-duty aluminum foil sheet. Freely salt and pepper. Place 1 bacon strip on each fillet. Raise aluminum sheet edges to retain liquids. Squeeze one large lemon over fillet, add 1 tablespoon butter and ½ cup white wine such as Wente Chablis (note, save remainder of bottle until the dish is served). Carefully fold foil and seal package well. Cook in hot coals (or a 325° oven). Stand by for about 60 minutes for a taste bud tickler."

FROM ARTHUR GODFREY'S GRILL

Arthur Godfrey is a seafood lover and if you didn't know it before, you know now that he's an avid, veteran diver who loves to cook his own catch. Confirming the statements of many others including ourselves (many times), Arthur says "The reason lots of folk are not turned on by fish is that they overcook it and it's not fresh in the first place!" To further quote Arthur, his exact instructions for his favorite fish recipe follow:
1. Catch your fish yourself so you know it's fresh.
2. Fillet it.
3. Cut into bite sized chunks and place with a square of REAL butter, pepper and salt in a piece of aluminum foil.
4. Place the package on a grill over hot coals.
"When the paper gets too hot to touch, take it off the fire—it's *done!*"

---

* For Bill's octopus recipe, refer to Mollusk chapter.

Poached Fish

Poaching is a favorite method of cooking fish. It can be used as an entree and simply served with a sauce, or used as the main ingredient of a casserole or other combination dish. Poached fish also makes an excellent salad when chilled and flaked and added to eggs and dressing over a bed of lettuce.

POACHED FISH WITH EGG SAUCE

You Will Need

2 pounds fish fillets or steaks	3 peppercorns
2 cup boiling water	2 springs parsley
¼ cup lemon juice	1 bay leaf
1 small onion, thinly sliced	Egg Sauce (below)
1 teaspoons salt	Paprika

Remove skin and bones from fish. Cut fish into 6 portions. Place fish in a well-greased 10-inch fry pan. Add remaining ingredients. Cover and simmer for 5 to 10 minutes or until fish flakes easily when tested with a fork. Carefully remove fish to a hot platter. Pour Egg Sauce over and sprinkle with paprika. Serves 6.

Egg Sauce

¼ cup butter or margarine	1¼ cups milk
2 tablespoons flour	2 hard-cooked eggs, chopped
¾ teaspoon powdered mustard	1 tablespoon chopped parsley
¼ teaspoon salt	
Dash pepper	

Melt butter. Stir in flour and seasonings. Add milk gradually and cook until thick and smooth, stirring constantly. Add eggs and parsley Heat again. Makes 1½ cups sauce.

POACHED SHEEP-HEAD

(Use any firm, white, mild fish flesh)

This recipe is good served hot as is, or can be used to cook sheep-head before using in salads or when substituting sheep-head for crabmeat. Save the broth!

You Will Need

2 thick sheep-head fillets	2 slices lemon
½ cup instant or fresh onions, minced	Fresh celery leaves
6 peppercorns	¼ cup tarragon vinegar
1 tablespoon thyme leaves	
1 tablespoon marjoram leaves	

Place enough water in a pan to cover the fish. Bring to a boil and add all ingredients to it except the fish, then let boil five minutes. Add fillets and boil for 10 minutes. Remove fish with slotted spoon and serve either as is for a main course or cool and flake for other recipes using cold crab or fish. Use the broth as a before-salad hot appetizer or save and freeze, using it when recipes call for fish stock.

CREAM SAUCE FISH BALLS

1 pound flounder fish fillets
½ cup light cream
4 tablespoons flour
½ teaspoon salt

For Sauce:
¼ cup butter
4 tablespoons flour
1½ cups dairy cream
1 egg yolk

Have blender or food grinder on hand. Cut fillets into small pieces (1-inch or so) and place a few pieces at a time into blender with a little of the cream, then blend to make a paste or puree. If grinder is used, use fine blade to grind up fish, then blend in a little cream to make the paste. Combine the fish mixture in a bowl with 4 tablespoons flour and salt, making it very smooth. Cover and chill for 4 hours or so.

Place two inches of water in a large fry pan and season with salt. Heat to boiling and reduce heat. Shape fish mixture into balls by pressing between 2 teaspoons—balls will be oval in shape. Poach a few of these balls at a time in the gently simmering water for 5 minutes, then remove with slotted spoon and keep warm on a serving dish. Save ½ cup of the liquid for the sauce.

Cream Sauce

Melt the ¼ cup butter in a small saucepan and stir in the 4 tablespoons flour, cooking and stirring constantly, cooking just until bubbly. Stir in the 1½ cups cream and reserved poaching liquid. Cook and stir until sauce thickens and bubbles for one minute. Beat the egg yolk slightly in another small bowl, then stir in half of the hot mixture. Return the complete mixture to the saucepan and cook, stirring constantly to keep smooth, for one minute or until sauce thickens again. To serve, pour Cream Sauce over fish balls and sprinkle with chopped parsley.

Steamed Fish

BASIC STEAM FISH RECIPE

Place 1½ pounds fish fillets, steaks, or pan-dressed fish in a well-greased steamer insert-pan or rack. Sprinkle with salt, cover, and cook over boiling water 5 to 10 minutes or until fish flakes easily when tested with a fork. Cool. Remove skin and bones. Makes 2 cups cooked fish.

HOM HA JIN YEE

*Another From Ray Cannon
Ray says this is truly the best fish dish he ever ate and that he learned it from a Cantonese family.
You Will Need
    2 cups very firm (even toughish) fish, diced into 1-inch squares
    2 tablespoons soy sauce
    2 tablespoons brandy or rum
    1 tablespoon water
1½ tablespoons salty shrimp paste (available at Japanese markets)
    Fresh ginger root (not dried) very thinly sliced
Mix the soy sauce, brandy or rum, and water. Marinate the fish in this for 15 minutes. Now place the fish in a deep, heat-proof bowl and spread up around sides. Then apply a thin coating of the shrimp paste and cover the surface with the sliced ginger root. Steam in a large pot for 20 to 25 minutes. Serve on cooked white rice.

FISH STEAMED IN GINGER
WITH BLACK BEANS

†From Paul J. Tzimoulis
Publisher, Skin Diver Magazine
Paul and Doris Tzimoulis gave us this great recipe for fish and bean lovers. It's a natural as a quick, tasty, homey, and informal dinner.
Have on hand:
A whole cleaned fish   Safflower oil
Scallions or green onions   Sesame oil
Garlic   Olive oil
Parsley
Grated ginger
Canned black beans
Place fish in steamer (or use a regular vegetable steamer) skin side down. Over this cut up scallions or green onions along with some mashed or minced garlic, some shredded parsley, grated ginger, and a small amount of the black beans. Simmer a short time until fish can be flaked

---

* For another of Ray's good recipes, refer to the Raw Fish recipes at the beginning of the recipe section.
† Another Tzimoulis recipe appears in the Crustacean chapter under shrimp.

easily with a fork. When done, place on a hot platter and pour over a little hot safflower, sesame, and olive oil, then add for garnish a little more garlic and parsley. Serve hot with huge chunks of hot Italian, French, or homemade bread and invite guests to feel at home if they wish to sop up extra sauce with their bread!

Baked Fish

EASY HALIBUT

You Will Need
  4 halibut steaks, about ½ lb. each
½ cup butter, melted
  2 tablespoons wine vinegar
  3 teaspoons lemon juice
  1 clove garlic, minced
¼ teaspoon dry mustard
¼ teaspoon each thyme and tarragon (use finely crushed leaf spices,
    if possible)
½ teaspoon salt and ¼ teaspoon pepper
    Few drops bottled hot pepper sauce

Place halibut steaks in single layer in shallow baking dish. Combine and mix well the rest of the ingredients and pour over fish, then turn to coat well on all sides. Bake in very hot oven—450 degrees—about 10 minutes or until fish flakes when probed with fork. Serves 4.

BAKED SHEEP-HEAD WITH RICE

From Larry Canfield and Carol Jacobs
(use any white, firm, mild flavored fish meat)
Fry sheep-head fillets until just golden—fry slowly.
Meanwhile, cook four servings of brown rice and add chopped onions and minced garlic. Stir well. Place fish fillets in a buttered casserole and cover them with barbecue sauce. Fill casserole to top with the rice, then pour over a little catsup and top with pats of butter. Bake at 350° 1 hour.

WALTER DEAS'S BAKED CORAL TROUT

Walter Deas is the author and photographer of many reef-life books on Australian species and is an expert underwater cameraman. Further, he can cook seafood almost as well as he can photograph it. We recommend this recipe with enthusiasm:

You Will Need

1 coral trout (10-12 pounds) or similar sized reef fish such as
schnapper or jewfish.

3 cups soft bread crumbs

1 large onion, finely chopped

2 rashers bacon, chopped

3 level tablespoons chopped green capsicum (green pepper)
Salt and pepper

1 egg, beaten
Milk to moisten
Oil, white vinegar, lemon, parsley

Trim fish and remove eyes. Rub inside of fish with a little salt and
cut lemon. Combine bread crumbs, onion, bacon, capsicum, and salt
and pepper with the egg and sufficient milk to moisten. Fill cavity of
fish with seasoning and secure opening with needle and thread or skewers.
Place on a large sheet of greased foil and brush with equal quantities of
oil and vinegar. Loosely wrap fish in foil and bake in a moderate oven
for 15 minutes per pound or until flesh flakes with a fork. Baste occasionally with oil and vinegar. Serve garnished with lemon and parsley.
Accompany with savory rice if desired.

ALMOND FISH

Use four portions fish fillets—about 2 pounds. Place fillets in buttered
casserole. Combine 3 tablespoons melted butter and 1½ tablespoons
lemon juice and brush on fillets. Sprinkle with ¾ teaspoon salt (freshly
ground rock salt if possible) and a sprinkle of freshly ground pepper.
Bake uncovered in 350° oven till fish flakes when probed with fork—
about 15 to 20 minutes. Brown ¼ cup sliced almonds in butter until
golden, stirring constantly. Remove nuts and sprinkle over the fish. Use
either the Scrumptedelicious Sauce, or combine a tablespoon lemon
juice, a little minced garlic, and some minced parsley with some melted
butter; drizzle over fish, then serve immediately.

HALIBUT ROYALE

2 pounds halibut steak
Lemon juice from 1 lemon
½ cup chopped onion
2 tablespoons butter
1 teaspoon salt
½ teaspoon paprika
Green pepper

Place halibut steaks in greased casserole. Marinate with the salt, paprika, and lemon juice for one hour, turning steaks over after first half hour. Sauté onion in butter until transparent. Drain marinating liquid from fish. Sprinkle the fish with onion and top with strips of green pepper, then pour the fat from the frying pan over all. Bake at 450° 10 minutes for each inch of thickness.

FISH AU GRATIN

Another one from Larry and Sharon Canfield.
You Will Need
2 pounds fish fillets
Slices of cheddar cheese
Oregano
Parsley
1 cup chopped onions
2 tablespoons flour
1 teaspoon salt, ¼ teaspoon pepper
1 cup milk

Cut fillets into serving pieces. Place a layer of fillets in greased baking pan and cover each with a slice of cheddar cheese. Make another layer of the same, continuing until fillets are used up. Sauté onions in butter, then add flour to thicken; season with salt and pepper. Stir and slowly add milk. Pour over fish and bake 30 minutes at 400° First comments of guests: "Oh, boy, is *that* good!"

BAKED HALIBUT OR SWORDFISH
FROM THE KITCHEN OF LLOYD BRIDGES:

You Will Need
A slice of swordfish or halibut 2 inches thick
Salt and pepper
Juice of 1 lemon
2 sliced onions
1 green pepper, minced (For halibut substitute 4 slices of bacon)
2 tablespoons butter

Wash fish and place in well-greased baking pan. Sprinkle with salt, pepper, and lemon juice. Place onion and green pepper (or onion and bacon strips if using halibut) on fish and dot with butter. For swordfish, add ½ cup water or white wine to fish. Omit if the liquid if using halibut. Bake in hot oven (400°) about 30 minutes, basting often. Serves 3 or 4.

"NEWSWORTHY" BREAM

From Ron and Valerie Taylor, Australia

This is a "bake-out" type of recipe that calls for just a fish, plenty of newspaper, and a book of matches. It can be used for bream or any firm fleshed fish and is delicious. Sam Miller, an old-time diver well known for his expertise with the preservation of sea life, says he used to cook fish this way with his father when the two went fishing together.

Use a whole fresh fish straight from the sea and wrap the fish neatly in 10 to 15 layers of wet newspaper until it resembles a soggy parcel. Place the package in the embers of an open fire. The newspaper will burn off sheet by sheet. After 15 minutes, turn the parcel over to cook for another 25 minutes. Try passing a knife through the parcel at this point and if it goes through easily, the fish is done. Remove the parcel from the fire and break open the remaining newspaper—skin and scales come away with the paper and the viscera has turned into a hard ball, which you discard. Gather 'round and eat the fish right from the paper. It will be sweet, juicy, and tender! Remove the backbone when it becomes exposed. Common sense will govern the amount of paper used and length of cooking time—a larger fish takes more of both than a smaller one, of course.

LEMONY STUFFED BAKED HALIBUT

You Will Need

Whole halibut, about 6 pounds or larger

½ cup chopped onion	1 lemon, peeled and diced
¾ cup diced celery	¾ teaspoon salt
¼ cup butter	⅛ teaspoon pepper
2½ cups bread cubes	½ teaspoon each thyme and tarragon
¼ cup chopped parsley	3 tablespoons melted butter
1 teaspoon grated lemon peel	1 tablespoon lemon juice
	Cayenne pepper

Lemon slices for garnish

When cleaning the halibut, fillet, but don't remove the skin. Sprinkle inside and out with salt and pepper. Sauté onion and celery in butter until translucent. Add bread cubes, parsley, lemon peel and lemon sections, and seasonings. Toss. Add about 5 tablespoons boiling water. Toss again and stuff mixture down the center of the halibut, inside two halves. Tie with string. Place halibut in buttered casserole. Combine melted butter, cayenne pepper, and lemon juice, then brush the fish with this mixture. Bake 40 to 50 minutes in 400° oven, basting from time to time with lemon-butter sauce. Serve with lemon slices arranged overlapping across the top. Serves 6 to 8 people.

JACK HALL'S BAKED TREEFISH

(Use any rockfish for this recipe)
This one is simple and you can apply the technique to any firm flesh fish. Melt some butter in a baking pan, then place fish fillets in the pan and sprinkle with lemon juice and 1 cup chopped onions. Other spices can be added if you wish, such as tarragon, thyme, and so forth. Bake at 350° for 20 minutes. Quick, easy, and delicious.

ORANGE APPLE PERCH

Roy Brizz, of Roy Brizz Advertising, is a food connoisseur and artist first and a diver second, but is well known in the world of diving and advertising for his ability to create an impact in graphic design with color, layout, and text. Roy's wife, Joyce, takes half the credit for this recipe.

You Will Need
 1 large perch (at least 3 pounds)
 1 stick of sweet butter
 ½ cup finely chopped scallions or green onions
 1 teaspoon salt
 1 teaspoon pepper
 2 teaspoons chopped parsley
 1 cup apple cider
 1 tablespoon flour
 2 cups peeled and diced apples
 1 tablespoon bread crumbs

In a large pan, sauté butter, green onion, salt and pepper. Arrange perch on top of this mixture and sprinkle with parsley and bread crumbs. Pour over the apple cider, cover, and bring to low boil. Remove lid and add diced apples. Place pan in a preheated 400° oven and bake for 10 minutes. Remove and arrange on a warm platter. Add flour to drippings in pan and heat a few minutes longer, stirring constantly until slightly thickened. Pour this sauce over the fillets and serve garnished with orange slices.

LOW-CAL BAKED FILLETS

From Ruth Brawley
Ed Brawley's Scuba Schools, Inc.
This is simple, very nutritious, delicious, and low in calories: Place enough fish fillets in a baking pan to feed the number of people neces-

sary. Now place in the pan some cherry tomatoes, cut up celery, cut up cauliflower, some mushrooms, pearl onions, salt, pepper, and paprika if desired. Anything else that sounds good to you can be added also. The surprise is that you now cover the whole thing with buttermilk! Bake in a 350° oven for 45 minutes to an hour.

FLOUNDER ROLL-UPS FOR SIX

You Will Need

12 large flounder fillets	½ teaspoon dried chervil
8 strips bacon, diced	½ teaspoon dried tarragon leaves
½ cup melted butter	Hot water
6 cups cornbread crumbs	Butter or margarine

Cook bacon until crisp. Drain on absorbent paper. Measure ¼ cup of bacon drippings and add to melted butter. Combine cornbread crumbs, bacon, herbs, and combined fats; mix well. Add enough hot water to make stuffing as moist as desired. Placed spoonful of stuffing on each flounder fillet; roll up firmly. Line baking pan with foil. Grease foil. Place roll-ups in pan; dot generously with butter or margarine. Bake at 375° for 25 minutes or until fish flakes easily with fork. Serve with the sauce of your choice, or Sour Cream Dill Sauce:

Sour Cream Dill Sauce

Combine 1 cup dairy sour cream, 1 teaspoon dill weed, 1 tablespoon wine vinegar, 1 teaspoon celery salt, and ½ teaspoon sugar. Chill to blend flavors.

Smoked Fish

CLEVELAND'S SMOKED FISH

This recipe is so good that it has been sought after by experts in the smoking field. It is great for smoking just about any fish and will make believers out of those who formerly rejected certain species for this purpose. The recipe comes from two close friends of ours, Gordon and Priscilla Cleveland, of Palos Verdes, California. Gordon is an avid big game fisherman. His record black marlin catch off Cabo San Lucas in Baja several years ago was written up at that time by Ray Cannon in his Western Outdoor News column. Gordon smokes his own catch and the recipe below was concocted by him to give the utmost in flavor.

You Will Need

1 cup Kosher salt	1½ cups brown sugar (granulated),
1 teaspoon ground cardamon	1½ teaspoons ground allspice
1 teaspoon garlic salt	1 teaspoon black pepper

Dry Cure Method:

Cut fish in slabs, coat heavily in above mixture and stack in crock or plastic (not aluminum) container. Marinate overnight. Next morning wash and dry with paper towels and let dry in air about 1 hour.

Brine Soaking Method:

Mix above recipe in two quarts of water and marinate overnight. Use a weighted screen or smoke rack to hold fish under water and stir occasionally. Next morning rinse and dry with paper towels and let dry in air about 1 hour.

Place fish skin side down on smoke rack.

Smoke 6 to 12 hours, depending on thickness of fish. For detailed information and smoking procedures, refer to Smoke Cooking in chapter one.

Fish Chowders

BASIC FISH CHOWDER

You Will Need

1 pound fish fillets, steaks, or pieces
2 strips bacon, diced
½ cup chopped onion
2½ cups diced potatoes
1½ cups boiling water
1 teaspoon salt
Dash pepper
2 cups milk or cream
1 tablespoon butter
Chopped parsley

Use only skinned, boned fish. Cut fish into 1-inch pieces. Fry bacon until crisp and add onion. Cook until onion is transparent. Add potatoes, water, seasonings and fish, then cover and simmer for 15 to 20 minutes or until potatoes are tender. Add milk or cream and butter. Reheat and sprinkle with parsley. Serves 6.

(For Manhattan style chowder, add 1 can tomatoes, some diced carrots, chopped celery, a little catsup, Worcestershire sauce.)

FISH CHOWDER FROM NOVA SCOTIA

You Will Need

2 pounds fish fillets (halibut, haddock, cod, etc.)
¼ pound salt pork, diced
1 chopped onion
2 cups diced potatoes
2 cups water
8 soda crackers, crushed
3 tablespoons butter
2 tablespoons minced parsley
2 teaspoons salt, ¼ t. pepper

1 quart milk or Half 'n Half   1 teaspoon crushed tarragon
⅔ cup evaporated milk   ½ teaspoon thyme

Cut fish into small hunks. Sauté the salt pork until golden, saving scraps for garnish. Sauté onions until transparent. Add potatoes and water and simmer until potatoes are tender. Add fish and simmer 5 minutes more. Combine milk, crackers, butter, and seasonings, heat just to simmer, then add to the fish mixture. Serve at once garnished with pork scraps.

QUICK N' EASY FISH CHOWDER

You Will Need
4 slices fat back pork, diced
1 onion, sliced
1 cup boiling water
3 pounds fish fillets
2 cups sliced potatoes
   Salt and pepper
   (Add anything else you like—vegetables, seasonings, etc)

Render the fat pork in a pot. Add fish and onions and cover with the potatoes. Season and add boiling water. Cook slowly until potatoes are done, about ½ hour.

SHEEP-HEAD CHOWDER

From Chuck Breslin, Lockheed Sea Stars Diving Club, California
You Will Need
  8 pounds sheep-head fillets
12 ounces frozen potatoes O'Brien (or home made)
  2 cups water   4 tablespoons flour
  2 cups cold milk   1 bay leaf
  ½ teaspoon salt   1 teaspoon Worcestershire sauce
  ¼ teaspoon pepper
  2 tablespoons butter

Place fillets, potatoes O'Brien, and bay leaf in deep kettle; cover with 2 cups water. Simmer over medium flame 10 minutes or until fish is easily flaked with fork. Add milk which has been blended into flour, also salt, pepper, Worcestershire sauce. Dot with butter. Heat to boiling point but do not boil. Serve with generous chunks of French bread and garlic butter.

Fish Salads

Fish salads are convenient to concoct when the cook is without shellfish meat but with plenty of fish on hand. They are great substitutes for crabmeat salads and just as impressive if the other ingredients render a zesty flavor to the dish. Fish that has been cooked in just about any manner may be used in fish salads, but be sure to remove any skin and bones that remain in leftover baked fish, etc.

SIMPLE SEAFOOD SALAD

You Will Need
    1 pound firm flesh fish fillets, cooked
    1 cup chopped celery
    ⅓ cup mayonnaise or salad dressing
    2 hard-cooked eggs, chopped
    2 tablespoons chopped sweet pickle
    Salad greens
Remove moisture from fish with paper towels and break into large pieces. Combine all ingredients except the salad greens and toss lightly. Chill and serve on the salad greens. Serves about 6.

MEAL-IN-A-BOWL SUNSHINE FISH

(Serves 6)
You Will Need
    1 head lettuce
    4 tomatoes, peeled
    1 large cucumber, peeled
    2 cups (cooked) frozen, or canned peas
    2 cups canned sliced mushrooms
    6 hard cooked eggs
    1½ pounds firm fish fillets, cooked
    Crushed tarragon
    Lemon juice
    Salt and pepper (fresh- or coarse-ground)
    Mayonnaise, salad dressings, or sour cream (dairy)
Tear lettuce into bite-sized pieces or larger, then distribute evenly between 6 individual (large) salad bowls. Cut tomatos into small chunks and distribute these pieces around the edge of the bowls on top of the lettuce. Do the same with the cucumber, placing the chunks in a ring inside the tomatoes. Make another ring inside this with the peas, using ⅓ cup peas or so to each salad. This should fill up the bowl to the center. Cut each egg into fourths lengthwise and break or cut the fish fillets into strips as much as possible, the rest in chunks. Divide the fish strips between the six salads, placing these across the middle and any chunks between pieces of cucumber or tomatoes. Decorate each in strategic

places with the mushrooms and egg wedges. Minced onion may be added if desired.

Mix just enough of the lemon juice with the dressing or sour cream to make a mixture that dips easily with a ladle, then mix in the salt and pepper to taste and crushed tarragon to make a nice mottled effect. Serve this dressing in a bowl on the side.

Poisonous Fishes

The fishes that contain a poison within their muscles, viscera, or slime (mucus) and that are orally toxic to humans are grouped under the big scientific name of ichthyosarcotoxism. This category includes all of the oral fish poisons recognized by leading world toxicologists and are as follows:
1. Scombrotoxism (tunas, mackerels, bonito, jacks).
    Refer to "Mackerel-Like Game Fishes."
2. Clupeotoxism (herrings, anchovies, tarpons, bonefish).
    Refer to "Herring-Like Fishes."
3. Cylostome poisoning (lampreys and hagfishes).
    Refer to "Eels and Eel-Like Fishes."
4. Tetrodotoxism (puffer-fish poisoning).
    Refer to "Puffer-Like Fishes."
5. Elasmobranch poisoning (sharks and rays).
    Refer to "Sharks and Rays."
6. Chimaera poisoning (ratfishes).
    Refer to "Chimaeras."
7. Gempylid-fish poisoning (castor-oil fish, snake mackerels). Refer to "Mackerel-Like Game Fishes."
8. Ciguatera poisoning (mostly tropical shore fishes).
9. Ichthyoallyeinotoxism or hallucinatory fish poisoning (tropical reef fishes).

The first 7 fish poisons are briefly described under specific fishes while the last 2 are general-type poisons and are described here.

* Ciguatera Poisoning

Ciguatera is a poisoning caused largely by tropical shore fishes and unusually large barracudas, jacks, and groupers during their reproductive season. More than four hundred species have been incriminated, the greatest concentration of ciguatoxic fishes having been found to be around the tropical Pacific islands and in the Caribbean area. Ciguatera is unpredictable and the edibility of the fish in an island area has been known to change suddenly. It is believed that many fish become poisonous because of their feeding habits. The ciguatoxin evidently originates in some marine plants, and vegetarian fishes, while unharmed by the substance, store it in their flesh. When these fish, or fish that have eaten these fish, are eaten by man, he will develop ciguatera poisoning. It has

Flatworm.

been recently reported that the flesh of some tropical fish have become violently toxic to man after the fish has eaten the colorful marine polyclad flatworm (Pseudoceridae).

Symptoms of acute poisoning begin any time within thirty minutes after ingestion and include numbness and tingling of the face and lips that spreads to fingers and toes. This may be followed by nausea, cramps, diarrhea, muscular spasms, loss of hair and nails, and paralysis. The fatality rate is said to be about seven percent. Ordinary cooking procedures do not destroy the poison.

The following fishes have been reported ciguatoxic in tropical areas:

Anchovies	Grunts	Permits	Squirrelfishes
Angelfishes	Halfbeaks	Pompanos	Surge fishes
Barracudas	Hawkfishes	Porgys	Surgeonfishes
Blennies	Herrings	Rabbitfishes	Sweeperfishes
Butterflyfishes	Horse mackerel	Sardines	Tangs
Cardinalfishes	Jacks	Scorpionfishes	Tarpons
Croakers	Ladyfishes	Sea Basses	True Eels
Damselfishes	Lizardfishes	Seahorses	Trumpetfishes
Dolphinfishes	Milkfishes	Sea Perches	Tunas
Flounders	Moray eels	Silverfishes	Unicornfishes
Flyingfishes	Mullets	Snake Eels	
Goatfishes	Needlefishes	Snappers	
Gobies	Oilfishes	Soapfishes	
Groupers	Parrotfishes	Spadefishes	

* Ichthyoallyeinotoxism

The flesh of certain types of reef fishes in the tropical Pacific and Indian Oceans have caused in man a relatively mild poisoning that is of a hallucinatory nature (trying to pronounce this toxin can cause a similar reaction!). This poisoning has the unlikely name of ichthyoallyeinotoxism, and is caused by sea basses (Serranidae), tangs (Acanthuridae), rudderfishes (Kyphosidae), mullets (Mugilidae), goatfishes (Mullidae), damselfishes (Pomacentridae), and rabbitfishes, (Siganidae). A common complaint from the victim of this poisoning is "someone is sitting on my chest," coupled with the conviction that he is going to die, or some other frightening fantasy. Ordinary cooking procedures do not destroy this type of poison, however no fatalities have been reported.

* Six Precautions

In order that precautions may be taken against eating poisonous fish, six steps have been suggest by the United States Naval Research Laboratory, Washington, D. C.:

1. Never eat the viscera, liver, gonads, or intestines of tropical fishes.
2. The roe of any tropical fish is potentially dangerous.
3. Large reef fishes, such as snapper, barracuda, grouper, and jack, should never be eaten.
4. Keep in mind that ordinary cooking, such as baking, frying, or drying does not render a toxic fish safe to eat.
5. Tropical moray eels should never be eaten.
6. Eat only open-water fishes (when in tropical areas.)

Spearfiishing Equipment

Pole Spears

Pole spears are most effective on small fish at close range and when hunting bottom fish in holes and crevices. They are simple and easy to use but have less range than a speargun. Don't count on spearing a fish

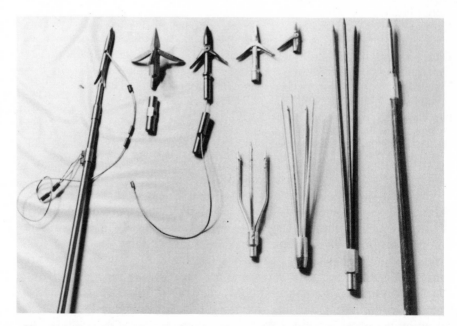

Slip-tip; three-barb detachable head; two-barb detachable head; two-barb fixed head; single barb; three-prong tip; five-prong tip, three-prong palayzer; single tip.

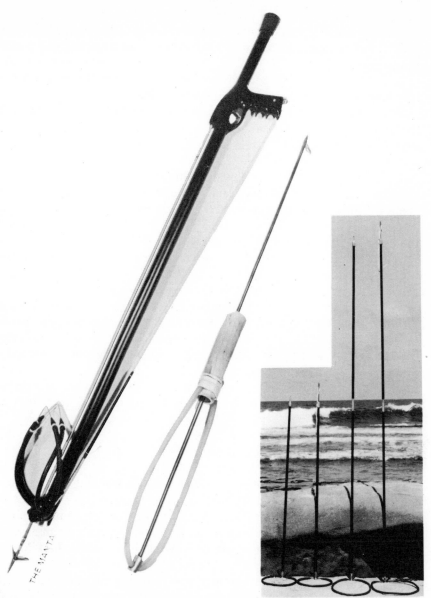

There are many types of spearfishing equipment. Shown are the speargun, the Hawaiian sling, and four different pole spears. COURTESY AQUA-CRAFT, INC., SAN DIEGO, CALIFORNIA.

more than three feet beyond the tip. For longer range blue-water fish up to twenty five pounds (much larger fish have been taken), use a long spear from seven to nine feet with a three-inch slip-tip. For medium range fish and from ten to twenty five pounds, use a spear from five to seven feet long with a slip-tip. A three-pronged "paralyzer" tip about twelve inches long can immobilize a twenty five pounder and is easier to use than a slip-tip. For pan-size fish up to ten pounds, or fish in dirty water, and fish in rocks and caves, use a short spear from four to five feet long with a regular three-prong spear head.

When replacing the rubber sling, get surgical tubing that is two-fifths the length of the pole spear and a diameter that tests your strength to stretch it to at least three times its relaxed length.

Hawaiian Slings

These are effective in very clear, shallow water on small, open-water game fish up to fifteen pounds, and large bottom fish that hole up after being hit. A rubber sling is used to fire a shaft through a tube held in the hand, much like a bow and arrow. It fires a free spear with no line attached. Hawaiian slings are not popular where the water is too dirty for free spearing.

Pneumatic Guns

These guns are best for small, open-water fish that do not hole up after they are speared. The pneumatics are very accurate and the power can be adjusted by adding or reducing air pressure. The gun is loaded by inserting a shaft into the barrel and forcing it in against the pressure until it locks. Sand or debris on the shaft or in the barrel will prevent loading or damage the barrel. A dent in the barrel or a bent shaft will prevent loading.

Rubber-Powered Spearguns

These guns are preferred by most divers for every species of fish in all kinds of water. The major considerations in selecting a speargun is the length of the gun and its rigging. A long speargun—six feet and over—is used in extremely clear water for blue-water game fish when range is important, and for extremely large fish where maximum penetration is necessary. The gun should have a three-eighth shaft for momentum.

A medium gun, around four feet with three-eighth shaft, is best for maneuverability in the open sea, in moderately dirty water, and for bottom fishing. Any fish from eight to thirty pounds and over are fair game for this gun. A one hundred-pounder can be taken with a medium gun if rigged with breakaway gear and detachable head.

A short gun, about two feet long with a five-sixteenth shaft, is needed when fishing in very dirty water or close in around rocky areas where maneuverability is important, and for small fish.

A breakaway rig is used when hunting large, fast blue-water fish of twenty five pounds or more, and when hunting extremely large fish. The

Valerie Taylor shooting sweet lips in Australian waters. COURTESY RON TAYLOR.

rig is made by attaching one hundred to three hundred feet of poly-ethelyene or nylon line (the reserve line) to the end of the shooting line. Poly floats and is easier to retrieve. Instead of tying the shooting line to the muzzle as you would normally, use fifty-pound test fishing line to attach the shooting line to the muzzle. This line will hold a small fish but will "breakaway" with a large fish. The reserve line is coiled into a line pack, or a reel, or is attached to a surface float. A CO_2 in-flatable float is attached to the end of the line in the pack. With a reel, the float is attached to the gun. A detachable head is usually used with a breakaway.

A riding rig will be necessary when hunting fish around oil rigs. Use a powerful gun with a straight slip-tip spearhead. The shooting line

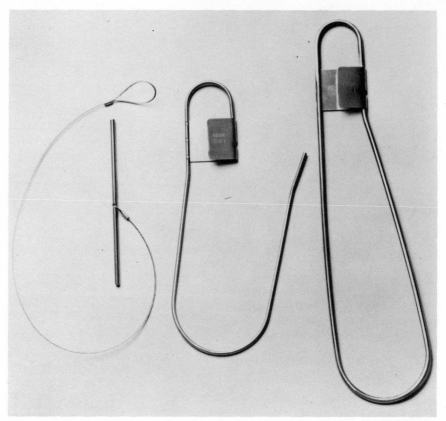

Various types of fish stringers. COURTESY AQUA-CRAFT, INC., SAN DIEGO CALIFORNIA.

should be twelve to fifteen feet of stainless-steel cable with a six-foot rope attached. A loop at one end permits a diver to hold on and ride the fish.

Use a fish stringer to hold your catch, and a diver's flag and float if boats frequent the diving area. Carry a diver's knife to cut line if ever necessary and sometimes to help remove spearheads. Use a compass and depth gauge to help you navigate to productive areas. Use gloves to prevent injury to your hands. Wear a vest or buoyancy compensator for efficiency on the bottom and safety on the surface. Most professional dive stores have the equipment described here and will be happy to explain any terms you don't understand.

5

Marine Reptiles and Mammals

The only three representatives of the class Reptilia in our marine environment are the sea turtles, sea snakes, and marine iguanas—unless the reader would care to speculate on the edibility of various mythical "sea monsters" (all of which seem to take the form of overgrown sea serpents. If you find one, it will serve a real crowd, utilizing our Serpent Supreme recipe!).

Turtles

The green, loggerhead, and hawksbill turtles are all good food turtles. The green turtle, however, is the one most well known and revered for its value in this regard. This is the one whose flesh is so highly esteemed for use in turtle soups, stews, and steaks, and we have found it makes excellent "turtleburgers." Turtles are an important food source but are now in danger of extinction due to poaching for both meat and eggs. Conservation in this respect is very important to the future of this beautiful animal. The green turtle (a threatened species) gets its name from the green-tinged fat under its shell, and this fat should be separated from the meat since it sometimes gives a disagreeable "soapy" taste to the meat. The hawksbill turtle is the source of popular tortoise shell and it is not as important a food source as the green turtle. The flesh is less acceptable to the palate, often having a very fishy flavor. It is also sometimes poisonous. The hawksbill eats jellyfish and the Portuguese man-o-war.

Turtles.

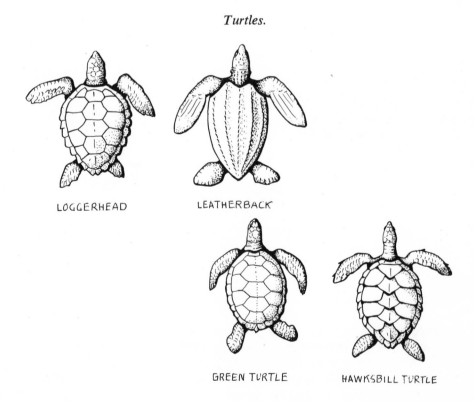

LOGGERHEAD   LEATHERBACK

GREEN TURTLE   HAWKSBILL TURTLE

* Turtles in the waters of Japan, India, New Guinea, the Philippines, and Tahiti may be extremely poisonous, and turtle liver is especially dangerous. The very edible green sea turtle, the rare leatherback turtle, and the hawksbill turtle have been reported as poisonous to eat in the aforementioned areas of the world. When in doubt, check with knowledgeable local inhabitants.

Most sea turtle meat resembles veal in flavor and needs ample seasoning to be at its best. Freezing must be done with care to preclude a dry, tasteless product when you are ready to use it. Don't overlook the cartilage between the upper and lower shells when cleaning the turtle; this "calipee" is the ingredient that gives your turtle soup its beautiful clear appearance and its slightly sticky quality, which indicates a genuine gourmet broth.

Cleaning Turtles

Sea turtles are cleaned by cutting apart the top and bottom (carapace and plastron) shells with the turtle on its back, then removing the entrails. Remove the eggs, if your turtle is a female, and save these for a delicious addition to your stew. Remove the cartilage (calipee) from the plastron and meat and be sure to get the meat from the flippers; something the layman often misses. Cartilage is also found in the space around the edge of the carapace. Cartilage from this top shell is called the *calipash*.

Turtle Dishes

Turtle meat is made into steaks, creamed dishes, soups, fondues, and also for "turtleburgers." Any of these dishes (except steaks and burgers) are improved greatly by utilizing the cartilage of the animal along with the meat. In the case of clear turtle broth, the cartilage, or calipee, is sometimes used exclusively, omitting the meat altogether. When all is said and done, turtle meat is used very much the way you would use beef.

CLEAR TURTLE BROTH

To make calipee stock for Clear Turtle Broth, bring 1½ quarts of water to boil. Add 1 teaspoon salt, ¼ cup calipee, and 5 peppercorns. Simmer 30 minutes. If liquid has boiled down below 4 cups in volume, add water to bring it back up to a quart and simmer 5 minutes more. To make the broth, bring the calipee stock to a boil. Add 1½ pounds turtle meat, 1 tablespoon dried tarragon leaves, salt and pepper to taste, and ½-cup minced onion. Simmer 30 minutes, add ¾-cup dry white wine, and cook 5 minutes more.

CAYMAN TURTLE STEAK À LA THELMA WELCOME

Thelma Welcome is a native of Grand Cayman and fed us some of the best turtle dishes we have ever tasted while we were visiting the Caribbean.

You Will Need

Turtle meat cut into 6 steaks	1 tablespoon chopped onion
Vinegar	1 cup Bordeaux
Flour	Salt and pepper
2 eggs beaten	Nutmeg
Breadcrumbs	Beef stock
Butter	½ cup sherry

Sliced mushrooms

Rub the steaks with a damp cloth dipped in the vinegar. Dip each steak into seasoned flour, then in beaten egg, and finally in the bread crumbs, coating each steak well. Heat ¼ cup butter and stir in 1 tablespoon finely chopped onion. Cook steaks in this to a delicate brown on both sides. Pour over 1 cup Bordeaux, season with salt, pepper, and a dash of nutmeg. Now cover and let simmer 15 to 20 minutes. Remove the steaks to a hot platter.

Reduce sauce over a hot flame to almost nothing and stir in ½ cup rich beef stock, ½ cup sherry wine, and 1 cup thinly sliced mushrooms. Taste for seasoning, then pour a little sauce over each steak. Serve the rest of the sauce in a sauceboat. Garnish with watercress if desired.

CARIBBEAN GREEN TURTLE STEW

(Courtesy of Mariculture Ltd., Grand Cayman)

You Will Need	10 cloves
2 pounds turtle meat	2 springs thyme
1 teaspoon salt	6 peppercorns
1 onion	3 tablespoons cooking oil
1 glass sherry or white wine	Juice of 1 lime
2 tomatoes	

Parsley

Wash the turtle meat with some lime juice, then sprinkle the lime juice over it and season with salt. Add sliced tomatoes and onion, cloves, thyme, parsley, peppercorns, and wine. Let stand for 15 minutes. Heat the oil and brown the meat; cover and allow to cook slowly for 45 minutes. Add all the seasonings and simmer until the turtle is tender. Add more onion if you wish. Serves 4.

Sea Snakes

True to their ancient and, to westerners at least, unique cuisine cul-

Frankie Hebert gingerly carries a sea snake in the South Pacific. COURTESY STAN KEISER.

ture, Japan consumes great quantities of sea snake meat. The meat of these reptiles is actually very nourishing and is as tasty as veal or chicken when prepared properly. Though the sea snake has an extremely poisonous bite, there is great variance in opinion as to how dangerous they actually are to human beings. There probably is a great deal of variation also in the toxicity of the venom from one species to another. Sea snakes are very shy cowards, to boot, so that reported bites from these tropical creatures are very rare. There is no antidote for the sea snake bite, nevertheless, and his poison is reported to be ten times more potent than the king cobra, so caution is certainly in order when hunting these small delicacies. They are numerous around Taiwan. These snakes can stay submerged for eight hours on one breath of air. They boast fifty-one species in the Pacific.

Sea snakes are hunted for their skins also, from which a good leather is made. Others are bottled and sold as an aphrodisiac and as a cure-all medicine. In Japan and Ryukyu Islands, sea snake is smoked and eaten as a delicacy.

To prepare a sea snake for cooking, first skin it by cutting the skin around the back of the head and pulling the skin down over the tail. A pair of pliers will help hold the skin. Clean out the viscera and cut the meat into six-inch long strips. The meat can then be utilized in any eel recipe. The Sea Snake Sandwich, however, is our favorite:

SEA SNAKE SANDWICH

Brown the snake meat in clarified butter, seasoning it with salt and pepper. Pour over a little claret wine and braise until the meat is tender. Slip out the bones (this can be tedious) and make sandwiches with very fresh white bread that has been buttered with dairy butter.

SERPENT SUPREME

You Will Need
2 sea snakes, about 2 feet long, cleaned
  Flour, salt, pepper, mixed
  Clarified butter
½ cup red wine
4 small onions, sliced
½ pound fresh mushrooms, sliced
1 lemon
  Butter
  Cayenne powder
  Parsley

Coat snake strips with flour mixture. Brown in clarified butter. Pour over the red wine and let simmer.

While the meat is cooking, brown onions in another pan, then add a little more wine. Braise until the wine cooks away. Pour onions in with the meat and add sliced mushrooms and more butter. Cut the lemon in quarters and squeeze the juice over the dish, dripping the juice around in circles. This cuts the butter and keeps the dish from becoming too rich. Sprinkle with a little cayenne and parsley. Serve with cooked white rice.

Marine Iguanas

The perpetually grinning marine iguana must carry this smile because he hides the secret of delicious meat under his tough, gnarled, ugly outer covering. All of tropical America prizes this delicate, tasty meat but the only place you'll find a live marine iguana in his natural habitat is on the rocks or in the waters of the Galapagos Islands or at Lake Nicaragua in South America. Iguanas are harmless friendly animals, somewhat oblivious to the fact that man could, in time, decimate their species. The land iguana is often kept as a pet in areas of its natural habitat. Be *sure* to check local laws with authorities before taking marine iguanas.

Marine iguana.

Cleaning Iguana

This lone representative of a marine lizard is cleaned by first skinning the animal, then removing the insides. Save the yellowish eggs, the liver, and the heart. Now with a sharp knife, cut the body in half by cutting along the back bone. Cut off the legs and cut each half of the body meat into three parts.

IGUANA AND RICE

Iguana and Rice is a stew-type dish, and by the time this dish is put together, the iguana's grin will have faded, but when you taste the finished concoction, your smile will have replaced his twofold!

Use one iguana and clean as above, cutting the meat into two-inch pieces. Brown the meat in coconut oil over a low fire. Pour water over to cover, then add some chili piquant and three mashed garlic cloves. In another pan, boil any iguana eggs (unshelled) you have in very salty water along with a chili pod for 30 minutes. Drain the eggs and add, shell and all, to the meat. Dice the liver, heart, and any yellow eggs without shells that you have found in the iguana and add these to the dish. Cook until the liquid is almost gone. In a warm bowl, mix 2 cups hot, cooked rice with one #1 can of heated kidney beans. Pour iguana liquid over the rice and beans, then heap the stew on top and serve with garlic bread and a cool salad.

Mammals of the Sea

There are three orders of the Mammalia class that live partly or wholly in the sea. These are the Cetaceans (whales and narwhal, dolphins and porpoises), the Sirenias (sea cows, manatees, dugongs), and the Carnivores (sea otters, seals and sea lions, and walruses.) All are edible. (Whether the mermaid is a mammal or a viviparous fish, or even edible, is a moot question, so we'll leave her—and King Neptune— out of this!)

Almost all mammals of the sea have felt the heavy hand of man, who, since the dawn of his race, has hunted them for their flesh, fur, and oil.

Most whales are on the endangered list. Whale meat is very good and no animal has been more remorselessly slaughtered by man. Almost every square inch of the whale is utilized for various products. In Japan, Russia, Norway, and other Scandinavian countries whale meat is a staple food item. The narwhal of the Arctic seas is still hunted by Eskimos for its meat, oil, hide, and ivory. Porpoises are eaten by Indians living on

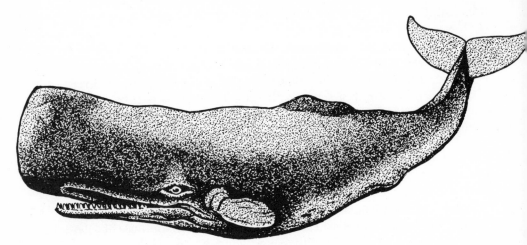

Sperm whale.

coasts of North and South America. In Normandy there was once an important porpoise fishery. The meat was eaten and the blubber rendered into oil for lighting. Porpoise flesh was considered a very royal dish in medieval England.

Two families of the sea cow (manatee or dugong) are known for their delicious meat containing high quality protein. They are also sought for their fine oil. Since mammals are protected in the United States, the numbers of manatees in Florida and the Gulf Coast have not changed in the last fifty years. The Florida manatee is an endangered species.

The Chinese hunt the sea lion and boil the blubber for oil, also render the bladder and bones for glue, process the reproductive organs for rejuvenating medicine, and even use the whiskers to make adornments for bridal costumes. Eskimos traditionally hunted the walrus for its meat and fat and made tools from the ivory tusks. This huge animal was once very abundant throughout the cold Arctic but was relentlessly pursued by hunters for its hide, oil, and its two-foot-long tusks.

The only mammal of the sea that seems to have escaped the exploitation of man is the dolphin. It is closely related to the valuable sperm whale and is undoubtedly edible and potentially valuable, but since ancient times, dolphins have been revered as almost sacred creatures because of their friendliness toward man. Sailors hold them in high esteem to this day and scientists are constantly studying the brain of this animal as well as its means of communication. No other creature has better or faster reflexes than the dolphin. It exhibits more intelligence and a better memory than any other creature on earth except man.

Porpoises are less playful than dolphins and rarely leap out of the water, nor do they follow boats as often as dolphins. Porpoises have more streamlined faces than dolphins, having blunt snouts and lacking the "beak" or "bottle nose" of the dolphin. The porpoise's back fin is small and fairly square while the dorsal fin of the dolphin curves backward to a point. However, the two names are used interchangeably.

Whales and dugongs have meat that resembles beef and the meat is used much the same way. Dolphins, seals, and sea otters come under the same category. Whale meat is a dark red color resembling beef, but is tough. It is especially delicious cut in long strips and barbecued over an open fire or patio barbecue and also makes very good steaks.

* The Australian sea lion which is confined to the coast of South Australia is said to have toxic flesh. The bearded seal (*Erignathus barbatus*) is circumboreal and has a poisonous concentration of vitamin A in its liver. *Circumboreal*, however, pinpoints areas within the Arctic Circle, and not many of us have the desire to fish or dive in this region, much less to bother with the liver of a bearded seal. Other mammals in cold climates have been reported poisonous to man for the same reason as the bearded seal—poisonous concentrations of vitamin A in their livers and kidneys.

Although the practice of sensible conservation is very important, state departments of fish and game in some areas say that seals and some other mammals on offshore islands are proliferating to the point of overpopulation. The resulting crowded conditions cause the death of many pups who are suffocated when adult seals sit or lie on them, yet the population of these mammals continues to rise. Sea lions breed from October to December, and they are usually quite tame except when defending their pups. The California sea lion (seal) breeds in June and July. Wherever sea lions live near a commercial fishery, they are blamed for damage to both fish and equipment. These animals are unpopular with fishermen even though most varieties of fish they eat are chiefly noncommercial.

Since the sea otters of Northern California have been declared a threatened species, these animals have been enjoying a trouble-free existence. They, too, are proliferating to the point of somewhat decimating the supply of shellfish in the areas where they are abundant. These animals feed mainly on sea urchins, clams, crabs, mussels, abalone, and occasionally on fish and octopus. Sea otters dive to depths of one hundred feet for food and require a great deal of it. It is estimated that they eat about a quarter of their body weight each day or about twenty pounds of food. Sea otters that find state protection and refuge in Monterey Bay, California, are a delight to tourists who can observe them from shore or boat. The otters are seen floating on their backs, pounding shellfish against a rock which they balance on their chests, thus breaking open the shellfish to get the meat inside. An amusing animal to watch, the sea otter's impish face grins at us as he gleefully wipes out the sea urchin and abalone population of Northern California!

6
Echinoderms

The Echinodermata phylum includes some pretty prickly sea creatures. The starfish, sea urchins, brittle stars, sea cucumbers, and sea lilies are

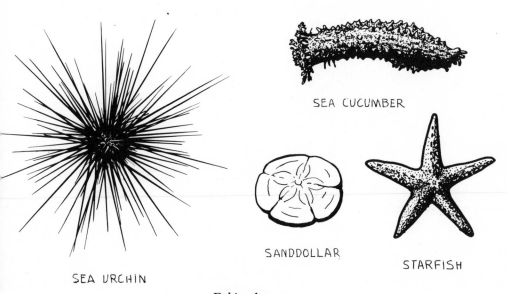

SEA CUCUMBER

SANDDOLLAR

STARFISH

SEA URCHIN

Echinoderms.

all members of this group and all have, in varying degrees, calcareous material that forms their body structure. Therefore, if it weren't for the very palatable qualities of the sea urchin's roe and the adaptability of the sea cucumber to delicious oriental dishes, this lowly group of bottom dwellers would head the list of unappetizing sea animals. Many members of this group are inedible because of the very high percentage of calcareous material their bodies contain. Some also contain toxins.

Sea Urchins

To gourmets the world over, the sea urchin is a delicacy of fine quality; indeed, many epicures consider it to be one of the finest foods to come from the sea. The roe of the sea urchin is not only of excellent flavor, but is extremely healthful and some even consider this roe an aphrodisiac. Actually the entire inner part of the sea urchin is edible, but it is the roe, or eggs, that are prized most as food. Well over a million urchins per year are supplied to the fish markets of Paris and Marseilles, but the supply is being depleted by overfishing. The California coast has choice sea urchins for the table and they are heavily harvested for other countries, but sea urchins are not as yet commonly eaten in the United States. However, their popularity is spreading rapidly throughout the world of scuba divers and beach-combers. The sea urchin has worldwide distribution, mostly in shallow waters, and boasts eight hundred representa-

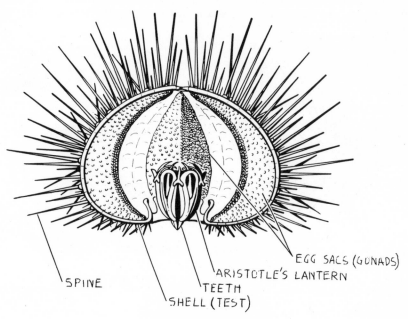

SPINE
SHELL (TEST)
TEETH
ARISTOTLE'S LANTERN
EGG SACS (GONADS)

Anatomy of a sea urchin.

Gathering sea urchins at White's Point, California. COURTESY DALE MC-NULTY.

tive species. Over two thousand years ago Aristotle wrote of sea urchin teeth resembling a horn lantern.

Eating Sea Urchins

Each urchin has five egg sacs nestled against the inside perimeter of the shell, or "test." Each egg sac has a shape somewhat similar to an orange segment. The eggs are sweet and at their best when they are full and orange colored. Sacs of the male are yellow and are edible but not quite as tasty as the orange female roe. The orange eggs are very good eaten raw. The yellowish, male eggs can be used for cooking and mixing with other ingredients in dips, spreads, and so forth.

Sea urchin roe is an exotic, delicious, and nutritious repast. It can be eaten right from the shell either straight from the ocean or boiled first; it can be fried lightly, quickly baked in a scallop shell, mixed for dips and butters, or used in a variety of other dishes such as the Japanese nori maki sushi (kelp rice roll). Nori maki sushi sometimes features sea urchin roe alone but often includes raw fish and scallops also.

To open a sea urchin, simply crack it open at the bottom or cut it in half with a heavy knife.

SEA URCHIN BUTTER
OR SEA URCHIN DIP

You Will Need
½ cup urchin roe
½ cup butter (for dip substitute ½ cup sour cream or mayonnaise)
   Garlic salt to taste

Start with the butter or sour cream in a blender and add the sea urchin roe until you have a definite sea flavor. Add garlic salt or whatever else pleases you such as minced onion, garlic, seaweed bits, and so forth. The more roe you add, the thinner the mix will be.

URCHIN TOAST AU GRATIN

Butter a lightly toasted piece of bread. French bread would be appropriate for this French recipe. Spread on a layer of urchin roe. Sprinkle with grated mild cheddar cheese and toast in the broiler or hot oven until the cheese is slightly melted or until lightly brown if you desire. These may be cut into wedges and served as dainty hors d'oeuvres or eaten as an open-faced sandwich.

BARBECUED URCHINS

Whole sea urchins may be broken open at the mouth, placed upon an open fire or grill, and barbecued about 10 minutes. Don't drain the juices before cooking. After cooking, the juices may be discarded or sipped from the shell Japanese style. The roe is eaten from the shell with a fork or fingers. A good dip will improve flavor for some. The roe is also good with potato chips or corn chips.

Slice through the sea urchin with a heavy, sharp knife.

Dump the watery viscera and carefully remove the five roe sacs.

BOILED URCHINS

Boil whole urchins in salted water for about 5 minutes over a low fire. Remove from water and cut out the mouth with scissors. Drain entrails, leaving yellow roe in shell. Dip pieces of buttered bread or toast into the roe around the inside of the shell. In Marseilles, the urchins are enjoyed raw this way, so if you're not squeamish, skip the boiling!

URCHIN PASTE

This is similar to anchovy paste, but much more exciting and a real aphrodisiac! Push urchin roe through a sieve, then mix in one teaspoon of salt for each ¼ cup of roe. Add 1 tablespoon melted butter for flavor. (One urchin that measures about 6 inches in diameter will yield about ¼ cup of sieved roe.) This paste will keep about a month in the refrigerator. Serve on crackers or toast.

URCHIN PUREE

Rub urchin roe through sieve. Add an equal amount of Bechamel sauce and simmer 5 minutes. Blend in 2 tablespoons of butter per quart. Use this paste to fill puff pastry, tarts, or to spread on buttered toast or French bread.

Bechamel Sauce: Put into electric blender ¼ cup softened butter, 1 teaspoon salt, ¼ teaspoon pepper, 6 tablespoons flour, and 2 cups hot milk. Blend for 30 seconds, first at low speed then at high speed. Pour into double boiler and cook over simmering water for 15 minutes, stirring constantly.

URCHIN ROE ESTRELLA

This is an attractive, delicious way to serve urchin roe as an appetizer and is straight from the country of Chile.

Remove the five roe sacs carefully to keep them in their original form and intact. Place the five egg sacs of each urchin on a plate or platter so that each group of five forms a star. One at a time, pour over each star some lemon or lime juice, then a little olive oil, and last about ¼ cup dry white wine. Surround each star with a circle of chopped black olives. Around the edge of the platter place lemon wedges and halves of purple grapes. Furnish a plate of crunchy crackers for guests to eat with (or alternately with) the urchin roe.

Urchin-kelp rice roll or Uni Nori Maki Sushi.

URCHIN KELP RICE ROLL

(Uni Nori Maki Sushi)

Little Tokyo restaurants in Los Angeles serve Kelp Rice Roll with urchins regularly along with other raw seafood hors d'oeuvres. Alice Hollenbeck, who used to supply sea urchin roe to many of these restaurants, listed the ingredients of the Japanese kelp rice roll for us and we developed from these the recipe that follows. This Urchin Kelp Rice Roll includes raw fish and scallops and is beautiful to look at as well as delightful to the palate. (Makes two rolls or about eight servings.)

You Will Need

¼ pound raw fresh fish fillets (bass, tuna, albacore)

2 cleaned scallops

6 large sea urchin egg sacs

1 package dried seaweed leaves (nori, laver, or porphyra)

1 cup uncooked rice

⅓ cup vinegar (rice vinegar preferred)

1 tablespoon sugar

½ teaspoon salt

Cut fish and scallops into long, thin strips, each strip about ¼-inch wide. Boil rice in 1¼ cups water, bringing to a boil, then reducing heat and steaming for 20 minutes with the lid on the pan. Set aside for 15 minutes. Fluff rice and pour into a large flat pan. Dissolve salt and sugar in the vinegar, then sprinkle the mixture over the rice, fluffing the rice with a spoon as you pour, so the vinegar mixture will coat each grain of rice—this keeps the rice from becoming sticky or mushy. Place a sheet of kelp on a folded paper towel (Japanese use a small bamboo mat) and spread rice evenly over the kelp, leaving a ¼-inch margin on each side of the kelp and a 1-inch margin at each end. Now place the fish, scallops, and urchin roe on the rice at the end where you will start the roll, nestling them nicely together for easy rolling. Start as for a jelly roll, using the napkin (or mat) to form the roll. Moisten the last inch of the kelp with vinegar to make it stick and seal. Slice roll crosswise into four or six individual servings. Serve with teriyaki sauce or lemon juice. These make interesting snacks and appetizers, and the variations possible are limited only by your imagination.

FRUIT OF THE SEA

Seafood specialty cafés in both Italy and France serve trays of shellfish with an entree. In the late fall months, one of the seafoods will always be sea urchin (*oursin* in France, *ricci di mare* in Italy). The Italians call this tray *frutta di mare* or fruit of the sea. The whole urchin, with the entrails removed, is served with the mouth cut away from the bottom of the shell. Small pieces of raw roe are broken off with a small fork and dipped into a vinegar and chopped onion mixture. After the roe has been eaten, the urchin juice is sipped right out of the shell as though it were a cup of tea. As a variation for the dip, use salted lime or lemon juice, teriyaki sauce, mayonnaise, or melted butter. The ancient Greeks and Romans often used vinegar, honey, and other strong seasonings.

Sea Urchin Poisoning

* Some sea urchins may be highly poisonous during their reproductive cycle. Eating the ovaries of these urchins will cause nausea, vomiting, and diarrhea. The male gonads do not seem to be affected. The species that are poisonous during the reproductive cycle are *Paracentrotus lividus* from Ireland to West Africa (used in Italy and France during the late fall months), the white sea urchn *Tripneustes ventricosus* from the West Indies to Brazil to West Africa, the sea needle *Diadema antillarum* from the West Indies. Other poisonous species are reported to occur in Japan. Local inhabitants of the area—especially in tropical regions—should be consulted before indulging in urchin roe.

Sea Cucumber (Sea Slug)

Certain species of sea cucumbers are taken in great numbers in some areas for use as food. They can be eviscerated, boiled, and used in soup, or sliced into rings and pickled. The genus *Stichopus* on the West Coast of the United States and the *Holothuria floridana* in Florida are edible but are exploited by few. The Greek philospher Aristotle gave the sea cucumber its name over two thousand years ago. They are found in all seas. The larger sea cucumbers are caught in the Far East and off Australia. They are eaten raw or boiled and dried and eaten as trepang or bêche de mer. A few Westerners eat the small muscle strips and throw the rest of cucumber away.

The sea cucumber ranges in length from six inches to more than two feet and in the South Pacific, particularly Australia, is called by other names such as teatfish, tiger fish, lolly fish, and mammy fish.

PICKLED SEA CUCUMBERS

In the Japanese settlements of California, the sea cucumber is indulged in during the Christmas and New Year holidays. It is pickled in rice vinegar and served as an appetizer; some like it with beer. Both ends of the sea cucumber are cut off, the viscera removed with a chopstick, or by cutting the animal in half lengthwise. It is then dropped in boiling water for about 15 seconds, removed, and brushed or scraped to clean the outer surface. The sea cucumber is then cut into $\frac{1}{8}$-inch slices and marinated in the following mixture for 24 hours:

To each cup of rice vinegar add:

8 tablespoons sugar

1 teaspoon salt or Accent

2 tablespoons lemon juice

2 slices lemon

Grated daikon

Trepang (Bêche-de-Mer)

Smoked and dried sea cucumbers are called *trepang* in China, the Philippines, and other areas of the Pacific, where they are used as a popular and tasty ingredient in soups and other dishes. In France they are called *bêche-de-mer*, and the Chinese call them *hai sen*.

In the Pacific Area, sea cucumbers are boiled until firm, smoked and dried, and packaged for storage and transportation. On Truk Island, sea cucumbers are dried for 2 days at 80 to 85°C, packaged in plastic bags, air-shipped to markets in Singapore and Hong Kong, and sold for as much as two dollars per pound. To use, trepang is reconstituted and used for many dishes such as stews, thick soups, filling for dumplings, salads, and with rice. Some of the soups are similar in taste to turtle soup.

QUICK-SMOKED SEA CUCUMBERS

The purpose of drying sea cucumbers is to add flavor and prepare them for long storage. This recipe uses the quick method of smoking where long storage is not necessary. Be sure to read "Smoke Cookery" in chapter 1 before preparing these. The total preparation and smoking time will range from 6 to 8 hours.

To insure freshness, put the sea cucumbers in cold sea water as soon as they are taken from the ocean. Keep them cool until you cook or freeze them, preferably within 24 hours. Some people add a little lemon juice or vinegar to the sea water.

Split fresh sea cucumbers lengthwise or cut in half and simmer for one hour in brine. To make brine add 1 cup of salt to each quart of water. Smoke the sea cucumbers with hickory chips or dry in the oven for 4 to 6 hours. If dried in the oven, set temperature control at 150°. Smoked or dried in this manner sea cucumbers will keep 4 weeks or more in the refrigerator. Use in any sea cucumber recipe after reconstituting. Smoked or dried sea cucumbers are called *trepang*.

Preparing Trepang for Cooking
Like most other dried foods, trepang must be reconstituted by soaking and boiling before eating. Soak dried sea cucumbers (trepang) in cold water for one day or overnight, then brush and clean them thoroughly. If you have not cut off the mouth end, do it at this point. Some recipes indicate soaking them for 3 days. Change the water and boil them one hour over medium heat, then cut in half and remove the insides. Wash thoroughly, quarter, and boil again until tender. Use in any sea cucumber recipe.

SEA CUCUMBER AND PORK SAUCE

The dried sea cucumber is sometimes referred to as "sea slug" and these animals vary in size, but they average about two inches in diameter and eight inches in length. They are sold by the piece and will keep indefinitely without refrigeration. This is an important seafood in the world of Chinese cuisine and this particular dish is fairly common there. Dried sea slugs are available in Chinese markets. Allow about four days before you prepare this dish, since most of the time involved is devoted to soaking of the sea cucumber, readying it for the pot.

You Will Need

    1 large dried sea slug about 8 inches long

    8 scallions or green onions, tied in a bunch

    2 1-inch pieces of ginger, peeled

    2 pounds fresh bacon with rind

    2 to 3 tablespoons soy sauce

    2 tablespoons sugar

      Salt to taste

    ½ teaspoon monosodium glutamate (Accent)

    8 dried black mushrooms

  1½ tablespoons shrimp eggs (at Chinese markets)

    2 tablespoons dry sherry or shao hsing wine

    2 tablespoons peanut, vegetable, or corn oil

    ⅓ cup bamboo shoots, thinly sliced

    2 green onions, including green stalk and cut in 2″ lengths

    5 thin slices fresh ginger, peeled

  1½ tablespoons cornstarch

    2 tablespoons rendered chicken fat

Hold the sea cucumber over a high gas flame or electric burner, turning frequently, about 1 minute. Place the sea cucumber in a very large bowl or utensil and add lukewarm water to cover. Soak 12 hours, then drain. Now place the sea cucumber in a pan and add water to cover, bring to a boil and simmer, covered, 1½ hours. Let cool in liquid, then drain and rinse. Cover with hot water and let soak 24 hours more. Drain and rinse again in warm water and carefully clean out the viscera. Wash well.

Now put the sea cucumber in a kettle with 4 quarts warm water and add the green onions (tied) and the ginger. Partially cover and simmer 1 hour or until tender. Cool in liquid.

While this cools, combine the pork, 5 cups of water, 2 tablespoons soy sauce, sugar, salt, and ¼ teaspoon monosodium glutamate. Bring to a boil, then simmer partially covered for 2 hours. Remove the pork and save. (This can be chilled and sliced to serve as a separate dish.) Set broth aside.

Place the mushrooms in a bowl, add boiling water to cover and let stand 15 to 30 minutes. Drain and squeeze to extract maximum moisture. Cut off and discard the tough stems.

Drain the sea cucumber thoroughly inside and out. Let stand at room temperature.

Combine the shrimp eggs and wine and steam these for 10 minutes. Heat the oil in a very large skillet (or wok) over a high flame and add the sea cucumber, then cook 10 seconds and add the shrimp eggs and bamboo shoots. Cook for 30 seconds more and add 2 cups of the pork broth and the mushrooms. Sprinkle with the remaining monosodium glutamate. The color should be dark brown; if not, add more soy sauce.

Salt to taste. As the sea cucumber cooks, spoon the sauce over it.

Transfer the sea cucumber to a large platter. Put the green onions (2-inch pieces) into the pan and thicken the sauce with the cornstarch mixed with 3 tablespoons water. Stir in the chicken fat and spoon the sauce over the sea cucumber.

STEWED SEA CUCUMBERS

This recipe from Hong Kong uses reconstituted dried sea cucumbers; fresh sea cucumbers would be too tough if cooked in this manner.

There is an old Chinese saying, "You must keep three things in mind when preparing food; it must have an appealing aroma, it must be pleasing to the eye, and it must be appetizing." This dish fills all those qualifications.

You Will Need
8 reconstituted sea cucumbers
1 tablespoon shortening
1 cup beef or chicken broth (stock)
1 teaspoon garlic, onion, and ginger each
¼ teaspoon monosodium glutamate, or Accent
1 tablespoon Chinese or white wine
1 teaspoon soy sauce
Salt to taste

Cut sea cucumber into ½-inch pieces. Heat shortening and add garlic, onion, ginger, wine, monosodium glutamate, broth, salt, and sea cucumbers and simmer for 10 minutes. Add about a tablespoon of cornstarch or arrowroot to a little cold water to make a thin paste. Stir slowly into stew to thicken. If arrowroot is used, do not boil again or the thickening property will be destroyed; however, arrowroot will give you a clearer stew than cornstarch.

Sea Cucumber Poisoning

* There have been some unconfirmed reports of poisoning from eating sea cucumbers in the tropical Pacific. Toxins of various strengths have been found in many sea cucumbers but it seems that the gastric acids of the stomach neutralize the toxins. Also, the process of soaking and boiling leaches out the toxins. The four most toxic of the many Indo-Pacific species are *Holothuria atra*, *H. aciologa*, *Stichopus variegatus*, and *Thelenota ananas*. All of these are found in Australia.

Starfish

The starfish, a universal favorite as an item of decor and study by beach combers, yields little in the way of edibility. Anything on the starfish for the purposes of this book probably falls into the category of "useless information," though starfish do have small strips of roe along each arm; but only a starving man would look upon this creature as a source of gastronomical benefit. Further, for survival purposes, there is very little reliable information on toxic starfish.

* Sometimes these have proven to be toxic during the summer months. The poison could possibly be concentrated while feeding on poisonous mussels and clams. Parker (1881) cited the death of two cats that had eaten a sunstar. One cat died in fifteen minutes and the other died in two hours.

Sea Lilies

These animals are very common to deep waters but the feather star or sea feather (Antedon) range in waters as shallow as one hundred feet in temperate zones. Sea lilies are of the class Crinida and are very plantlike, having stemlike stalks. Inedible, they are also known as the stone lily and have bodies that are ninety percent chalk.

Equipment Tips

Sea Urchins

Pry sea urchins off rocks by using a diver's knife. It is wise to wear gloves to protect your hands from the sharp spines. You will need a bag in which to gather them.

Sea Cucumbers

These should be handled carefully after they are picked up from the bottom, merely to keep them from eviscerating themselves. Place them in a small amount of seawater to which lemon juice or vinegar has been added to keep them fresh during transportation. Sea cucumbers that do rid themselves of their entrails are every bit as good as those that hang onto them until you get them home, but some Orientals feel they stay fresh longer if they stay intact until you are ready to clean them.

7

Seaweeds and Seawater

Beach-combers who stroll along the glistening wet, steel-gray sand are greeted by ruffles of brightly colored, satiny seaweeds strewn along the beach where storms have tossed them. Spring greens, olive and dark greens, purples, browns, brilliant pinks, bluish-green, and even white seaweeds decorate such beaches as though a pirate's treasure chest had spilled colorful swatches of exotic satins and silks as it washed ashore. Few of these beach-combers realize that the beauty of these seaweeds is matched by their delicate sea flavor when added to salads, either as they are or dried to make a seasoning.

Most seaweeds are edible and nutritious, though some are difficult to eat or have an undesirable flavor unless they are dried, cooked, or chopped finely first. A few tiny seaweeds, such as Desmarestia in Japanese waters, are poisonous, but we are not concerned with the very small species here.

Seaweeds are algaes and contain all the elements the body needs for healthy growth. Also they are an excellent vitamin source, containing fifty times more iron than that of wheat. Their ascorbic acid (vitamin C)

238

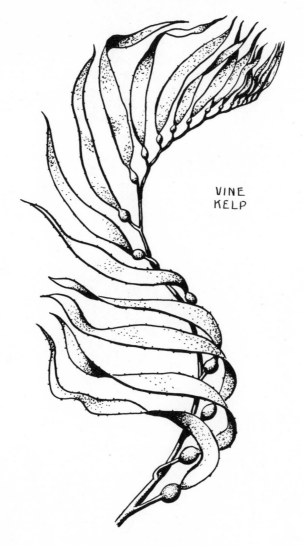

VINE
KELP

Seaweed (vine kelp).

content compares well with that of green vegetables and, all in all, sea-weeds can be compared with land plants as a source of dietary nutrients. Most seaweeds are a relatively high source of protein, though due to their shortage of amino acids this protein may be less easily assimilated by the body than animal protein.

Seaweed has been farmed for generations by the Orientals. Many other countries, including the United States, now farm seaweeds to a great extent. These seaweeds are then processed by commercial compa-nies and made into a powder that is used in hundreds of drug and food

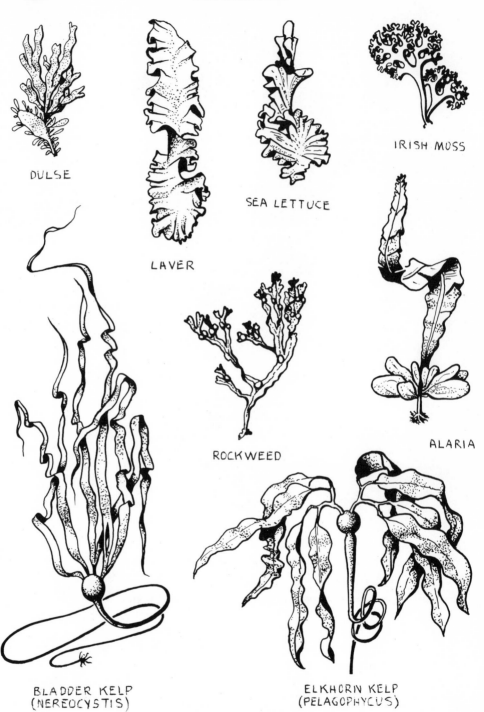

DULSE

LAVER

SEA LETTUCE

IRISH MOSS

ROCKWEED

ALARIA

BLADDER KELP
(NEREOCYSTIS)

ELKHORN KELP
(PELAGOPHYCUS)

Various seaweeds.

products. It would be difficult for anyone to get through a day without eating food that does not contain some form of algin processed from seaweed.

Dulse (Rhodymenia)

Dulse is a red algae found in the temperate zones from shallow to deep water and is usually eaten after it has been dried. Children in New England have chewed on dried dulse for generations between meals.

Dulse can be shredded and stewed in milk as soup, fried in butter, then sprinkled with pepper and dropped over a dull vegetable; is delicious added to cooked oatmeal or mashed potatoes; ground up with clams for clam recipes; or added to eggs and other dishes. In its dried form, dulse can be stacked, pressed down, then shredded and added to salmon or other fish loaves or casseroles.

Dulse Recipes

Fletcher W. Harvey, of Lake Dark Harbour, New Brunswick, Canada, has been distributing dried dulse throughout the world for many years. The product he distributes is merely washed and dried dulse, a process that the seafood fan can easily perform himself. If the reader would like to order Mr. Harvey's product, however, for a trial run with some of the recipes he gave us below, write to Fletcher W. Harvey, Lake Dark Harbour Brand Dulse, Seal Cove, Grand Manan, New Brunswick, Canada.

STEWED DULSE

Chop and simmer gently in milk until the dulse is tender. Add butter and serve with crackers.

FRIED DULSE

Fry dulse in melted butter until it turns color. Add pepper.

DULSE SANDWICH

Make a sandwich filling of dulse leaves and lettuce. Simple, but both tasty and healthful.

SEAWEED CAKES

Mix some dulse that has been boiled a few minutes to tenderize with a little butter and cream, then add raw oatmeal (Quick oats) to stiffen. Shape into flat cakes and fry in bacon fat or butter.

MASHED POTATOES WITH DULSE

Cook dulse slowly with a very little water, mashing with a wooden spoon. Add salt, pepper, and butter and serve with mashed potatoes or mix in with the potatoes.

Dulse can also be added to dressing for any fish, chowders, or tossed with green salads.

Laver (Porphyra or Nori)

Laver, another red algae found in most oceans in shallow water, is comparatively tender and can be used as is or dried like dulse, then shredded and used in the same way. Fresh, it is just a little tough and should be shredded very fine. The Japanese sauté laver (nori) after softening it by soaking it in oil with a little garlic about 30 minutes. After sautéing, they add a little teriyake sauce for zest and pour it over hot, cooked rice.

Sea Lettuce (Ulva)

A green algae found in most oceans in shallow water, sea lettuce is dried, ground to a fine powder, and used as a delicious seasoning. Once you have made sea lettuce seasoning with this simple method you'll worry about gathering another fresh batch to make sure you won't run out!

SEA LETTUCE SEASONING

Rinse a good bunch of sea lettuce well in cool water and pat with a towel. Heat your oven to about 150°. Spread the sea lettuce out on a cookie sheet and let it dry in the oven for several hours until crisp and dark. It should be crisp enough to roll easily into a fine powder. Use as a unique, tangy seasoning over salads, fish, or any dish that suits you. Experiment!

Sea lettuce can be gathered by divers easily or picked up near shore where it has floated in on the tide. It resembles nothing so much as a piece of bright green, smooth, ruffled plastic.

Irish Moss (Chondrus)

Irish moss renders a high viscosity extract that is used to thicken, emulsify, suspend, and stabilize various fluids such as beer, fruit syrups, chocolate milk, ink, cosmetics, and shampoos; and is also used to smooth and thicken products such as ice cream, facial creams, and so forth.

Domestically it is used mostly as a thickening agent and for making blancmange in the eastern seaboard states of the United States. It is found in shallow water in temperate zones.

BLANCMANGE

Gather about two cups of Irish moss. Use one cup of Irish moss to two quarts milk. Place the moss in a double folded and tied cheesecloth bag and place it in the top of a double boiler. Cover with milk, put the lid on the pan, and cook about 30 minutes, stirring from time to time to keep the gelatin product that exudes from the moss well mixed with the milk. Each time you stir, press the bag to push out the extra gelatin. After 30 minutes remove the bag and flavor the milk with anything you like—fruit flavoring, hunks of fresh fruit, or bouillon if you want a jellied bouillon treat. Chill and enjoy.

Rockweed (Fucus)

The brown algaes include the kelps which are extremely rich in potassium, and some species contain as much as twenty five percent protein.

Rockweed is a small brown algae and is used mostly as a flavor-exuding bed for cooking fish and shellfish dishes. Its best use is for the clambake. To use rockweed for a clambake, alternate thick layers of it with layers of vegetables such as corn and/or seafood in the kettle or sand pit until the cooking container is full. Be sure to place a bed of rockweed on the bottom first. Rockweed is also great in the bottom of the steaming kettle for steaming mussels or clams. You can find rockweed on rocky shores in the tidal zone of cold water seas.

Bladder Kelp (*Nereocystis*) and Elkhorn Kelp (*Pelagophycus*)

These two kelps, sometimes called "Sea Pumpkin," are found among the giant kelp beds of California. These magnificent kelps grow to around one hundred feet tall and their hollow stipes, or stems, as well as the huge bladder balls at the top, are delicious candied or pickled.

KRAZY KELP KANDY

Use the hollow stipe and large bladder ball at the top of sea pumpkin, elkhorn, or bladder kelp. These kelps have different common names in various locals, but are the two species *Nereocystis* and *Pelagophycus*. Peel the kelp with a potato peeler, then cut into bite-sized pieces. You will need on hand:

> 2 or 3 quarts of white vinegar
> Sugar

Cinnamon
Red food coloring

In a large pan, cover the kelp with vinegar. Cover and boil 15 minutes. This removes any bitterness and softens the kelp. Drain, rinse, and let stand in a plain water bath for 4 to 6 hours, changing the water every hour or so until no vinegar can be tasted upon sampling the kelp. Drain. Use two cups sugar to two cups kelp pieces: Pour sugar over kelp and stir with a large spoon. The sugar will liquify. Add 2 teaspoons cinnamon and about 2 teaspoons red food coloring, or enough to give the syrup a bright red color. Bring to a boil, then turn down to simmer. Cook 1 hour. Spread a layer of granulated sugar over a cookie sheet or sheet of waxed paper. With slotted spoon, dip kelp candy from syrup, drain slightly, and place on the bed of sugar. Roll pieces of kelp in sugar, separating them as you mix, until each piece is well coated with sugar. Place the candy in a single layer on waxed paper to cool. You may want to roll it again in sugar when it is cool. Store the candy in a covered container in the refrigerator and it will keep indefinitely. Be sure to save the syrup and utilize it for several batches, then strain small pieces of kelp from it and store it for the next candy making. Better yet, use it as a delicious topping for ice cream. The syrup is clear, beautiful, and also keeps indefinitely in the refrigerator.

Pickled Kelp
(Plan on at least two weeks storage time before serving)

Use the same kind of kelp as for Krazy Kelp Kandy; pumpkin, elkhorn, or bladder kelp (*Nereocystis* or *Pelagophycus*), and utilizing the upper portion of the stipe that is at least 2 inches in diameter, and the bladder ball.

Using a potato peeler, strip off the thin skin of the kelp. Cut the bladder into one-inch pieces and slice the stipe into thin rings. Make a mixture of ¼ cup coarse-medium salt to 1 quart water and cover kelp pieces with the solution. Soak overnight. Drain and rinse the kelp.

In a large pan, cover the kelp with vinegar, cover, and boil 15 minutes. Drain, rinse, and let stand in a plain water bath for 4 to 6 hours, changing the water every hour or so until no vinegar can be tasted in a taste test. Drain well.

The pickling recipe below will be enough for about 4 cups of kelp pieces:

¾ cup apple cider vinegar
2½ cups sugar (use natural sugar for an extra healthy snack!)
5 whole cloves
1 tablespoon pickling spice
1 drop green food coloring (for appealing tint)

Mix the above ingredients together and bring to a boil. Simmer about 5 minutes and pour over one quart of prepared kelp. Let stand 12 hours or overnight. Drain off syrup and heat again to boiling, pour again over kelp and let stand another 12 hours. Drain off syrup into a container that has a pouring lip.

Sterilize jars, then fill each with kelp pieces (rings and pieces may be separated into different jars for uniformity if desired). Pour hot syrup over, filling jar to top. Seal and let stand from two weeks to a month before serving.

Alaria

This is the seaweed that is known in Japan as *Komba* and is utilized as a seasoning. It grows to fifteen feet in cold water.

Wonderful experiments can be made with seaweed the next time you have the opportunity to wander along a rocky shore, or to pick up some underwater while diving. Pluck a piece here and there, then taste it. See if it's tough, tender, rubbery, or brittle. If it seems bitter, take it home and dry it or boil it in acetic acid (vinegar) to remove the bitterness or to tenderize it for palatability. You'll find you will enjoy chewing on some seaweeds right on the spot and they will impart a tangy, salty sea flavor.

SEAWEED-SHELLFISH SOUP

From Okinawa

David B. McCreary is a well-known author of diving articles from several areas of the world, and he gave us this Okinawan recipe for Seaweed-Shellfish Soup to try. It is not only delicious but appropriate to most areas of the world in regard to the accessibility of its ingredients.

You Will Need
  4 cups water
  ¼ cup dried shrimp
  1 tablespoon soya sauce
  1 teaspoon salt
  ¼ teaspoons monosodium glutamate (Accent)
  Enough shellfish so that the meat itself gives you roughly 3 to 4 cups meat.
  2 cups "tangle" seaweed ("Wakame" or any dried seaweed)
  Lemon slices

In a large kettle, bring first 5 ingredients to a boil. Scrub and clean the outer shells of the shellfish still in their shells. Drop into the boiling soup and simmer for 15 minutes. Add the seaweed and boil for 2 minutes more. Serve hot garnished with lemon slices. Serves six.

Note: It may be necessary to add more water as shellfish are simmering. Dried shrimp and soya sauce are available in Japanese food stores and some super markets at the Oriental food counters.

Seawater

The sea is basic to all life—moderator of the climate and provider of water, food, and nutrients. The nutrients of the sea are so conveniently available that marine life forms can take it right into their systems and get the oxygen and carbon dioxide needed for life and the nutrient salts and minerals needed for growth. Just as land plants depend upon minerals in the soil for their growth, sea life depends upon the salts and minerals in seawater.

Minerals from the Sea

Due to its particular composition, the sea may be a fountain of youth to man. A very interesting fact that has been known for a long time is that seawater is a close equivalent to human blood. Seawater has actually been used for blood transfusions when blood was not available—with excellent results. In view of this fact, it would seem practical to obtain mineral needs of the body from the sea. When we have a steady diet of land-grown foods, which usually are grown in mineral-starved soil, we should eat food from the sea regularly to avoid mineral deficiencies that may develop in our bodies.

It is now known that many deficiency ailments are caused by a lack of essential trace elements instead of by the invasion of a germ or virus. We find that seawater is the only medium left to us that contains all water-soluble trace elements, and most of these elements are known to be essential to good, vibrant health. It is not surprising that many people state that they are finding tremendous beneficial results from taking a little seawater every day as a supplement to make up for the lack of natural elements in their daily diet. Some people claim relief from various diseases and allergies by taking from two to four tablespoons of seawater daily. There is certainly nothing very new about these allegations; Hippocrates and other physicians of his time advised drinking small doses of seawater several hundred years before the birth of Christ.

Purifying Seawater for Use

Seawater collected for the purpose of consumption should be obtained far enough out to sea to avoid possible pollution and should not be taken from the surface or the very bottom of the area. Fill a container in about fifteen or twenty feet of water or about halfway between the surface and the bottom in clear water. Very clear water usually doesn't have to be purified if it is to be used immediately since it is cleaner than most tap water. If you intend to store the seawater so that you can use a little each day as suggested earlier, however, it should be purified.

The Institute of Marine Sciences at the University of Miami in Florida recommends the following methods of purification:

Seawater may be sterilized by boiling, autoclaving, or filtration. While only a few minutes of boiling is necessary to kill the vegetative forms, the destruction of spores requires water to be boiled from 30 minutes to an hour. Sterilization may also be accomplished by autoclaving at 15 pounds for 15 minutes. Boiling seawater will cause calcium carbonate to precipitate. Continue boiling will cause sodium chloride and other minerals to precipitate as volume is reduced.

Perhaps the simpliest technique, and the one which produces the least alteration of seawater is sterilization by filtration. If seawater is passed through a membrane filter (millipore, HA, 0.45 u pore size) into a clean flask, it will effectively remove the bacteria and other particulate matter.

Membrane filters with a 0.45-micron pore size and a diameter of forty seven millimeters can be purchased from the Millipore Filter Corporation, Bedford, Massachusetts. Filtering the water through this extremely fine pore size takes about twenty four hours per gallon and one filter per gallon.

Uses for Seawater

Filtered seawater can also be used for seasoning foods, for storing frozen seafoods, seawater aquariums, laboratory studies, and for many other applications. T. W. Thornhill, president of Charleston Oil Company of South Carolina, had the city water department test deep seawater from fifteen to twenty miles out. Analysis of the seawater proved that it was just as pure for drinking as tap water of the city. Mr. Thornhill has been using deep seawater since 1959, and in our correspondence with him he has laid down some of his suggestions for the use of seawater:

1. Do not use as a medicine. Use as a supplement for salt and water. Salt and water are present in most things we eat or drink.
2. Water for drinking; add ½ teaspoon per glass of water. Also the same for milk.
3. Grits, rice, oatmeal, cream of wheat, and so forth; 2 tablsespoons per person.
4. Cold cereals using milk or cream; use 1 to 2 teaspoons per person.
5. Salads with fruits; 1 to 2 teaspoons. Sprinkled on with any other dressing, but leave off the table salt.

If you don't have a seawater source, the next best thing to use will be whole sea salt, seaweed, kelp tablets, or some kind of sea food. Commercial table salt is no substitute—it contains only sodium chloride. Too much table salt causes the body to store water whereas whole sea salt or seawater will not. A balance of sodium (salt) and potassium in the body will preclude water storage in the body and let it drain off naturally. There is enough potassium in seawater and whole sea salt to maintain this balance.

Dr. George W. Crane, Ph.D., M.D., highly recommends seawater and states that his patients have had great success from using seawater or sea salt in their diets. Arthritic problems among other ailments have improved greatly from this treatment, says Dr. Crane.

MERMAID'S SEAWATER BREAD

This recipe is not only extremely healthful, but very convenient to use, especially if you travel aboard a boat or wish to have some real homemade bread on a beach camp-out, for it's made atop the stove and can be made successfully even over a campfire.

You Will Need

1½ cups seawater

1 tablespoon sugar

1 tablespoon dried yeast (1 envelope)

4 cups plain flour

2 teaspoons minced seaweed (parsley can be substituted)

Melt the sugar and yeast in the seawater and mix well. Add the flour and stir well. (No kneading is necessary.) Mix seaweed with flour.

Grease well and flour a pressure cooker or heavy sauce pan that has a snugly fitting lid. (If a pressure cooker is used, leave the valve open.) Put the dough into the pan and cover with a towel, then let it rise in a warm place for two hours (on a good hot day you can set the pan in the sun on a picnic table or utilize your boat deck for this!). Put the lid on the pan and cook over a low flame on top of the stove for one half hour, then remove the loaf, turn it over, and replace it in the pan. Cover and cook for another half hour.

You'll find that the seaweed or parsley gives this old-fashioned bread real character in appearance, and the texture of the bread itself will be hardy and welcome for out-of-doors lovers. Needless to say this is one of our favorites and we make it on most dive-club campouts or overnight boat trips we go on.

Toxic Seawater

* Although taken in small amounts seawater can be very beneficial, it can be toxic under certain conditions. It is unsafe to drink when it is highly polluted, especially when it is polluted from sewage outfall. A very high percentage of dinoflagellates, which cause the "red tide," could also render seawater unsafe for drinking. Anyone who must restrict their salt intake should consult their physician before using seawater in their diet, according to the International Oceanographic Foundation of Miami.

Too much seawater may cause a laxative effect and, if this occurs, the amount taken should be reduced to the point where the effects disappear. The amount of seawater taken daily can vary from two to eight tablespoons and should be taken with three times as much fresh water in order to dilute the sodium concentration in the seawater. The human kidney can eliminate about three grams of sodium per liter (or about one tenth of an ounce of sodium per quart), and seawater contains that much sodium per cup. Therefore, a ratio of one part seawater to three parts fresh water or other sodium-free liquid would provide the balance.

Survival at Sea

Clean, uncontaminated seawater may be taken in amounts of up to two cups a day in emergency conditions such as being stranded at sea. Contrary to popular belief, survival on the ocean can be prolonged by drinking seawater, according to Dr. Harbans Lal, a Chicago research scientist. Some people who have died from dehydration on the open sea could have been saved if they had taken small quantities of seawater. Earlier conception of survival at sea and some fiction stories have caused some people to believe that swallowing seawater even in very small amounts increases one's thirst and causes the tongue to swell; also that seawater is poisonous. Recent research on survival, however, has indicated that about 400 cc of seawater (about two cups) a day will prolong survival. Ingesting more than two cups may cause dehydration of the body cells.

It is suggested that survivors do not drink any water at all for the first two days. This allows the kidneys to become accustomed to the shortage and trains them to conserve the little water they will receive. Thus the survivor's body gets *some* water to live on during its time of strife. The only noticeable side effect that this amount of seawater seems to create in some cases is a tendency to become irritable, excited, or depressed—but persons rescued after being adrift at sea felt it was worth the temporary discomfort to their emotional outlook.

ELEMENTS PRESENT IN SEAWATER

MAJOR ELEMENTS—MORE THAN 100 PPM

Chlorine	Sulphur	GASSES:
Sodium	Calcium	Oxygen
Magnesium	Potassium	Hydrogen

MAJOR ELEMENTS—FROM 0.5 TO 100 PPM

Bromine	Silicon	GASSES:
Carbon	Fluorine	Argon
Strontium	Nitrogen (Comp)	Nitrogen
Boron	Aluminum	

MINOR ELEMENTS—LESS THAN 0.5 PPM

Actinium	Francium	Manganese	Rhenium	Titanium
Antimony	Gadolinium	Mercury	Rhodium	Uranium
Arsenic	Gallium	Molybdenum	Rubidium	Vanadium
Astatine	Germanium	Neodymium	Ruthenium	Wolfram
Barium	Gold	Nickel	Samarium	Xenon
Beryllium	Hafnium	Niobium	Scandium	Ytterbium
Bismuth	Holmium	Osmium	Selenium	Yttrium
Cadmium	Indium	Palladium	Silver	Zinc
Caesium	Iodine	Phosphorus	Tantalum	Zirconium
Cerium	Iridium	Platinum	Technetium	Tungsten
Chromium	Iron	Polonium	Tellurium	GASSES:
Colbalt	Krypton	Prasodymium	Terbium	Helium
Copper	Lanthanum	Promethium	Tallium	Neon
Dysprosium	Lead	Protactinium	Thulium	
Erbium	Lithium	Radium	Thorium	
Europium	Lutecium	Radon	Tin	

8

Edible Et Ceteras and Combinations

There are an odd assortment of sea creatures, as well as recipes, that just won't fit into a particular category for our purposes in this book. We found that attempting to categorize them was rather like trying to find a word that rhymes with "orange." No category came quite close enough.

There are some sea animals that are generally thought of as being absolutely inedible and/or poisonous; these are jellyfish, sea anemones, sea worms, plankton, and sponges. Many of these are actually inedible but some have a geographically limited use as food and this book would be incomplete without discussing them. These are covered in the first part of this chapter.

The second part is devoted to recipes for the many sauces that can be used with various types of seafood dishes as well as recipes for such things as bouillabaisse and cioppino, which do not align themselves with any particular seafood, utilizing all at once various species of fish and shellfish.

When all is said and done, and with deep respect for the lobster, crab, sea urchin, halibut, and red snapper dishes throughout the world, it is

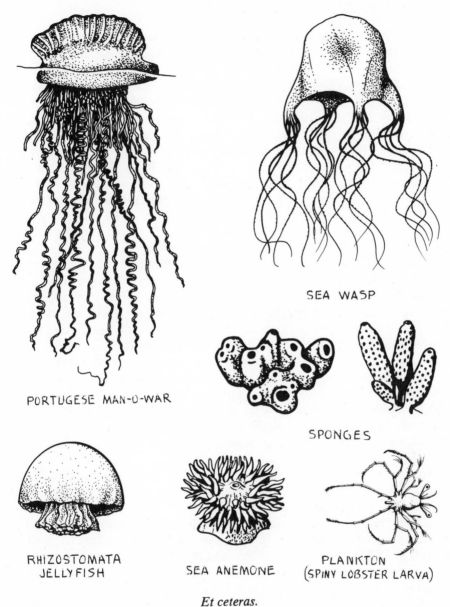

PORTUGESE MAN-O-WAR

SEA WASP

SPONGES

RHIZOSTOMATA
JELLYFISH

SEA ANEMONE

PLANKTON
(SPINY LOBSTER LARVA)

Et ceteras.

the bouillabasses and cioppinos that give us the real aroma, zest, and flavor of our bountiful Mother Sea.

The inseparable combination of seafood and wine concludes the book. Just by turning to the last page, you can conveniently find the right wine for your seafood dining pleasures.

Coelenterates

This phylum includes jellyfish, corals, and sea anemones. Surprisingly, some of these are quite edible, but others can be highly toxic and deadly.

Jellyfish

No attempt should be made to eat a fresh jellyfish, due to its stinging cells. Those that are eaten in a few parts of the world are first processed. Two species of jellyfish (*Rhizostomata*) are utilized for the table in Japan and China. One species (*Stomolophus meleagris*) of the *Rhizostomata* is abundant in the Pacific around San Diego and in the Atlantic from the Carolinas southward; they are also found in the Gulf of Mexico. Jellyfish are preserved by brining and drying. Orientals preserve the *Rhizostomata* in salt and alum or place them between steamed leaves of oak. When ready to use, the jellyfish are soaked in water, flavored, and cut up for serving. Many jellyfish are toxic even after cooking.

The use of gloves is important when handling a jellyfish, as contact with the bare skin will produce painful stings. A weak solution of ammonia or baking soda sometimes helps. There are a few jellyfish which might be considered dangerous just from their stings. These are the box jellyfish (*Chironex fleckeri*), sea wasp (*Chiropsalmus*), sea nettle (*Dactylometra*), and sea blubber or lion's mane (*Cyanea.*) The box jellyfish and the sea wasp are probably the most venomous marine organisms known and their stings may cause death within minutes. The *Cubomedusae*, so called because of its thin, squarish shape, ranges in size from as small as grapes to as large as pears and have four tentacles or four groups of tentacles. They prefer shallow waters on warm beaches and are troublesome around Northern Australian coasts, the Philippines, and Japan.

Sea wasps can kill in as short a time as half a minute but usually in about a quarter of an hour, the victim dying in excruciating pain. The Portuguese man-o-war is among the common stinging hydroids. Over three hundred years ago sailors began calling this jellyfish a caravel, or Portuguese man-o-war, since it resembles the Portuguese caravel, a ship of 100 to 150 tons with a broad bow and high narrow poop. The sting of this animal can cause cramps, nausea, or, very rarely, death. Even the dried stinging cells are dangerous when handled carelessly. The dangerous jellyfishes are usually found in tropical seas. The box jellyfish has been identified around the islands of southeast Asia and tropical waters of Australia.

Dried jellyfish are sometimes found in the refrigerator section of a store. These come in one-pound tan slabs sealed in a plastic bag and is somtimes labeled "Salted Jellyfish." This will keep in the refrigerator for several weeks. This recipe for jellyfish with chicken shreds is from China and is really quite good.

SHREDDED CHICKEN WITH JELLYFISH

You Will Need
 1 one-pound package dried jellyfish (available in Chinese markets)
 1 whole chicken breast skinned and boned
 4 teaspoons cornstarch
 1 tablespoon beaten egg white
   Salt to taste
 ¾ teaspoon monosodium glutamate (Accent)
 1½ teaspoons sugar
 2½ cups (scant) vegetable oil
 1 tablespoon water

Wash jellyfish to remove salt and place in a bowl. Cover with water to about 1 inch above the jellyfish. Set aside several hours or overnight, changing the water several times.

Drain the jellyfish and cut into fine shreds, then put into mixing bowl and pour boiling water over to cover. Let stand 30 seconds and drain well, immediately running cold water over, then draining again.

Cut the chicken into very thin slices then into very thin shreds. (Partially freezing the chickens first will facilitate this procedure.) Place the shreds in a bowl and add the 1 tablespoon cornstarch and the egg white, salt, ¼ teaspoon monosodium glutamate (Accent), and ½ teaspoon sugar. Blend with fingers and refrigerate for at least 30 minutes.

In a skillet (or wok if you have one) heat 3 tablespoons of the oil, then add the jellyfish and cook over high heat about 10 seconds, stirring constantly. Add salt to taste, ¼ teaspoon Accent, and ½ teaspoon sugar. Cook over high heat about 2 minutes, again stirring constantly. Drain. (Jellyfish gives up a lot of water as it cooks.)

In another skillet, warm the 2 cups of oil and add the chicken, then cook briefly just until the shreds separate and the meat is white. Drain, catching the drippings in a bowl, then wipe out the pan. Heat 3 tablespoons oil to almost smoking and add the chicken. Stir constantly and add salt to taste, the remaining ¼ teaspoon Accent, and the remaining ½ teaspoon sugar. Add the jellyfish and cook over high heat, stirring constantly and tossing a little, about 30 seconds. Blend the 1 teaspoon cornstarch and water to make a thin paste and stir in to thicken. Serve hot. Serves 6 to 8.

Sea Anemones

Many anemones are edible after cooking and preserving. Sea anemones are preserved by boiling in brine and drying. Cooked sea anemones are eaten in the Mediterranean area and are also commonly eaten by natives of Samoa, the Philippines, New Guinea, and other tropical Pacific areas. Many anemones seem never to be poisonous, although some have dangerously venomous stinging cells that could envenomize

* a person attempting to eat them raw. Two species (*Rhodactis howesi* and *Physobrachia douglasi*) eaten by the natives of Samoa are considered poisonous raw, but safe to eat when cooked. Some are toxic even after cooking and consumption of anemones in some areas has caused gastrointestinal and neurological disorders. These animals have sometimes been used for criminal purposes— as a method of "getting even" with an adversary!

Seaworms

At the end of April when tides are abnormally low on several islands in the Palau group, worm diggers can usually be seen on the vast sand flats where they are gathering two species of edible worms. The natives call these two species *ngimr and kleu*. Both are white and about fifteen inches long, but *ngimr* are more highly prized as they become tender when cooked; the *kleu* species get tougher.

Our research in this area has been highly limited and little is known about the edible qualities of other sea worms.

Plankton

Plankton includes all the living organisms, plant or animal, usually minute, that drift or swim weakly about in the ocean. These minute creatures exist in countless swarms and form the basic food in the food chain for a host of marine creatures.

* For all practical purposes, plankton is potentially poisonous for human consumption, regardless of the fact that plankton can be commercially processed into a "basic protein" product. This process requires cooking as well as careful selection of ingredients. For the layman, the real danger in eating plankton taken from the ocean is the possibility of ingesting poisonous organisms. Some of these organisms, such as some of the dinoflagellates, are quite deadly. These dinoflagellates, which are the most numerous of the poisonous organisms, are the ones that poison clams and mussels during the warm summer months on some open coasts.

Human test subjects, used by the Air Force in attempts to determine the edibility of plankton under life-raft survival conditions, became violently ill after eating plankton.

Sponges

Sponges are made up almost entirely of microscopic fibers of either calcium carbonate, silicon compounds, or spongin. Each fiber is covered with a thin, slimy, odiferous skin. Tiny plants and animals are sucked into sponges and are engulfed by the fibers. Although most sponges

Sponges at Grand Cayman Island (about fifty feet deep).

taste and smell badly and are protected by sharp spicules, they are eaten by some nudibranchs and sea spiders.

*   Nothing is known about the effects to man of eating sponge extracts, although laboratory animals have died from it.

Bouillabaisses and Cioppinos

Bouillabaisses and cioppinos can be called "seafood stews" for all practical purposes, but this mundane term doesn't nearly do them justice. Though both (so goes the story) originated as dockside sustenance for hungry fishermen, they have evolved into two of the most popular sea-food dishes. The very bosom of the sea visits itself upon the diner through three of his strongest senses: smell, taste, and touch—not neces-sarily in that order but certainly with the sense of smell coming into play first. As the dish is brought to the table it seems to be wafting in on a heavenly aroma of robust mixtures—seafood, garlic, and wine—and the taste buds come suddenly alive. The very best of olive oils should be used for this dish to compliment the subtleties of fennel, saffron, and bay leaf that are an integral part of the delicate flavors.

These dishes can be served in one of two ways. Some prefer serving the soup first and the meat and vegetables after; others like the whole thing served up in deep soup plates. Good chunks of French or Italian bread with plenty of dairy butter is served alongside either for eating with the dish or for "sopping." When soup and vegetables are served together, some will attempt to be neat and start with a spoon or even a fork; but this will never crack it (literally, for there are shells to be contended with in this seafood "stew"). Seafood can be shelled first, but that, in the opinion of most gourmets, is the coward's way and denies the diner of the privilege of bringing into the experience the ever important sense of touch—using his hands to obtain the delicious morsels of meat from the shells himself.

Bouillabaisse originated in Marseilles, France, and in Marseilles it is believed that the only true bouillabaisse must be prepared there, for one of the fish used in the dish there is the *rascasse*, which cannot be found anywhere except the Mediterranean. Good substitutes for this fish, however, seem to work out well in other parts of the world.

Cioppino is an Italian concoction. It has been rumored that cioppino was actually born right in San Francisco (and that bouillabaisse was invented in a French convent!). Whatever their origins, these wonderful dishes are gustily flavored, highly nutritious, and provoke warm, chuckily conversation between bib-bedecked guests.

And—they are fun to prepare.

BOUILLABAISSE MARSEILLES

You Will Need

9 or 10 pounds of fish—various species: red snapper, halibut, eel, bass, and whiting

5 pounds shellfish consisting of: *crayfish, shrimp, clams, lobster, and mussels

2 medium onions, chopped

2 leeks, chopped

4 skinned, chopped tomatoes

1 ounce (about 6 cloves) crushed garlic

2 tablespoons cut up parsley

Pinch of fennel

1 bayleaf

Small pinch saffron

4 tablespoons olive oil

Salt and pepper (freshly ground)

Clean fish and cut in crosswise pieces. Wash shellfish; cut shrimp in half and lobster in chunks, removing intestinal veins. In a stewpan, place the onions, leeks, tomatoes, garlic, parsley, fennel, bayleaf, saffron, the

* If available.

fish, crustaceans, shellfish, and fish. (Fish such as bass and whiting that have tender flesh should be added later.)

Fifteen minutes before you begin to cook the stew, cover the whole thing with boiling water and add salt and pepper to taste. Begin to cook 15 minutes later and boil very rapidly for 7 minutes (rapid boiling keeps the oil circulating.) Now add the tender fleshed fish and cook another 8 minutes. Pour the liquid portion into a heated soup tureen over thick slices of French bread—enough bread to make the soup thick as it is absorbed by the bread. Place the fish on a shallow dish and sprinkle them with parsley, then surround them with the shellfish. Serve soup and seafood at the same time with lots of French bread on the side.

BOUILLABAISSE PARISIAN

You Will Need

½ cup olive oil
1 large purple onion
2 leeks, thinly sliced
3 cloves garlic, minced
1 bay leaf
2 cups peeled, chopped tomatoes
2 cups liquid (fish stock or water and clam juice)
1 cup dry white wine
½ teaspoon fennel seed, crushed
⅛ teaspoon crushed saffron

Salt and pepper
2 teaspoons minced parsley
2 lobster tails, cut into 2-inch chunks
1 pound red snapper (cut up)
1 pound sea bass (cut up)
12 shrimp
6 dungeness crab legs (or other large crab)
8 mussels (if available)
6 clams
6 oysters

In large stew pot, heat oil and add the onion, leeks, garlic, and bay leaf. Sauté until onion is tender. Add tomatoes and stock, wine, saffron, salt and pepper, and parsley. Simmer 15 minutes and add lobster and fish. Cook 10 minutes. Add washed shellfish and cook 5 minutes, or until clam, oyster, and mussel shells open. Ladle into deep soup plates. Serve with plenty of French bread—(garlic bread is superb).

ROCKFISH CIOPPINO (ROCK COD)

You Will Need

6 tablespoons olive oil
¼ cup chopped onions
2 chopped green onions
1 #1 can solid pack tomatoes
1 cup water or fish stock

¾ cup dry white wine
2 pounds rockfish, cut up
1 crab (dungeness or cancer crab) chopped up
2 pounds unshelled clams

Salt and pepper   1 pound shrimp or prawns
                                   Parsley

Heat olive oil in large pot. Sauté the onions and smaller green onions until transparent. Add tomatoes, water and seasoning. Stir, then add the wine, crab, clams, and shrimp or prawns. Simmer 10 minutes, then add the rockfish. Simmer another 10 minutes. Shake the pot now and then while cooking, but do not stir at this point. Sprinkle the chopped parsley over and serve in large soup plates.

CIOPPINO ITALIANO

You Will Need   1 8-oz. can tomato puree
3 tablespoons high quality   ⅛ teaspoon dried thyme
   olive oil   1 bay leaf
5 cloves garlic, minced   Salt and pepper to taste
1 medium onion, diced   2½ cups dry, white wine
1 bell pepper, diced   10 small clams, 6 oysters,
1 green onion (with green   6 prawns, 2 small lobsters,
   stalk), diced   1 large crab or 2 small crabs
1 leek, with leaves, diced   2 pounds rockfish and sea bass,
1 #2 can solid-pack tomatoes   (total)

Wash clams and oysters, still in the shell and alive. Clean and shell prawns (or shrimp). Wash lobsters and cut into quarters. Split the crabs and disjoint the legs. Cut fish into 3-inch pieces.

Heat the olive oil in a pot and sauté the garlic, onion, bell pepper, green onion, and leek until all are lightly browned. Add the tomatoes, puree, thyme, and bay leaf. Cover and simmer for 2 hours, stirring often. Add salt and pepper, then the wine. Cook 10 minutes more.

Place all shellfish and fish in the pot and cook, covered, over low flame, simmering for 15 minutes, adding more white wine if necessary. Serve in large soup dishes. Garnish with chopped parsley and provide plenty of garlic Italian bread. Best wine to serve is Riesling or chablis— either one, chilled.

PAELLA

Originally, paella was a picnic food, but into it went anything besides the basic chicken and rice that happened to be available—or just close at hand—and the fishermen in Spain often contributed to the dish with an unbelievable variety of seafood. Here's a recipe that has just about everything—and it's delicious. It was given to us by Richard R. Spencer, a NAUI diving instructor and devoted seafood fan from Southern California.

You Will Need

2 1¼-pound to 2-pound lobsters
½ cup olive oil (use top grade)
1 cup dry white wine
6 large shrimp, deveined
12 littleneck clams
12 mussels
½ pound lean pork cut into ½-inch cubes
6 chicken breasts, boned
2 red onions, diced
3 red peppers, diced
4 large tomatoes, peeled and chopped
1 package Chicken Flavour'd Rice
⅛ teaspoon saffron
2¼ cup water
5 Spanish sausages (chorizos), sliced to ¼ inch
1 cup frozen peas, cooked (don't overcook)

Remove tail from lobsters (also claws if using clawed lobsters.) Cut tails into 4 pieces. Sauté over medium heat in half the olive oil and season with salt and pepper. Cook about 3 minutes, then add 2 tablespoons of the wine and set aside.

Steam mussels and clams in deep kettle with salted water just until they open, about 5 minutes. Remove from heat and cut out the muscles; these will be very tough and can be discarded.

Roast pork cubes dry, without any liquid, for 20 minutes at 375°, stirring often to prevent sticking.

In a large casserole that is flame-proof, sauté the chicken breasts in 2 tablespoons olive oil just until golden, then remove the chicken from the pan and set aside. Add onions, red peppers, and tomatoes to the pan juices and cook over medium heat just until the onions are transparent. Add the remainder of the olive oil and the contents of the rice envelope. Sauté just until golden brown, then add saffron, contents of spice package accompanying rice, the water, and the remainder of the wine. Bring to a boil.

Arrange the lobster and shrimp around the edge of the pan. Arrange the chicken breasts in the center. Cook 15 minutes at 375°, then add clams, mussels, pork, and chorizos. Cook another 10 minutes or until liquid is absorbed and rice is tender. Sprinkle peas over all. Serves 6.

Other Seafood Combinations

Clambakes and other conglomerations are usually mistitled either through carry-over terms or practical reasons such as title space. "Clambakes" usually utilize as the main ingredient, for instance, lobster and fish with clams thrown in if there happens to be any on hand. Other seafood conglomerates include many varieties of seafood though the titles may reveal something as vague as "seafood" to enlighten the cook as to ingredients. Almost all, however, call for crab and/or shrimp and it is important that the cook realizes he can substitute any seafood he desires for any of the specific types designated in these recipes. The clambake, of course, is something special and if at all possible, lobster should take a prominent place in the pit.

CAPE COD CLAMBAKE

Not for you if you're a time-conscious worrier. The clambake takes on all the aspects of a miniature sea festival and several hours are needed for proper preparation and good conversation and fun in the process, plus languid dining when the pit is ready to open.

Dig a pit about 2 feet deep and 2 feet wide by 3 feet long in the sand. Line the bottom and sides near the bottom with rocks (preferably the porous type) about 7 inches in diameter each. Over these build a wood fire and stoke it occasionally for 2 or 3 hours. This will heat the rocks through. Let the fire die. Place a thick layer of seaweed at the bottom of the pit over the hot rocks. Atop the seaweed place your seafood and other goodies. Corn on the cob is usually included along with lobster and clams and other vegetables such as sweet potatoes and onions are also used—even hotdogs and sausages are sometimes thrown in to delight the children (and other hotdog lovers.) The food that takes the longest to cook should be placed on the bottom of the heap. Clams and potatoes might be easier to handle if they are placed in cheesecloth wrappings.

Cover the food with more wet seaweed and cover the pit with a wet tarpaulin—cover the entire pit to hold in the heat and moisture. A combination of hot rock baking and steaming from the wet seaweed does the cooking. Start checking for doneness after an hour. The hotter the rocks, the quicker the cooking, and it will take up to two hours for the complete process.

When cooking is completed, lift the tarpaulin and enjoy the delicious aroma! Then remove the top layer of seaweed and fill up plates—paper plates are used, along with plastic or foam cups for convenience in cleaning up, but be sure these are tossed into a proper recepticle and not left to float out with the tide. All shells and seafood leftovers can be left to return to the ocean if you're near shore—these will help, rather than to harm, the ecology. The clambake—a truly "finger-lickin' good" experience—is an aromatic feast worth the work and waiting for.

(You can carry on a clambake in your own kitchen if you use a large pot instead of a pit. For authenticity of flavor, however, be sure to use fresh seaweed at the bottom of the pot to steam and flavor your seafood.)

GOURMET SEAFOOD CONGLOMERATE

You Will Need
  1 red pepper (capsicum), sliced
  4 ounces green (raw) shrimp
    Small mushrooms, cut in half
  1 lobster tail (raw), chunked, meat only
  4 ounces scallops
  1 medium fish fillet, cut in strips
  1 cooked chicken breast, cubed
  8 steamer clams (optional), steamed just enough to open
  1 tomato, peeled and center removed, chopped
1¼ cup fish stock
  1 onion, chopped fine
  1 garlic clove, mashed
  1 cup raw rice
  1 cup rosé wine
1¼ cup fish stock
  1 bay leaf
    Crushed, dried thyme
  1 tablespoon arrowroot
1½ tablespoon cream

Sauté red pepper in clarified butter, then add the shrimp. Add mushrooms, turning in butter until they glisten. Add lobster meat, scallops, fish, and clams (if used.) Sprinkle chopped tomato over top and add 1¼ cups fish stock. Simmer while you prepare the rice.

Sauté the onion and garlic in clarified butter in skillet. Add the raw rice and stir. Add the wine and the other 1¼ cup fish stock and stir again. Add the bay leaf and sprinkle the thyme over the top so it can be scraped off later. Bake the rice in a 350° oven until done, about 30 minutes. Remove the herbs and place on a warm plate. Spoon the seafood mixture over, reserving the liquid to thicken it with the arrowroot and cream, mixed. Pour the thickened sauce over all. Serves 4.

Sauces

Two important items to have on hand at all times for the seafood lover are fish stock and clarified butter. Both are simple to make and keep and are most effective in producing for the cook a gourmet touch to the finished flavor of seafood dishes. Both, however, cause some inconvenience if they have to be prepared at the time the recipe is put together. Fish stock can be frozen in a plastic container, then removed and wrapped in a plastic bag or foil and replaced in the freezer. The amount needed for a given recipe can then merely be chipped off and the remainder returned to the freezer. Clarified butter will keep in the refrigerator indefinitely, since the substance in butter that makes it rancid is removed in the clarifying process. Clarified butter is much better for sautéing than whole butter as it will not scorch and blacken.

BASIC FISH STOCK

You may use a fish head or fish scraps to make your stock. Cover the fish pieces with 1 quart water and 2 cups dry wine. Add several peppercorns and 2 or 3 bay leaves. Cut a cheesecloth square about 7 inches wide and into the center of it place some crushed tarragon, several sprigs of celery, and small thin slices of carrot. Various recipes for fish stock call for parsley, onion, thyme, and so forth. Suit yourself. Tie up the corners of the cheesecloth square and drop into the pan. Simmer for about an hour, until liquid has reduced to almost ½. Strain and remove cheesecloth bag. This stock can be used now for fish sauce recipes, poaching fish, or even as a first course broth as is.

CLARIFIED BUTTER

Place one pound of butter into a saucepan on medium to low heat and let melt. Watch carefully so as not to scorch. When the butter is all melted and a scum has formed on top, skim off the scum (save this for buttering vegetables if you like), then slowly pour off top of melted butter into the dish you will store it in. When sediment at bottom begins to look as though it will let itself into the container, stop. Discard the sediment. Store the clarified butter, covered, in the refrigerator.

TANGY CALIFORNIA SAUCE

(For Lobster, Shrimp, Fish, Barnacles, Scallops)
You Will Need
¼ cup butter, melted
1 clove garlic, chopped
1 medium onion, chopped
¼ cup flour
1 10½ oz. can condensed chicken broth
2 tablespoons soy sauce or teriyaki sauce
1 navel orange, peeled and diced

Sauté garlic and onion in butter until tender and golden. Stir in flour to blend, then gradually stir in chicken broth and soy sauce or teriyaki. Cook over low heat, stirring constantly, until sauce thickens. Fold in diced orange. Serve hot over broiled, grilled, or barbecued lobster, with scampi; with solid, white-fleshed fish; over barnacles; or over diced, raw scallops.

VELOUTÉ SAUCE

(Use with any fish dish)

Melt 3 tablespoons butter or margarine in a saucepan. Stir in 3 table-spoons flour and continue stirring and cooking to make a roux. Take off the heat and add ⅛ teaspoon Accent, then gradually stir in 2 cups fish stock. (If you haven't yet made your stock for storage, use 1½ cup water, ½ cup dry white wine, and a pinch each of salt, pepper, tarragon, thyme, and celery salt.) Cook and stir until the sauce is thickened. Sprinkle with chopped parsley.

FISH CURRY SAUCE

You Will Need

¼ cup butter	¾ cup fish stock
4 teaspoons minced onion	1½ teaspoons curry powder
3 tablespoons flour	5 tablespoons cream

Sauté onion in butter until onion is transparent and slightly browned. Stir in flour gradually to make a roux. Add the fish stock gradually, stir-ring constantly. Add curry powder and stir well, then add the cream a little at a time, stirring well after each addition.

SAUCE REMOULADE

You Will Need

3 tablespoons finely chopped capers
¼ cup finely chopped dill pickles
1 tablespoon prepared dijon mustard (mild)
1 tablespoon chopped parsley
1 tablespoon dried, crushed tarragon
1 tablespoon chervil
½ teaspoon anchovy paste
2 cups mayonnaise
Freshly ground pepper
Dash mutmeg

Drain chopped pickles and capers well. Mix all ingredients. Remou-lade sauce is served chilled with, or mixed with, fish or shellfish.

HOMEMADE TERIYAKI SAUCE

This is a top recipe straight from the Orient. You'll find it easy to make in large quantities by doubling or quadrupling the recipe and much better than any ready-made teriyaki sauce found in markets.

You Will Need
⅔ cup soy sauce
¼ cup sake or meering
2 tablespoons sugar
½ teaspoon powdered ginger
1 clove garlic, chopped

Mix all ingredients well and use to marinate eel for barbecuing, marinating abalone or scallops for eating raw, or as a dip for raw seafood. (We make this by the gallon and use it not only for seafood but for steaks and barbecued or baked chicken also.) This recipe makes about 1 cup teriyaki and the longer it is stored, the better it gets!

Bechamel Sauce: (Refer to chapter 6 under "Urchin Pureé.")

CHABLIS LOBSTER SAUCE

Sauté ⅓ cup each chopped green pepper and onion in 2 tablespoons clarified butter until tender. Add 1 teaspoon crushed leaf tarragon and cook 1 minute. Add ½ cup chablis wine and cook another 3 minutes. Beat 1 egg yolk slightly and add a little of the hot mixture to it, then stir this back into the sauce. Cook, stirring constantly, until thickened— at least 3 minutes. Serve with lobster or shellfish as a dip or pour-over sauce.

SPANISH MAYONNAISE

(All-i-oli)

This is a great recipe from John H. Harding, former editor of Fathom magazine, Australia. It's a beautiful accompaniment to grilled or fried fish; also good with lobster, sea urchins, and seafood salads.

You Will Need
2 cloves garlic
2 egg yolks
  A few drops cold water
1 tablespoon lemon juice

1½ cups olive oil
  (at room temperature)
Salt to taste

Put a few drips of cold water and a few drops of lemon juice in a mortar with the garlic. Mash the garlic well. Add the raw egg yolks and blend. Add the olive oil very gradually, stirring like mad at the same time. Blend in additional lemon juice, salt to taste. Makes approximately 1½ cups sauce.

Seafood and Wines

The Edible Sea would not be complete without a wine list in connection with seafood. Some discussion is also in order since wine and seafood is one of the most misunderstood areas of preparing various menus of foods from the sea. Coupling white wine with seafood for many years was a stock answer to the question and many people wouldn't dare serve anything else, so deeply ingrained is this belief. The real answer lies only in serving and drinking any wine that suits your palate along with any type of seafood. Once over the hangup of foolish rules, etiquette, and ritual (happily almost totally a thing of the past), more people are ready to enjoy wine for what it is, not for what someone else says it should be.

There are six thousand years of history and ritual involved with wines. The Greeks were enamored totally with wine and created a god, Dionysus, to preside over the grape and the orgiastic religious rites accompanying its use. Seafood and wine are powerful sexual stimulants, especially when used together. Accompanied with fine marine cuisine, soft lights, and romantic music, the warm, alcohol-induced glow lays a path straight to the boudoir. Taken with discretion, wine adds greatly to dining pleasures, but keep in mind that the secret in affairs of the cup is moderation. Overindulgence provokes the desire—but takes away the performance!

Dr. Lucia writes in *Wine and Your Well-Being* that wine contains half a dozen vitamins—5 of the B-complex and P, 13 major minerals—and there is easily assimilable iron in red wine. The natural sugars of wine are easily assimilated, its pH resembles that of gastric juice, and its acid stimulates appetite.

Wine nourishes, refreshes, and cheers. It is foremost of all medicines and aphrodisiacs. "Eat, drink, and be merry" is more than just a saying; it is a promise. Wine is constant proof that God loves us and loves to see us happy. Enjoy your favorite wine with seafood or select from the following suggested list, which is the traditional recommendation of connoisseurs:

LOBSTER, SHRIMP, BARNACLES
  Johannisberg Riesling, Chablis, Pinot Chardonnay
CRAB
  Chenin Blanc, Chablis, Chardonnay
CLAMS, MUSSELS
  Johannisberg Riesling, Chablis
ABALONE, CONCH, OCTOPUS, SQUID
  Sauterne, Chablis, Chenin Blanc

OYSTERS
  Pinot Chardonnay, Chablis, Johannisberg Riesling, Grey Riesling
SCALLOPS, COQUILLES ST. JACQUES
  Chenin Blanc, Green Hungarian, Brenache Rose
FISH, SHARK, RAYS, SKATES
  Johannisberg Riesling, Pinot Chardonnay, Chenin Blanc
FUGU
  Sake
TURTLE, WHALE
  Burgundy, Claret, Chianti

Index

Page numbers in *italics* refer to illustrations.